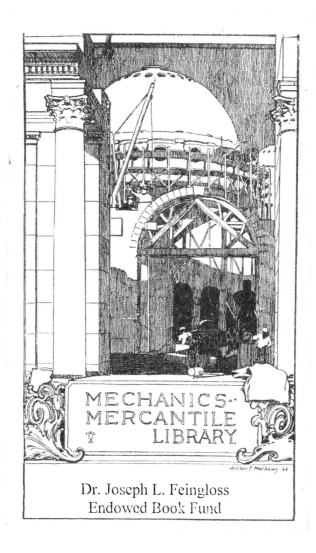

Non-Consensus Investing

DISCLAIMER

The views expressed herein are my own and should not be imputed to any other person or to any organization with whom I may be affiliated at any time. Also, the views expressed in this book do not purport to meet the objectives or needs of specific individuals or types of investment accounts but rather are intended to describe, based on my experience, how active investing can succeed by conducting differentiated fundamental research which proves the prevailing consensus view wrong as well as by using behavioral finance concepts to one's advantage. However, financial markets may change dramatically in the future and in a manner that makes the precepts or experiences described herein either irrelevant or counterproductive. The author neither guarantees the accuracy or completeness of the information contained herein nor does the author have any responsibility to update any material contained herein.

The purchases and sales of securities described in the book and the investment strategy pursued with respect to such purchases and sales are for illustration purposes only and based solely on the experience of a single individual. Nothing in this book should be construed as providing information reasonably sufficient upon which to make an investment decision and should not be considered a recommendation to any person to adopt (or refrain from adopting) a specific investment strategy or to purchase or sell (or refrain from purchasing and selling) a particular security, class of securities, index of securities or any other asset or asset class.

No one should make an investment decision based on the contents of the book. The author's past experience is not a guarantee of future success of the investment strategy or concepts described in the book. All investment decisions have risk of loss and may not be appropriate for everyone in all circumstances. Readers considering making investments are encouraged to conduct independent due diligence to determine if a particular investment is suitable for them given their unique circumstances including, without limitation, their investment objectives, investment experience, risk tolerance and investment time horizon.

The author, publisher, distributor, and their affiliates of this work do not assume, and specifically disclaim, any liability for any loss or damage howsoever caused resulting from any act or omission, directly or indirectly, in whole or in part, based on any information, description, suggestion, methodology, or explanation contained in this book. Any reference herein to a specific company, class of securities, index of securities, or asset or asset class does not imply that the author, at any particular time, held those securities or that they constituted a holding in a portfolio which she managed or that the reference to any company, class of securities, index of securities, or asset or asset class constitutes an investment recommendation with respect to them.

Non-Consensus Investing

Achieving Low Risks
and High Returns

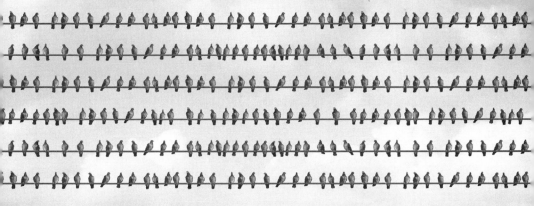

RUPAL J. BHANSALI

Columbia Business School
Publishing

Columbia University Press
Publishers Since 1893
New York   Chichester, West Sussex
cup.columbia.edu
Copyright © 2019 Contrarian Intrinsic Value Investing, LLC

Library of Congress Cataloging-in-Publication Data
Names: Bhansali, Rupal J., author.
Title: Non-consensus investing : achieving low risks and high returns /
Rupal J. Bhansali.
Description: New York : Columbia University Press, [2019] | Includes
bibliographical references and index.
Identifiers: LCCN 2019021924 | ISBN 9780231192309 (cloth : alk. paper) |
ISBN 9780231549769 (e-book)
Subjects: LCSH: Investments. | Investment analysis. | Investment advisors.
Classification: LCC HG4521 .B495 2019 | DDC 332.6—dc23
LC record available at https://lccn.loc.gov/2019021924

Columbia University Press books are printed on permanent
and durable acid-free paper.
Printed in the United States of America

Cover Design: Fifth Letter

This book is dedicated to my father, a retired stockbroker and investor who unknowingly gave me my first taste of equity markets and contrarian value investing—its ups and downs, ins and outs, and everything in between. An independent thinker, he marches to his own tune to most things in life, including investing. Since my childhood and beyond, I have witnessed vicariously and first hand the triumphs and tribulations of being a non-consensus investor and the fortitude it takes to go against the grain. His successes and failures have shaped my investing thinking in subliminal and explicit ways. It is only fitting that I dedicate this book to the man to whom I owe my personal and professional existence.

Contents

Contents

Acknowledgments

This book owes its existence to the support and encouragement of many colleagues, professional acquaintances, friends, and family. They are too many to name, but you know who you are—thank you! Alongside them, my editors Myles Thompson, and Maggie Stuckey, as well as book agent Cait Hoyt at CAA deserve a lot of credit for the final version of this book. All your expert critique and diverse view points have made this a far better literary effort than prior to your involvement.

A special thanks to all my bosses. You brought out the best in me by setting the bar high and skewing the curve up—I would not have it any other way. You helped me stretch and fulfill my potential in ways that I could not have on my own.

My deepest gratitude goes to my clients who stuck with me through thick and thin—it means more to me than I can express.

But I reserve my biggest thanks for my husband, Jayesh. Without your support in everything I do, I would not have been able to accomplish half of what I have. Thank you for figuring out how to stand by me and still let me stand on my own.

Non-Consensus Investing

1

How My Passion Became My Profession

My personal and professional lives are so highly intertwined, it is futile to discuss one without the other. My unconventional upbringing and eclectic work experiences have shaped my investment philosophy in many subtle and significant ways so it seems appropriate to share that personal journey with you before I describe my philosophy.

In this opening chapter, I tell the story of where my fascination with equity markets began, and how my passion went on to become my profession.

The Early Years: Unusual and Unconventional

From the beginning, my life took an unconventional path.

Most kids grow up on fairy tales and fables. I grew up on stock stories. My father owned a stock brokerage business, and since my childhood bedroom doubled as his home office, I often heard him talking to his clients. When the market or a certain stock was not performing well, they needed a lot of hand-holding. I remember how cogent he sounded as he laid out his investment views. Even though I was too young to fully understand what he was saying, I figured out that investing is a lot about managing expectations and emotions, not just money.

My dad became an accidental entrepreneur at the age of twenty-one, straight out of college, to support himself and his siblings. Even though he had no investment skills to speak of at such a young age, his timing was great—it was the early 1960s and stocks were rising—so he was able to build up a good roster of clients eager to invest. Flushed with success, he decided to go the next step and advise clients rather than simply execute their instructions. His business flourished.

Then, after years of success, he took a step too far and, by the early 1970s, started to trade on his own account instead of only on behalf of clients. This exposed our family to the vagaries of the stock market and transformed our lives into a roller-coaster ride on the "mark to market" train. If markets were down (as they often were in the mid-1970s and '80s), money became tight, and I was late paying basic bills such as tuition fees. It is not an exaggeration to say that the vicissitudes of the stock market became the backdrop of my existence. I was not sure I would be able to finish high school, let alone go to college. Thus, at the age of nine, I learned the meaning of the expression "Bills don't come due at market tops." It was a harrowing lesson, but also the beginning of a counterintuitive way of thinking about investing: not losing money is as important as making it—if not more so.

The saving grace amid this volatility was that my dad had the fortitude to hold steady in the face of setbacks. Thankfully, many of his stock picks eventually made money, allowing me to finish my schooling at Queen Mary High School and graduate in business and finance from Lord Sydenham College in Mumbai, India. This bittersweet journey taught me the importance of patience and not letting short-term pressures torpedo sound long-range decisions.

Despite the turmoil, I was fascinated by the markets and followed every twist and turn with the intensity teenage girls usually devote to makeup and boys. I noticed that not only did many of his stocks go up, several were genuine hits. I remember two in particular: Philips India Ltd., the Indian subsidiary of the Dutch consumer electronics conglomerate, soared from fourteen to eighty-four rupees, and Great Eastern Shipping from twenty-four to seventy-five, in a few years. I can vividly recall the thrill of watching those prices rise, knowing that my father's ideas were being vindicated and he was giving his clients peace of mind as well as profits. This is what led me to appreciate the power of active investing: you can get a lot of bang for your research buck. I knew then that I wanted to make this my vocation, a profession in which I could do well *and* do good.

I could not wait to start. By the age of sixteen, I had learned accounting in high school, so I could qualify for internships on Dalal Street (India's Wall Street). Alongside college in the mid-1980s, I worked part-time or summers as an apprentice at various firms to learn different facets of finance—from the foreign exchange desk at Citibank to the corporate finance and leasing department of an investment bank. By the time I was twenty-one, I had edited prospectuses, calculated residual values on leasing portfolios, and learned how to read balance sheets. I took on any assignment I could lay my hands on, from mundane tasks such as proofreading marketing material to complex ones involving researching regulatory barriers to venture capital financing in emerging markets. It may not sound like scintillating work, but I was drinking from a fire hose and it felt exhilarating!

During my undergraduate years, I noticed that when my classmates began planning their future, most took the conventional path of looking for a job. But through my dad's stockbroking business, I had firsthand exposure to the possible benefits of entrepreneurship, and I wanted them to at least think about it. So, I organized a competition called "Mind Your Own Business" in which students would present their original business plans and review business models, not just financial models. I guess you could say this was my first attempt to challenge conventional wisdom.

As irony would have it, I walked away from my own family business in India. I dreamt of going to New York, where I could practice money management as a profession. I knew if I wanted to be a top athlete in my chosen field, I had to compete in the Olympics. In investing, the Olympian battleground was not India but the United States of America, where the most sophisticated investors proved their intellectual worth by competing against benchmarks such as the S&P 500. Little did I realize I was signing up for an epic battle—the one between active and passive investing.[1]

But my dream to manage money quickly faced its first of many obstacles—money itself. The surefire way to secure a visa to America was to be a graduate student, but tuition for an out-of-state student (especially an international one) was prohibitively expensive. I began to look for a scholarship. My prospects looked bleak: I did not qualify for a need-based scholarship, and one based on scholastic merit seemed like a long shot. Then I learned about the Rotary Foundation and the scholarships it offered to well-rounded individuals. I was on pins and needles during the multiple rounds of interviews for the limited number of scholarships available. I felt daunted by the stiff competition but ecstatic when I made the cut. Finally, I was on my way to America.

But I almost didn't make it.

In the summer of 1991, just days after I bought my ticket to America, the Indian rupee devalued by 40 percent, which meant my expenses in dollar terms shot up by 66 percent! My heart sank. Fortunately, in reading the fine print, I discovered my scholarship was denominated in dollars, not rupees, so the devaluation did not affect my plans. But you can bet that ever since that gut-wrenching moment, I have read financial footnotes with an eagle eye and paid close attention to currency risk.[2]

---

1. Throughout this book, I use the terms "active" and "passive" as they are applied in the profession, as a kind of shorthand for "active management," "active investment philosophy," or similar expressions. In that sense, the two words, which in grammatical terms are adjectives, have become widely understood as nouns, rather like "liberal" and "conservative" in the political arena.

2. If sales are denominated in one currency but expenses in another, any adverse fluctuations between the two currencies can put one at risk. Currency risk—a common problem in the import/export world, where manufacturing costs are incurred in one currency but revenues earned in another.

Shortly after landing in America, I had my first taste of culture shock. I had chosen to do my MBA at the University of Rochester because it was in New York, the financial heartbeat of the world. I did not know that the university was in the *state* of New York, not the *city* of New York. In India, the names of cities and states are different, and I had assumed that to be the case everywhere else. It never occurred to me to check. If only I had triangulated information, instead of assuming it![3]

The Formative Years: What to Do and What Not to Do

I had hoped to work on the buy side of Wall Street rather than the sell side. The buy side comprises analysts and portfolio managers who manage money and buy stocks; on the sell side are brokers (like my dad) who execute trades placed by their buy-side clients. But of course, timing is everything, and mine was not good. I expected to graduate from my MBA program in March 1993, so I started looking for a job in 1992, which happened to coincide with a deep recession. Equity, bond, and property markets were all crashing, Wall Street was downsizing, and buy-side jobs were in short supply.

My specific circumstance was even tougher. I needed a work visa when my student visa expired. To get a work visa, I needed a job. Without a job, I had to leave the country. My dream was evaporating before it could even start.

I could not let that happen. After a disheartening search that seemed interminable, I managed to get a job at a boutique sell-side firm, Crosby Securities, which specialized in emerging markets. To be frank, it was not my dream job, but it was the only one

---

3. My daft mistake had a delightful ending. When I traveled for job interviews, my seven-hour train rides between Rochester and New York were spectacularly scenic, bringing the song "America the Beautiful" to life as I soaked in the majestic mountains, colorful wildflowers, and mesmerizing fall foliage that dotted the landscape.

I could get that would let me stay in the country, so I took the position and gave it my best. In hindsight, it turned out to be a terrific launch pad. My colleagues were great role models, and my clients included the who's who of money managers in North America (JP Morgan, Capital Guardian, Templeton, Wellington, Tiger, Soros, and countless others). This gave me a ringside view of their investment successes and failures, philosophies, and processes, as well as their product strategies and organization structures, and exposed me to a wide range of macro views, investment styles, and stock debates.

> **"The signature element of my upside-down investment process: it focuses on what can go wrong, not just what can go right."**

This amazing experience proved instrumental in shaping my own investment philosophy—not just what to do, but what *not* to do. By learning from the best and leaving out the rest, I was able to develop a counterintuitive discipline (non-consensus investing) which I have honed and applied over a career spanning twenty-five years.

The other interesting aspect of my first stint on Wall Street was that hedge funds were also my clients. Hedge funds make money by buying stocks that go up (going "long") as well as "shorting" stocks that are expected to fall (going "short").[4] As a result, not only did I have to produce "long" ideas, but I had to come up with "short" ideas as well. This experience of thinking about both the long and short sides of the trade has become the signature element of my upside-down investment process: it focuses on what

---

4. Here is a simplified scenario: Say you have identified a stock whose price is likely to fall. You presell shares (without actually owning them) in anticipation of negative developments that will cause the price to sink. When it does, you can buy them at the lower price and pocket the difference. If you presell XYZ stock at $100, watch it fall to $80, and then buy it, you have made a 20 percent return on your "short."

can go wrong (and how much the stock can go down), not just what can go right (and how much the stock can go up).

Then my life took a momentous turn. One of my clients at this first job was the hedge fund Soros Fund Management. They made me an offer, and I jumped at the opportunity, even though it meant a 50 percent pay cut. This was my chance to shift to managing money rather than brokering stocks. It has been among my best decisions ever. Over time, my learning, earnings, and career prospects vastly improved compared to the bleak future I would have confronted on the sell side. I see it as a profound reinforcement of the lesson I learned watching my father's career: if you choose long-term gain over short-term pain, you come out ahead in the end. It has served me well in investing and in life.

As the years rolled by, my roles and responsibilities expanded. My next stint was at Oppenheimer Capital, and my remit expanded from emerging markets to developed markets, from international equities to global equities, and from analyst to portfolio manager. Later I went from being head of international equities to chief investment officer of global equities. Clients expanded from multibillion-dollar private and public pension plans to trillion-dollar superannuation and sovereign wealth funds. Assets under management also grew from the millions to billions of dollars.

There were other changes, too: from receiving breaking stock news via fax and research reports via snail mail to consuming them online; from being tethered to a PC in the office to traversing the world with a laptop and a smartphone; from emerging markets and junk bonds being revered to reviled and back to being revered again; and from active investing going out of favor to coming back in vogue to going out of style again.

The one thing that did not change was my resolve to deliver superior investment results and solve for the seemingly mutually exclusive goals of achieving higher returns with lower risk. All my learning and experiences culminated in my unconventional investment discipline: non-consensus investing.

Non-consensus investing is not simply doing the opposite of what everyone else is doing. It is deeper and broader and requires its practitioners to develop skills to recognize when widely held investment views are likely to be wrong. It is consciously trying to establish whether you have a differentiated point of view on a company's fundamental prospects and intrinsic value and then courageously taking the unpopular side of the trade—buying when others are selling and vice versa. Non-consensus thinkers are not simply contrarians in a psychological or behavioral sense. They are analytical and independent thinkers who try to figure out what is misunderstood about the business and mispriced in the stock.

Non-consensus investing adopts an upside-down investment approach—doing things contrary to convention, such as examining the counterfactual instead of reviewing the facts or conducting research in an atypical sequence. For example, most investment processes typically try to shortlist securities that meet some preset criteria, usually minimum growth rates or maximum valuations. My approach is the opposite. Instead of trying to *select* companies, I look for reasons to *reject* them. By first and foremost looking for things to dislike and identifying what can go wrong, I proactively try to reduce the risk of being blindsided if adversity arises. Even if it does, I am prepared for it and can insist on getting paid for it. Those who look for things to like end up overlooking things that can go wrong and assuming more risk than they bargained for. Also, most conventional investment processes revolve around seeking returns; non-consensus investing aims first to identify and manage risk. It is a counterintuitive approach, but in my experience, the correct one.

They say there is nothing worse than being poor. I disagree. The worst thing is being poor after you have been rich. My childhood was a roller-coaster ride on the money train, with as many wrecks as riches. This explains why I pay so much attention to not losing money (risk management), instead of simply making it (return management). Few people realize that investing is a paradox: *to enhance returns one must reduce risks.* In fact, risk management is so important, so fundamental to the themes of this book, that I devote an entire chapter to it—chapter 6, "Do No Harm."

The Prime Years: Succeeding Against the Odds

Fast-forward to today—I am a woman of Asian origin managing billions of dollars of assets for institutional investors. The mutual funds I managed have received the coveted five-star Morningstar Rating (I think of them as the Academy Awards in my field), from time to time over my twenty-five-year career. For perspective, a five-star rating equates to a top decile performance among peers in the category.[5]

The most unconventional aspect of my career is that I have succeeded in a competitive, male-dominated profession. More than 90 percent of mutual fund managers in the United States

---

5. Note that Morningstar Ratings™ for funds or "star ratings" are assigned to mutual funds (with at least a three-year history) based on their *risk adjusted* returns, not returns alone. That is, they pay attention to both risk and returns. The Morningstar Rating does not include any adjustment for sales loads. The top 10 percent of products in each product category receive five stars, the next 22.5 percent receive four stars, the next 35 percent receive three stars, the next 22.5 percent receive two stars, and the bottom 10 percent receive one star. Ratings are objective, based entirely on a mathematical evaluation of past performance. The act of assigning a star rating on a mutual fund or ETF or stock by Morningstar does not constitute nor imply an endorsement or recommendation of the same by them. They are a useful tool for identifying funds and ETFs worthy of further research but should not be considered buy or sell signals. Also, I would add that you should not expect a fund to receive a high star rating every year. In fact, as you will see in chapter 11, it is fairly typical for a five-star-rated manager to *underperform* three straight years in a row, over any ten-year period. My own experience corresponds to this.

are male and typically white.[6] I am neither white nor male—living proof that the glass ceiling can be broken. I believe that if I can do it, anyone can do it. In the chapters ahead, I walk you through the right and wrong turns I took and what I learned along the way.

Sharing What I Have Learned

All my exposures and experiences—from growing up with the beat of the stock market to my formal education to my real-world training on the job—coalesced into a philosophy of investing that is the bedrock of my work today. And that is what I wish to share with you here.

"I wrote this book to help you make the transition from consensus to non-consensus thinking, from conventional to unconventional frameworks, and from rote rules to profound principles."

While applying my upside-down investment discipline can be rewarding and right, it is neither easy nor intuitive. I wrote this book to help you make the transition from consensus to non-consensus thinking, from conventional to unconventional frameworks, and from rote rules to profound principles. This mental pivot was difficult even for me, but the monetary payoff has been worth it, which is why I thought I should share my own real-life experiences. My own investment acumen was built on the shoulders of those who came before me, so in the spirit of passing it on, I wrote this book. But before consuming its contents, please

---

6. According to a study done by Morningstar in 2016, https://www.morningstar.com/articles/781996/women-fund-managers-are-scarce-worldwide.html.

be sure to read the disclaimer on page ii, if you have not already done so.

Unlike quant[7] disciplines that depend on computers and number crunching, non-consensus investing is a framework, not a formula. It relies on creativity as much as analytics and on art rather than algorithms. It comprises a series of principles, not rules, because I believe an investment process should *define* but not *confine* a craft. The ideal way to learn this philosophy is through osmosis, by working alongside great investors who can bring its core concepts and precepts to life. But for those who cannot do so, I offer this book as a surrogate.

Instead of investment jargon and abstract theories, I provide real-world applications, drawing from the many counterintuitive and non-consensus calls I have made throughout my career. It was not an easy decision to focus on my own experiences. I am concerned that it may seem as though I am trying to toot my own horn. But to fully embrace what may seem an entirely new way of thinking, it helps to see how to put the principles of non-consensus investing into practice, and my own anecdotes are what I know best.

Furthermore, I have made my share of mistakes too, as you will see—I discuss many throughout the book. In fact, more than half of the calls made by any investor, including me, can be and often are incorrect. No investment philosophy or framework—no matter how sound or rigorous—is error proof or guaranteed to make one money, in the short or long run. However, it can help *improve the odds* of making money and *reduce the odds* of losing money—for that reason alone it is important to use a discipline as a compass. I discuss mine because that is what I know best and it has worked for me. However, it may or may not appeal to or

---

7. The word "quant" is short for quantitative investment approaches, in which programmers write code to back-test data and try to identify relative mispricing among securities to beat the market. Quant strategies tend to be more trading oriented with a shorter time horizon than traditional fundamental research-oriented strategies.

be appropriate for you, because investors have a variety of needs, constraints, goals, and motivations, and one size cannot fit all.

Few investors realize that investing is about what *not* to do, rather than only knowing what to do. It is about mastering emotions and withstanding pressures, not just conducting fundamental analysis. This is why, throughout this book, I candidly share my failures as well as my successes, my triumphs as well as my tribulations.

This book is not just about seeking higher returns; it is also, and especially, about lowering risk. I believe that *return management should not come at the expense of risk management.* This book shows you how to be more right than wrong in conducting fundamental research and how to keep the cost of mistakes low—the latter is crucial if one is to have any hope of achieving the dual objectives of enhancing returns *and* reducing risk.

Warren Buffett, an active manager (stock picker), has made billions of dollars by recognizing the simple truth that just because stock markets are *frequently* efficient does not mean they are *always* efficient. Likewise, just because active managers can *frequently* underperform, does not mean they will *always* underperform. Society's failure to appreciate this subtle difference has given the entire profession of active management and the art of stock picking a negative reputation it does not deserve. I wrote this book to explain the power and payoff of differentiated fundamental research and active stock picking. In it, I describe how it is possible to *beat* the market, not just *match* the market—which is the whole point of active money management.

It is not my goal to champion one asset class or investment approach at the expense of all others, but to ensure that all sides are heard. It is true that not *all* active managers can outperform the market after deducting fees and expenses; by definition, the sum of all active is passive, which is the market itself. However, this notion has been taken too far to imply that *no* active manager can outperform markets. This is what I take exception to.

There is also a deeply personal reason for writing this book. Throughout my life, I have been inspired by other people's wisdom, often encapsulated in their writings. Books have been among my finest teachers, my passport to transcend time and space to learn from the best. I have come to realize that by only reading and not writing, I have taken knowledge but not given any in return. I owe a great debt to all those writers before me. If I can repay that in some small measure, I will feel my burden lightened.

Getting the Most from This Book

Investing is not just one big complex puzzle with many interlocking pieces, but a *kaleidoscope* of puzzles, where slight shifts in one element or angle can create an entirely new picture. To unravel the puzzle requires an understanding of many different but interdependent concepts and principles. However, a book, by definition, is structured linearly and cannot explain everything all at once. Each chapter, therefore, tackles only a piece of the puzzle. In a sense, this is artificial. In the real world, the concepts and principles described in a chapter do not operate in a vacuum; they are interrelated and connected to ideas outlined in other chapters. Thus, while they are written sequentially, they need to be applied simultaneously.

Furthermore, the concepts in any given chapter are not only incomplete, they are often counterintuitive. This puts an extra burden on me, the author, as well as you, the reader, because both of us are wrestling with a partial puzzle. I ask you to have faith that as the book progresses, the full picture will reveal itself with clarity and conviction. In the meantime, to make this task easier, here is a preview of the organization of the book, so you know what to expect.

The chapter immediately following reminds us of the history and power of counterintuitive thinking in solving humanity's most intractable problems with breakthrough solutions. Investing is no less a challenge, which is why I have found that unconventional thinking must be applied to solve the seemingly mutually exclusive goals of achieving higher returns *and* lowering risks.

The next chapter contrasts the risks and rewards of investing in stocks versus bonds. This might seem like common knowledge, but I bring an uncommon perspective on the trade-offs and pay-offs of one asset class versus the other. I also address how risk differs from volatility and how volatility can be the investor's friend instead of foe.

Chapters 4 through 11 dissect the core principles of non-consensus investing, ranging from the need to stand alone to stand apart, to how misunderstanding quality can be the mother of all mistakes but also the mother lode of all opportunities. I then detail how to be a victor instead of a victim of our innate behavioral biases; how value can only be intrinsic, not relative or conditional; and how patience is the only free lunch in markets.

The concluding chapter 12 summarizes the core facets and tenets of non-consensus investing. Think of these principles as a north star, pointing you toward success. I also underscore how it takes character and courage, not just intellectual curiosity and contrarian thinking, to succeed in investing. Keeping with the spirit of the contrarian theme that permeates this book, I often discuss what *not* to do and how *not* to do it.

Finally, as a woman who has succeeded in a male-dominated profession, I would be remiss not to encourage young women to join this profession and share some insights on what you can do to rise through the ranks. There is a special message from me to you, after chapter 12.

2

"And" Not "Or"

In investing, conventional wisdom dictates that you can have either high returns or low risk, but not both. You can have either capital appreciation or capital preservation, but not both. I did not want to settle for such a suboptimal compromise.

I looked around and realized that civilization has overcome many intractable challenges with non-consensus thinking. In fact, unconventional thinking and counterintuitive concepts have resulted in groundbreaking discoveries and outsized success in science, society, sports, and Silicon Valley. So, I thought to myself, why not apply the same problem-solving approach to overcome the seemingly mutually exclusive goals of achieving higher returns and lower risk in investing? This is what I have spent a lifetime trying to do.

Contrarians refuse to give up or give in. They prefer to aim high and fail than aim low and succeed. They develop breakthrough solutions that solve for "and" instead of settling for "or." Non-consensus investing aims for the same. Of course, as in any pathbreaking endeavor, success is never assured, but I found my mental reset got me closer to my desired destination. This chapter highlights how to secure "and" and not settle for "or".

Power and Payoff of Non-Consensus Thinking

If you trace the origins of many major advances in human history, you will find they have come from people who challenged conventional wisdom, often in the face of ridicule and disbelief.

Centuries ago, Magellan proved the consensus wrong when he set sail and did not fall off the edge of the world, decisively proving that the Earth was round.

Edward Jenner turned prevailing wisdom on its head when he injected a cowpox virus into patients to protect them from the smallpox virus. His counterintuitive approach of inoculating the human body to prevent deadly diseases has saved more lives than the work of any other human in history.

Professor Muhammad Yunus, founder of the Grameen Bank, lifted millions of people out of poverty by making small loans to the poor without collateral, defying prevailing wisdom that only large loans to the rich secured by collateral could be profitable. His pioneering microlending program for impoverished people (especially women) started in Bangladesh, but the concept has flourished worldwide. It has become a model of success on both commercial *and* humanitarian grounds—twin attributes which are usually regarded as mutually exclusive. His unconventional approach to solving poverty, one of society's most intractable problems earned him the Nobel Prize, the Presidential Medal of Freedom, and a Congressional Gold Medal.

In Canada, at the Toronto Film Festival, Piers Handling changed the business of film awards when he instituted the People's Choice Awards. Before this, an elite jury decided who won. Their verdict provided prestige but not necessarily profits at the box office. By making the viewers also the critics, Handling ensured that critical acclaim would also signal commercial success.

Here in the United States, Oakland Athletics general manager Billy Beane transformed the business of baseball when he used statistics instead of clairvoyance to find misunderstood and mispriced talent. He proved that, with smart evaluation and trading of talent, a small payroll could still achieve outsize payoffs.[1]

---

1. After he became renowned for his use of data over intuition, Billy Beane received many lucrative offers and spurned them all. "I made one decision in my life based on money and I swore I would never do it again." Beane gave up being the highest paid GM in sports history to be near his daughter. A reporter once asked him, "If you didn't get money out of it, what did you get?" His answer: "I changed the game."

Silicon Valley is none other than a community of contrarians, who constantly bet against the status quo and change our world forever. Steve Jobs was the poster child of this phenomenon. He transformed the mobile phone from a low-tech phone to a high-tech smartphone by upgrading the iPhone instead of dumbing it down, making the average person feel like a power user instead of a Luddite. He rejected conventional market wisdom on product design and embraced a "think different" mantra to make the iPhone an unprecedented success and Apple among the most valuable companies on Earth.

"And" Not "Or"

If you look closely at contrarians, you will find that they refuse to give up or give in. They often appear stubborn and unreasonable, but their push for change is driven by a desire to solve the intractable or to take on the impossible. To them mediocrity is a sin, if not a crime. Being the tallest among seven dwarfs is of no interest. Deep down, they are driven by the pursuit of truth or perfection, not fame or fortune. They want to change the world for the better and are not afraid to spend a lifetime doing so.

The hallmark of contrarians in fields as disparate as sports and science is that they develop breakthrough solutions that solve for the "and" proposition instead of settling for "or." For example: Selling groceries or household necessities that are low quality *or* low cost is easy to do; offering merchandise that is both high quality *and* low cost is tough to pull off. Yet Costco, the successful U.S. retailer, has done exactly that. Making a phone that is both powerful *and* playful could have been an oxymoron, but the iPhone delivered both. Lending to the poor with no collateral or track record could have been a financial disaster, but Yunus proved you can do good *and* do well. People, products, and companies that deliver the *"and"* proposition are game changers and become the benchmark to beat. Those that settle for delivering *"or"* are soon left in the dust.

Risk or Reward?

In investing, conventional wisdom traps you into making a poor trade-off: If you want high returns, you must accept high risk; if you have a low risk appetite, you must accept low returns. I did not want to settle for this suboptimal compromise. I wanted both—high returns *and* low risk—so I developed a non-consensus investing discipline to improve my odds of doing exactly that.[2] I have applied this investment approach since I became a portfolio manager in 1996 and regard it as the lynchpin and fountainhead of my professional success.

However, early in my career, many of my colleagues thought I was crazy to even attempt to square the circle of achieving higher returns *and* lower risks. My superiors were also skeptics. If you are among those, remind yourself that until Magellan, Jenner, Yunus, and Jobs proved the impossible possible, nobody believed they could pull off those feats. But here we are, flying around the world, getting vaccinated, lifting people out of poverty, and incessantly using our iPhones. While not every attempt will meet with similar success, there is a lot of truth in the old adage, nothing ventured, nothing gained.

I call my active investment approach "non-consensus investing" because the epic battle between passive and active is none other than being a contrarian. The greater the disagreement with the

---

2. Note I said "improve my odds," not "guarantee the outcomes." No investment discipline is foolproof or failsafe. But having a compass makes it far more likely to get you to your destination. View the contents of this book as a guiding light pointing you in the right direction, not some silver bullet that hits the bull's eye.

market, the more *non-consensus* your portfolio. The greater the difference versus the benchmark, the more *active* your portfolio. The greater the disconnect between your thinking and prevailing wisdom, the more *contrarian* your portfolio. Viewed from that lens, a truly active investor is implicitly, if not explicitly, a non-consensus thinker and contrarian investor.

"The epic battle between passive and active is none other than being a contrarian."

Contrarians defy conventional wisdom by turning it on its head. Throughout this book you will see examples of how non-consensus investing does things differently if not downright counterintuitively. For instance, instead of being afraid of market volatility, it takes advantage of it. Instead of denigrating the human mind as a source of bias, it leverages its horsepower and willpower to triumph against the odds. Instead of accepting the status quo of being average and getting average returns, it upends prevailing wisdom to secure higher returns with lower risk.

Passive: lower returns and higher risk?
Active: higher returns and lower risk?

In my opinion, while the *need* for higher returns and lower risk remains high, the *ability* of equities or bonds to offer either—let alone both in the next decade or so—is low.

Given today's lofty earnings levels, stretched balance sheets, and rich valuations, I believe we are likely to experience extremely low or even negative returns in equity markets for an extended period. I am not alone in this expectation. Methods and metrics used by Nobel Prize–winning economist Robert Shiller to invest-ment guru Buffett point to the same bleak projections (more on this in chapter 12, "North Star").[3]

Also, ten-year bond yields are so low (or negative) in most markets around the world that people cannot live off interest income anymore. Worse still, many bond gurus have voiced their concerns on valuations being too rich and not offering much protection against credit or inflation risk, which means bond prices could fall instead of going up.

These are all signs that investing *passively* in either equity or bond markets is unlikely to yield much by way of positive returns. Not only do the return prospects look unattractive, so do the risks. Passive investing may expose you to a litany of risks that you may be overlooking. I have outlined some of them below:

"You are exposed to a litany of risks with passive investing that are being glossed over."

1. *Crowded-trade risk*. The *Wall Street Journal* recently reported that money invested in index funds had reached 48.1 percent of all U.S. stock-fund assets as of November 30, 2018, up from 44.6 percent in the prior year, as the vast majority of flows go into passively managed index funds. Morningstar analyst Kevin McDevitt noted, "If present trends continue, index funds could exceed active funds by mid-2019."[4] Such herd behavior is symptomatic of a crowded trade, which typically sets up for inferior future performance.

2. *Valuation risk*. Who will buy the expensive stocks owned by passive investors when they want to sell? A wide divergence between what active investors are willing to pay

---

3. See https://moneyandmarkets.com/buffett-shiller-long-term-sp-500-prediction-method/.

4. Here is a snapshot of ten-year bond rates in major developed markets around the world as of December 2018: 2.65 percent in the United States, 1.12 percent in the UK, 0.40 percent in France, 0.07 percent in Germany, negative 0.4 percent in Switzerland, and negative 0.04 percent in Japan.

(based on fundamentals) versus the price (bid up by flows) at which passives have valued their portfolios could set the stage for big markdowns, aka losses.

3. *Redemption risk.* If everyone rushes to exit at the same time, how will passive easily liquidate its underlying assets into cash? Who will take the other side of the trade? Will a liquid asset class turn illiquid, causing passive managers to curtail redemptions?

4. *Liquidity risk.* To avoid restricting redemptions, passive managers may have no choice but to dump stocks in a disorderly fashion, causing them to gap down, which I describe as the cost to exit positions. These high exit costs can be many times higher than the low entry costs, potentially making it a penny-wise, pound-foolish trade.

5. *Front-running risk.* Passive managers such as Vanguard and Blackrock are mammoth players, so they cannot hide or disguise their trading activities. This could make them sitting ducks for nimble traders who front run (the practice of stepping in front of large orders to gain an economic advantage). In bull markets, nobody notices or complains about front running because it pushes prices up, creating the illusion of making money. On the way down, it can turn into a house of cards, as selling begets more selling by the front runners, paving the way for larger losses.

6. *Permanent-impairment-of-capital risk.* Cheap beta (which is the promise of passive) is only desirable in bull markets. Passive cannot protect you against capital loss.

7. *Behavioral risk.* Passive is not the negation of human neuroses or biases, but the aggregation of all neuroses and biases that exist in a market.

8. *Momentum risk.* Lacking self-correcting mechanisms, indices can swing wildly from greed to fear as momentum cuts both ways. On the way up, it turbocharges returns;

on the way down, it turns into a vicious downward spiral. Such roller coasters can be nerve-wracking, and investors may feel compelled to redeem instead of riding it out, exposing them to many of the risks described previously.

9. *Reflexivity risk.* If you think that passive is unemotional, objective, and rational, think again. Going passive is itself an active decision. It is humans who make the decision to choose or quit passive, and they can be every bit as emotional and biased (which are accusations typically leveled against active managers).

10. *Market-inefficiency risk.* Because passive does not care whether a market price reflects fair value or not (and therefore the efficiency of the market itself), all of society suffers. Active investors hold managements' feet to the fire, buying or selling specific stocks to send a signal that they agree or disagree with a business strategy. They make judgment calls about right and wrong. They do extensive work in figuring out the fair value of a business and stock. All this effort takes resources and money, but it helps society at large. To incentivize such costly and arduous efforts, markets provide rewards to active managers and their clients, making it a win-win proposition (more on this in chapter 4). Passive managers such as Blackrock and Vanguard may argue that they take proxy voting seriously and actively participate in corporate governance to ensure shareholder interests. But this pales in comparison to the ongoing dialogue and feedback that active managers can provide, including the threat of voting with their feet and selling the stock (which passive simply cannot do).

So, passively investing in equities or bonds may offer neither high returns nor low risk. This could not come at a worse time.

The wealthiest societies in the developed world are aging rapidly, meaning that many people will soon start living off savings and investment income rather than monthly wage income.[4]

The solution is not to give up on your investment goals of securing higher returns and lowering risk, but to reconsider the means of achieving them. This book talks about those means: active investing and more specifically non-consensus investing. To be clear, my investment discipline is an intellectual framework, not some magical formula that can be readily duplicated. Its principles are classic, but their application is dynamic. The best way to understand the philosophy is by practicing it. This is why I wrote the book as a series of foundational concepts and used stock examples as case studies to illustrate them.

However, before we can understand how to practice any form of active investing, including non-consensus investing, we must understand investing itself. How is it different from speculation? How do we choose between equities and bonds? What are their risks and rewards? How is risk different from volatility? I start answering these crucial questions in the next chapter.

Top Takeaways

1. Unconventional thinking and counterintuitive concepts have resulted in groundbreaking discoveries and outsized success in science, society, sports, and Silicon Valley. I have tried to apply the same problem-solving approach to overcome the equally intractable challenges of achieving higher returns *and* lowering risk in investing.
2. If you trace the origins of many major advances in human history, you will find they have come from contrarians who challenged conventional wisdom.
3. The epic battle between passive and active is none other than being a contrarian. The greater the disagreement

with the market, the more *non-consensus* your portfolio. The greater the difference versus the benchmark, the more *active* your portfolio. The greater the disconnect between your thinking and prevailing wisdom, the more *contrarian* your portfolio.

4. In investing, conventional wisdom has dictated that you can have either high returns *or* low risk, but not both. I refused to settle for "or" and developed an investing framework to improve my odds of achieving both: higher returns *and* lower risk.

5. Over the next decade or so, passive may offer neither high returns nor low risk. The solution is not to give up on your investment goals, but to reconsider the means of achieving them. This book talks about those means: non-consensus investing.

3

Stocks or Bonds?

This chapter addresses the investor's common question in an uncommon way: How do I weigh the risks and rewards of investing in equities (stocks) versus fixed income (bonds)?

It also addresses other questions that are not on everyone's mind but should be. How is investing different from speculation and risk different from volatility? Can volatility be an opportunity instead of a threat?

Spooked by the financial crisis of 2008, many investors have shunned equities due to their volatility and instead embraced bonds for their stability. My contrarian point of view is that not only could this bring disappointing returns, it may actually prove riskier.

Investing is Not Speculation

The key difference between investing and speculation is how the odds are set. In speculation—gambling—the odds of winning and losing are preset. You win or lose by chance, not choice. In investing, you have the power to alter the odds, if you are willing to do the work. This means you win or lose by choice, not chance. This is a crucial distinction. If you play an *active* role in investing, you can influence the outcomes through skill. In speculating, you are reduced to a *passive* position where luck prevails, and skill does not matter.

"In investing you win or lose by choice, not chance."

There are primarily two elements you need to consider when making an investment: the risk it exposes you to and the reward you can expect from it. You should always insist on knowing the odds of making or losing money in any investment proposition. To do that, you start by understanding the true nature of risk and reward. That is the purpose of this chapter: to help you pull apart some common misconceptions and see the risk/reward balance with clarity.

What exactly do those two words, "risk" and "reward," mean? I think of risk as the potential for permanent loss of money, and reward as the compounded rate of return over a full market cycle, typically ten years or more.

This leads me to address a big question that should be on everyone's mind: Should I invest in stocks or bonds? Which give the better returns? Which have lower risk?

Fixed income (bonds) and equities (stocks) are core building blocks of any investment portfolio, but they have vastly different risk/reward profiles, and determining the right mix between them is the most important decision you can make. Conventional wisdom would have you believe that bonds are low return but also low risk, while equities bring high return but with high risk. Unconventional wisdom suggests that bonds may actually be *higher* risk and stocks may be *lower*. Let us explore the risks and rewards of both, so you can choose between them with eyes wide open.

Investing in Stocks: Risks, Rewards, and Volatility

The "Nasdaq Crash" of 2000–2002 and the financial crisis of 2008 knocked the wind out of the sails of many investors, seducing them into the presumed safety of bonds and scaring them away from the apparent risks of equities. Indeed, bonds are so coveted that even junk bonds (those rated below investment grade, implying they are riskier) are venerated as high yield.

It is a tragedy that there is an entire generation of investors who do not appreciate the rewards of equities and instead singularly fret about their risks. At the same time, they display an unhealthy predisposition toward bonds and an underappreciation of their risks.

There is an important corollary about equities. Many investors shy away from them because they misunderstand—and therefore mistrust—their volatility. Volatility is not the same as risk; in fact, volatility can work in your favor, as we shall see shortly.

Rewards of Equities

Equities offer something that bonds simply cannot: the greatest opportunity to make a lot of money in the long run. It is true that bonds offer the greatest opportunity to *not lose* a lot of money, but that is not the same as *making* a lot of money. The top-ranked billionaires of our generation, such as Warren Buffett, Bill Gates, Sam Walton, and Jeff Bezos, all made their billions owning equity—in Berkshire Hathaway, Microsoft, Walmart, and Amazon, respectively. More impressively, they did this in a single lifetime.

Please do not think I mean you need to be rich to invest in equities. In fact, the best part of equities is not just their ability to build wealth, but that they offer that opportunity to anybody. Whether you are a blue-collar or white-collar worker, young or old, male or female, black or brown or white, upper- or lower-income bracket, you can get a piece of the action— by, for example, owning equity mutual funds—for as little as $1,000. Equities are an equal-opportunity asset class. In addition, you can invest in equities on any day or every day, regularly or sporadically, with a big or a small amount. Nothing is more flexible and inviting than that. There is really no excuse to not join this club.

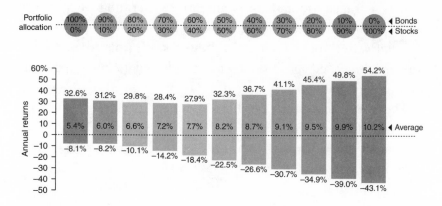

FIGURE 3.1 Best, worst, and average returns for various stock/bond allocations, 1926–2016. *Source*: Vanguard Fund, "Vanguard's Principles for Investing Success," figure 5, https://personal.vanguard.com/pdf/ISGPRINC.pdf.

In fact, if you want to make your money work as hard for you as you have worked for it, few things beat investing in equities in the long run. Notice I said, "in the long run." To understand the risk/return profile of any asset class, whether equities (stocks) or fixed income (bonds), you must look at a horizon that equals life spans, not quarters or years or even decades. Seen through that lens, equities have beaten bonds handsomely. Figure 3.1 illustrates this difference: the greater the allocation to equities, the larger your returns—by a factor of 2. If history repeats (there is no guarantee that it will), a nest egg of a million dollars, invested in stocks, would have earned an extra million dollars. Differently put, not owning equities is like potentially leaving a million bucks on the table.

Remember that equities have performed well over periods that spanned some truly trying and terrifying times—through war and peace, terrorism threats and espionage scandals, trade wars and trade pacts, loose and tight monetary policies, inflation and deflation, boom and bust years. Equities know how to scale a steep wall of worry.

Volatility of Equities

The biggest pushback on equities is that they may offer higher returns, but they also come with higher volatility.[1] Their prices swing wildly, changing a lot in short order.

My response to this gripe is, *So what?*

Volatility (short-term or temporary losses) is not the same thing as risk (long-term or permanent losses). Risk is serious, potentially fatal. Volatility is merely a short-term sacrifice you make for long-term gain. In fact, volatility can be an ally and opportunity. Here's how.

Let's indulge in a thought experiment. Imagine you are standing at the edge of a wilderness forest and you spot a brush fire in the distance. If you were a firefighter, you would be tempted to run to it and put the fire out. And that is exactly what firefighters did for many years. However, much to their astonishment, they saw that the fires not only came back, they also came back as bigger fires that lasted longer. Gradually, firefighters realized that small fires flame themselves out naturally; more importantly, because they remove brush, they serve to keep small fires from ballooning into a catastrophic wildfire. So, firefighters finally took the *contrarian* approach of ignoring frequent but short-lived fires.

In the same vein, volatility is the frequent but short-lived price fluctuations that cleanse the market and prevent the sharp plunge that could wreak major havoc. Think of volatility as the small brushfire that flames itself out, while risk is a catastrophic wildfire that rages on. And that is why I want you to embrace the idea that instead of doing harm, volatility can do some good.

---

1. In a literal sense, the term "volatility" means large oscillations in stock prices. It could describe a sudden upswing as well as a heart-stopping drop. But since it is the occurrence of precipitous drops that causes distress, that will be our focus here.

Volatility Can Be Your Friend Instead of Your Foe

Just as a brief illness builds your immune system, learn to think of volatility as a healthy interlude on the road to a stronger market eventually. If you have determined, with careful research, that the underlying business is resilient or building resilience, the setback in price will prove temporary. More than that, it now presents a terrific investment opportunity. Let me explain.

If the fundamentals of the business have not materially changed and its intrinsic value—what the business is worth—is not impaired, a sinking stock price is an opportunity to gain even higher returns at lower risk. This is how the opportunity to invest in American Express stock came about. In 2016, the company faced an unexpected loss of a large credit card contract with Costco. Fearing the large air pocket in earnings would bring price volatility, investors dumped the stock, and its price sank from the mid-80s to the mid-50s in a matter of months. My research told me that it was only a matter of time before the company replaced the lost revenue stream by signing up new clients. I had estimated the intrinsic value at about $100 under a base-case scenario, while my downside risk in a worst-case scenario was in the $50 range. When the stock fell to $55, the upside calculation rose to 82 percent [(100–55)/55], while the downside was a mere 9 percent [(55–50)/55].

Several things are worth pointing out here. Notice how the share-price volatility dramatically improves the upside/downside ratio, which is none other than the risk/reward ratio. The risk has been reduced because the share price has gone well below the base-case intrinsic value. (Remember, my assessment of this intrinsic value had not changed.) Note, too, that the greater the discount to intrinsic value, the larger the margin of safety and the greater the reward. As the price falls, there is a bigger reward *and* lower risk.

This is the crucial difference between volatility and risk: the former is temporal and short-lived, while the latter is structural and impairs the business permanently. Volatility is an opportunity because it only affects the stock price, while risk is a threat because it affects the intrinsic worth of the business.

"Investing is not a confidence game: it is about being more correct, not being more confident."

I do realize that making this shift in thinking can be difficult. Watching prices crash is excruciatingly painful. All of us would like to avoid pain if at all possible. But if you make hasty decisions in the face of volatility solely to avoid short-term pain at all cost, you risk leaving too much money on the table.

I learned this the hard way when I swapped two stocks because of currency volatility. At 5:35 a.m. on January 15, 2015, I was rudely awoken from my deep sleep when my trader called to tell me that the Swiss National Bank (SNB) had scrapped the currency's peg to the euro, causing the Swiss franc to shoot up by 30 percent intraday! As over 40 percent of Swiss exports go to the euro zone, firms across Switzerland warned of a hit to earnings. I feared that the SNB would continue to manipulate the currency, hurting the earnings of *exporter* stocks such as Nestle while helping *domestic* stocks such as Swisscom. So, I added to my Swisscom position and pared back my position in Nestle. That call proved shortsighted. Once the knee-jerk reaction subsided and the currency stabilized, the volatility evaporated, and over the next few years, Nestle stock performed much better than Swisscom. In hindsight, I should have looked past this noise and focused on the long-term earnings power and staying power of the respective businesses.

Volatility: Can Be an Opportunity Instead of a Threat

Volatility has another benefit for investors: it helps clarify the distinction between conviction and correctness and nudges them toward the latter. Conviction (aka confidence or hubris) will lead people to make a decision about a certain stock based on some sort of gut feeling—a whim, a hunch. But investing is not a confidence game; it is about being more correct, not being more confident.

"Volatility is an opportunity because it only affects the stock price, while risk is a threat because it impacts the intrinsic worth of the business."

Smart investors know they need to research the fundamental intrinsic value of equities they are considering; that research is what gives them correctness. And that's where volatility comes in. When a stock suddenly drops in price, everyone "feels" there is a big problem with the company. But if you have done your homework, in the form of painstaking research, and have verified that the underlying value is intact, suddenly the balance beam tips in your favor. Your research proves everyone else's assessment is wrong. Now you are looking at a bargain.

In summary, then, an undue focus on avoiding volatility because of short-term pain often proves counterproductive to your long-term gain. Yes, equities come with some short-term volatility. This does not mean you should turn your back on their long-term superior returns. Your investment focus should be on reducing risk, not reducing volatility.

There is another reason to invest in equities. It is your invitation to an awesome party—a seat at the table to celebrate innovation, the struggle to overcome challenges, and the ingenuity to solve problems. Silicon Valley, to use just one example, is built on equities, not bonds. From Google, which put the world's information at your fingertips, to Amazon, which brought a gigantic assortment of merchandise to your doorstep, business is predominantly funded by equity.

Risks of Equities: First in Line to Take the Bullets, Last in Line to Get the Goodies

Now let me walk you through the relevant risks in equities, because I do not want to sugarcoat what can go wrong. You may wish you did not know the downside, but ignorance or denial is not going to help you overcome your fear of risk—only knowledge and understanding will. So, let's first acknowledge and understand the risks of equities, before we turn to non-consensus investing to help mitigate them.

Equity shareholders—people who own stock in a company—occupy a "worst of all worlds" when it comes to claiming a piece of the financial pie. Their piece must come out of what is known as free cash flow. Free cash flows represent the surplus cash flows a company generates after:

1. Paying all expenses of the business
2. Reinvesting in the business to support ongoing operations or growth
3. Setting aside money to pay back long-term liabilities

After all those business needs have been dealt with, whatever is left is available to distribute to shareholders in the form of cash dividends or share buybacks. Take note of what this means: equity shareholders are last in line to get cash out of the business—*if* any is left over.

Consider the Hershey Company, makers of chocolate. First, Hershey has to pay the vendors who supply the raw materials such as cocoa, sugar, oil, flour, milk, and eggs. Then it has to pay employees in the factory who make the chocolates. The company incurs depreciation on its manufacturing facilities to account for wear and tear. It has to pay for marketing and advertising programs that remind us how much we love candy and entice us toward new delicacies. It incurs transportation, sales, and distribution costs to ensure its chocolates get onto the retailers' shelves, so we can buy it when we go grocery shopping. It has to pay taxes to the government, and incurs capital expenditures and other investments such as research and development to keep the business in good operating condition and to position it for growth. Finally, the company needs to set aside money to meet the working capital needs of the business and repay long-term liabilities such as pensions and debt.

Clearly, being last in line means there is a risk that equity shareholders may not get any or all of their investment back. And that's not all. Equity shareholders are also first in line to be called to put up additional money needed by the business or the bankers. If the business experiences a setback and makes a loss, or bankers need the company to put up more equity capital to reduce financial leverage ratios, it is the shareholders who provide that additional capital.

This is why I earlier described owning equities as "the worst of all worlds." Equity shareholders are first in line to absorb losses and last in line to be paid. Obviously, this is a very risky position to be in, so people who are willing to invest equity capital must be given a sufficiently significant incentive in the form of large upside potential to attract necessary investment dollars to fund the business. And therein lies the positive side of being an equity investor: you get a chance to make outsize returns if you choose well.

This is exactly what my investment approach strives to do. It tries to take advantage of both the volatility and the value-creation potential of equities and helps me choose well, to make higher returns without taking higher risk.

By the way, this explains why the United States is among the most successful and prosperous countries in the world: it is built on the shoulders of entrepreneurs and small-business owners who are none other than equity shareholders. The only difference is that they own private companies while our focus is on public equities, but the principle is the same. Equities enable you to become extraordinarily wealthy if you choose well. To realize how mammoth the rewards of equity investing have been for America, consider this: The United States dominates the global equity benchmarks when different countries are given a weight in proportion to the size of their respective equity markets. Measured this way, as of December, 2018, the United States has a weight of 54 percent, while forty-five other countries have a *combined* weight of 46 percent. America epitomizes the power and payoff of equities.

Investing in Bonds

No discussion of stocks is complete without discussing their opposite: bonds. Given that so much attention has been focused on the appeal of bonds—their stability and steady interest income— let me give you the other side of the coin: their risks.

Inflation Risk

Bonds may represent an optical illusion. I say illusion because many investors focus on nominal prices (which matter less) instead of real prices (which matter more). Here's an easy way to understand this important distinction. Imagine you get a 5 percent raise, and your boss tells you that you should be happy because your wages have gone up 5 percent. However, if your cost of living—inflation—also goes up 5 percent, your real purchasing power is unchanged. For you to come out ahead, wage growth must exceed inflation. In the same way, if you want to maintain, let alone improve, your standard of living, your savings (aka nest egg) must outpace inflation.

If your nest egg is invested in bonds, and if inflation grows faster than what bonds are pricing in (meaning that inflation expectations are implicitly embedded in the price), you risk losing your real purchasing power and thus eroding your standard of living.

Therefore, you *are* taking a risk in owning bonds, except the risk has a different name: inflation risk instead of volatility risk. By owning bonds, you have not reduced risk, you have only swapped it. Risk by any other name is still risk.

The reason people fear equities is that their volatility is easily visible. Investors are seduced and soothed by bonds because inflation is less visible. This is what makes inflation risk (and therefore the risk of owning bonds) even more sinister—you do not see it coming. It is a bit like putting on weight: it is not noticeable on any given day because it happens very gradually, almost imperceptibly. You may think bonds are not risky because they have gone up in price in the past few decades while inflation has fallen (inflation and bond prices are inversely correlated; when one goes up, the other falls). However, if the opposite happens and inflation rises, bond prices will fall.

And that's not all. In addition to inflation, other risks are embedded in bonds. One is credit risk. If the credit metrics (akin to credit scores) are low or deteriorate, then credit risk goes up, the bond becomes riskier, and a higher interest rate must be charged. Since the price of the bond is inversely correlated with interest rates, if rates go up, the price of the bond falls, and vice versa.

Credit Risk

Here's an easy way to think about this. A credit card loan is unsecured and therefore has a greater credit risk than a mortgage loan, which is secured (collateralized by a house). In 2018, credit cards charged around 16 percent interest on unpaid balances (tantamount to a loan); secured mortgages came with an interest rate of about 5 percent. The difference in rates (also referred to as credit spreads) for the two types of loans reflects the difference in credit risks.

Of late, in 2017 and 2018, amid rising budget deficits, relatively robust economic growth, and inflationary pressures building in the U.S. economy, the Federal Reserve Bank had started to raise rates. This caused longer-dated bond prices to fall, creating losses for investors who owned the bonds before the rate increases. Government Treasury bonds or bills often pay the lowest interest rates because they are viewed as the lowest-risk investment; in fact, they are frequently referred to as risk-free return. However, this can be a red herring. If the creditworthiness of the U.S. government is called into question, the price of U.S. Treasuries can fall. Then the presumed risk-free return morphs into return-free risk.

Right about now, many would protest that the creditworthiness of the U.S. government is absolutely sound. Not necessarily. Note that one of the three main rating agencies, S&P, downgraded the United States from AAA to AA+ in August 2011, for the first time in more than seventy years. Recent corporate tax cuts and other forms of spending or stimulus have resulted in a $1 trillion budget deficit in 2018. These deficits continue to add to our debt obligations, which now amount to about $15 trillion. If we add the $45 trillion estimated present value of future liabilities such as Medicare, Medicaid, and Social Security, the total liabilities amount to $60 trillion. This is a ginormous debt burden to shoulder, let alone repay, and it exposes bond investors to heightened credit risk.

Default Risk

You need to be aware of debt risk and its implications: the greater the indebtedness, the worse the creditworthiness. Bonds are not risk-free in and of themselves. If someone—a consumer, company, or country—borrows too much, then bonds can become very risky. In the aftermath of the 2008 financial crisis, the U.S. Federal Reserve Bank tried to resuscitate the economy by engaging in quantitative easing, forcing interest rates lower than they would otherwise be. This led many to go on a borrowing binge. Then, as interest rates go up and risk appetite goes down, many borrowers may have difficulty repaying their debt. This is called default risk.

These examples describe some of the different types of risks bond investors are exposed to. When these risks unfold, the dream of stability associated with bonds may turn into a nightmare of volatility. This is what happened in the UK, whose bonds (called gilts) show eerie parallels with U.S. Treasuries.

Throughout the first half of the twentieth century, the United Kingdom was the world's superpower, and the pound sterling was the reserve currency (meaning the one most people preferred to trade in, just as U.S. dollars are today). For sixty years, interest rates were range-bound between 2 and 5 percent; then, in just over twenty years, they shot up to 15 percent (see figure 3.2). The UK never regained its former glory. The trigger for this instability was the record fiscal deficits and liabilities that the government

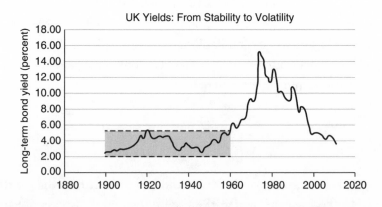

FIGURE 3.2 UK government bond yields. *Source*: ONS Bank of England.

simply could not meet. The United States is fast confronting such a predicament with its pay-as-you-go policies on important social programs such as Social Security and Medicare. These liabilities are not funded and therefore do not show up in the official debt statistics, but they are real, and coming due.

Liquidity Risk

Another risk that is ignored by many bond investors is liquidity risk. If you cannot sell something to generate cash, it is an illiquid asset, and it is worth far less than a liquid one. I learned about liquidity risk firsthand. My dad made an astute but illiquid investment in buying a seat on the Bombay Stock Exchange (India's equivalent of the New York Stock Exchange). That single investment of a few thousand rupees appreciated to several million rupees several decades later, but in the meantime, it brought little solace to our family because we could not liquidate it to pay for day-to-day expenses.

Most bonds, especially corporate bonds, are far less liquid than equities. If you need to sell them, you may not find a buyer right away, and you may have to offer significant discounts to their fair value to entice bids. With quantitative tightening underway (the Federal Reserve is tightening the money supply in the economy), the illiquidity risk of bonds may become more severe as easy money disappears. Investors got a taste of how big and unexpected this risk can be in December 2015, as signs of stress grew in credit markets. The $788 million Third Avenue Focused Credit Fund blocked clients from redeeming their money, as the alternative was a fire sale with a significant markdown on their realizable value.

Of course, not all bonds are illiquid, but most are. On one hand, U.S. Treasuries are very liquid, but on the other hand, say, sovereign or corporate debt issued by countries or companies in emerging markets can be fraught with illiquidity risk.

Valuation Risk

Another associated risk in bonds is that, because of their less liquid nature, they are harder to value accurately. Few transactions occur, so prices cannot be validated but are assumed to be what is quoted by two dealers. However, these quotes represent an indicative price, not a guarantee. You will only know their true value when you sell them. This takes us right back to the illiquidity risk. If you cannot liquidate, you cannot establish real value. Illiquidity risk exacerbates valuation risk.

Most bond managers underplay this risk, claiming they will hold the bond to maturity. But what if you need the cash before then? Consider the plight of people who had invested in a bond fund managed by GAM. When irregularities in the risk-management and record-keeping procedures were found, the portfolio manager was suspended, and bondholders were prevented from redeeming their $7.3 billion investment.

In November 2016, ratings agency Fitch warned that a mismatch within open-ended bond funds offering daily liquidity while holding less liquid securities had increased to a record high. Fitch analyst Manuel Arrive cautioned, "Drawdowns resulting from fire sales in illiquid markets increasingly put fund capital at risk, as bond carry returns have become insufficient to offset volatility."[2]

Capped Upside Risk

There's one more type of risk, and it is a big one: Bonds can expose you to large losses but cannot offer large gains (unless you buy them in the secondary market at a huge discount to their

---

2. Quoted in Gemma Acton, "This Is What Could Disrupt the Bond Market: Fitch," CNBC, October 17, 2016, https://uk.finance.yahoo.com/news/could -disrupt-bond-market-fitch-131800164.html.

face value). That is because a bond's upside is capped at par.[3] Let's say you hold a bond with a par value of $100. At any point before its maturation date, that same bond can fall in price to $70 or $60 or even lower. If you have to cash out when the price is down, you lose. But even if you hold the bond to maturity, you cannot get repaid a cent over $100. This asymmetry means that if you do not buy bonds at a significant discount to their par value in the first place, there is no upside, but there is always a chance of downside. Buying bonds at par can represent return-free risk instead of risk-free return. Why would you bother?

Conclusion: Stocks or Bonds?

In the short term, you may not perceive bonds as risky because inflation has fallen, not risen, or because companies whose bonds you own have not defaulted. But there are significant risks embedded in bonds, even if they are not immediately apparent, and you ignore them at your peril. When these risks manifest themselves in the future, bonds may prove to be an inferior investment choice. Bottom line: It is naive to think that bonds do not come with *any* risk. They just come with a *different* risk.

On the other hand, choosing equities is a bit like parenting—there are more ups and downs (volatility), but they are also worth it in the fullness of time (value creation). Think of owning stocks of quality businesses akin to raising a child whose best days are still ahead of her. Sure, she may act up now and then, but you do not give up on a child just because of a few stumbles. Children, like stocks, may not offer joy every day, and on some days, they may bring pure nuisance and annoyance, but you would not decide

---

3. No, not golf. A bond entails repayment of a fixed principal amount called its par value. The maximum amount you are repaid when the bond becomes due at maturity is this fixed, capped amount.

not to have kids because some bad comes with the overwhelming good. Just as helping your children grow can be among the best rewards of life, investing in stocks can be among the best investment decisions you can make for your family and those who entrust their investment decisions to you.

I am not saying bonds do not have a role in your investment portfolio, or that stocks should occupy prime position for everyone or at all times. Each investor should consider the suitability of allocating to stocks versus bonds based on their own circumstances. I wrote this chapter to call your attention to the risks of bonds and the rewards of stocks because popular perception is the opposite. A contrarian investor should always consider alternative perspectives, especially when they are being overlooked by others.

Top Takeaways

1. Investing is about winning by *choice*, not *chance*.
2. Volatility is not risk.
3. Bonds are neither risk free nor low risk. They come with *different* risk, not *no* risk. Bonds expose you to inflation, credit, default, illiquidity, and valuation risks. Stocks may depress your mood occasionally, but bonds may depress the returns of your nest egg permanently.
4. In *theory*, equity investors assume more risk; in *practice*, by owning high-quality businesses and not overpaying for them, you can dramatically lower that risk.
5. Non-consensus investing strives to take advantage of both—the *volatility* and *value creation* attributes of equities, to improve the odds of generating superior risk-adjusted returns.

4

To Stand Apart, You Must Stand Alone

In most things in life, if your answer is correct, you score points or win the prize. Not in investing, where not only must you be correct, but your correct call must also be non-consensus. That is, you must be right *and* prove others wrong. To achieve exceptional results, you must do something that makes you stand apart from the rest.

Standing apart means you opt for the lonely trade, not the crowded trade. Markets do not reward copycat research that leads to consensus conclusions that are already built into the current stock price. They reward differentiated research that results in the discovery of a new and correct fair price that restores market efficiency.

This chapter also describes how going passive is not a panacea and in fact may prove to be a problem. It includes an exposé on gimmicky marketing strategies masquerading as genuine investment strategies and how you can distinguish between the two.

Think Different, Be Right, and Prove Everyone Else Wrong

Active investing is a tough vocation in which losers can easily outnumber winners. In this chapter, I will address why winning (beating the market) is so uncommon and how you can improve the odds. The solution is simple but not straightforward, because not only are the rules of engagement *different*, they are *asymmetric*.

In most situations in life, a correct answer usually implies success. Not in investing, where even if you are correct, you may not make any money. To succeed, not only must you be right, you must prove everyone else wrong. That kind of asymmetry can be tough to understand, let alone accept, so let us take a deeper look.

**"In investing not only must you be right,
you must prove everyone else wrong."**

Research Analyst or Regurgitation Analyst?

Imagine you are an analyst researching a company. With painstaking precision, you estimate how much money that company is going to make in a given quarter or year. When the numbers come in and they match your expectations, you feel pleased with yourself—you were right. But if everyone else came to the same conclusion, you will not make any money because those expectations were already priced into the stock.

Let us say you are researching Clorox and conclude that it is a company that makes high-quality bleaching products and charges a premium over store brands. Few people would disagree, but neither would they learn anything new—and therein lies the problem. If research does not uncover anything original or differentiated, it is not value-added research but simply regurgitation, the investment equivalent of reinventing the wheel.

On the other hand, if I told you that Tim Hortons in Canada makes high-quality coffee using a more expensive blend of 100 percent Arabica beans, yet sells it at a low price that appeals to frugal Canadians, it would qualify as differentiated research if you did not already know this.[1]

---

1. This research proved doubly rewarding. Not only did I uncover a profitable investment opportunity with an "and" proposition of a quality product *and* value pricing, I also discovered Timbits, mini donuts sold at Tim Hortons that are decadently delicious.

Markets do not reward research that discovers or proves what others have already discovered or proven. All the midnight oil burnt; frequent flyer miles logged; and arduous meetings with management, suppliers, customers, and competitors to conduct fundamental research amounts to zilch if you do not uncover anything new or different. Active investors who are unskilled in their research efforts are rightly facing an existential wake-up call: differentiate or die. It is not a market conspiracy but a market objective to weed out such undifferentiated active investors who add transaction costs in the form of high fees for their efforts but generate no value.

The Asymmetry: Penalty Points

Being correct is hard enough in markets; being correct and non-consensus is harder still. But it gets worse. Just when you thought you understood the rules of the game, markets throw you another curveball. In your imaginary life as a research analyst, let us say you concluded that the company you were studying would make more money than the consensus estimated, and you valued it accordingly. If that does not happen, it is you who will be proven wrong, instead of the consensus, and you will end up losing money. This is because incorrect answers result in price distortion and market inefficiency, and to discourage such activity, markets impose penalties (losses) on such participants. This is what makes investing not simply *different* but *asymmetric*. You may not make any money for being correct if your correct views are consensus, but you will lose money for being incorrect. Figure 4.1 depicts this asymmetry:

Here are some examples:

1. Correct but consensus call: Disney. A great company, but most people agreed. Unsurprisingly, the stock has traded

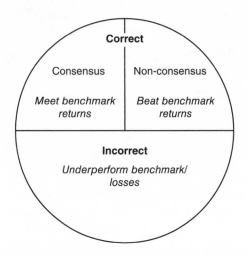

FIGURE 4.1 Asymmetric payoff of being correct or incorrect

in a narrow range between 2015 and 2018, proving that even when a call is correct, if it is also the consensus view, there is no significant mispricing to arbitrage or money to be made.

2. Correct non-consensus call: Ahold Delhaize. I regarded this food retailer with stores in Netherlands (Albert Heijn) and the United States (Stop & Shop, Giants, Hannaford, and Food Lion, as well as Peapod) as a well-managed company with good profit-growth potential. However, most investors were skeptical, valuing it as an ex-growth company with unstable earnings. When that consensus view was proven wrong, the stock doubled, from around €11 in 2012 to €22 in 2018.

3. Incorrect non-consensus call: Pitney Bowes. This was literally a money-minting business because it had near-exclusive rights from the U.S. Post Office to print digital stamps. As a quasi-monopolistic business, it made

eye-popping profits and returns on capital invested. Correct research would have led to the conclusion that these high returns would not last. Anyone who thought otherwise would lose money: the stock fell by 66 percent, from $28 in 2014 to under $7 in 2018. Sadly, I was among those investors. I made this mistake earlier in the mid-2000s when I bought Pitney Bowes's European counterpart, Neopost. Its lucrative profit margins and cheap valuation metrics (low PE and 5 percent dividend yield) seduced me into thinking I had found an investment bargain. But those numbers proved illusory when digital disruption came along: the profits collapsed and, along with them, the dividends that I had counted on. I lost money (penalty points for my incorrect albeit non-consensus call) and some sleep, but I also recognized that every mistake can be a learning opportunity.

What I learned was that to find a treasure instead of a trap, an investor must first be a *business* analyst and then a *financial* analyst. If you do not understand the business (and what can go right or wrong in it), your numbers will be wrong no matter how detailed your spreadsheet or precise your estimates (more on this in chapter 7, "False Positives and Negatives").

> **"To find a treasure instead of a trap, an investor must first be a business analyst and then a financial analyst."**

If undifferentiated or incorrect active investing is not the recipe for success, is investing passively the winning strategy? Not necessarily. The answer depends on what the *markets* want, not what *investors* want.

Markets Want and Reward
"Fair Price Discovery"

Just as nature has a singular and simple endgame—to reproduce—markets also have a singular and simple endgame—to uncover the fair price for an asset. Fair-price discovery is just another name for uncovering the correct intrinsic value of a business. It serves as a mechanism of exchange through which an asset can be converted into cash, or vice versa, at a price where neither side profits or loses.

> **"Fair price discovery is just another name for uncovering the correct intrinsic value of a business."**

The more it comprises stocks that are fairly valued, as opposed to under or overvalued, the more efficient the market becomes—and vice versa. In inefficient markets, the side that is correct and non-consensus will profit from the side that is not. This is the market's way of encouraging us to express and challenge different points of views: we will ultimately arrive at the fair price, which restores efficiency.

Markets do not play favorites. Anyone can take part and earn rewards if they give the market what it is trying to solve for: fair-price discovery. Markets do not care if they achieve efficiency on the shoulders of a man or a woman, bottom-up investors or top-down, growth or value, quant or fundamental, active or passive. All are means to an end. This explains why many distinctive styles of investing can coexist in a market, so long as they serve the market's purpose of discovering fair prices and restoring efficiency.

Markets Do Not Want
"Price Distortion"

On the flip side, markets severely penalize participants or strategies that perpetuate price distortion, because not only do they not create efficiency, they contribute to market inefficiency. The market does everything it can to sabotage such efforts, if not initially then eventually. Price-distorting participants and strategies find themselves exposed to a massive accumulation of penalty points (losses) smashing together like a massive car pileup on a crowded expressway.

I think of strategies that do not contribute to fair-price discovery (market efficiency) as "gimmicky" asset-gathering or "sham" strategies, while those that do are "genuine" investment strategies. I believe it is important for investors to invest in "genuine" investment strategies that are likely to contribute to market efficiency in the long run, and avoid slick asset gathering strategies that do not.

Asset-gatherers tend to package gimmicky investment concepts to pander to the desires of investors but are usually not in their best interests. "Sham" strategies often appear to generate good returns for a period of time, but winning a battle should not delude you into thinking you will win the war. Their superior performance could be short-lived. Let me show you how these strategies initially work but eventually fail.

Markets need diversity of participants and views to discover the fair price, and to encourage that, they will reward each participant just enough to keep them in the game. To the naïve observer, such occasional, sporadic successes will masquerade as a "proven" way to make money forever, but eventually they will prove to be illusory and temporary. This is because many "sham" strategies work as self-fulfilling prophecies. If enough people believe something— whether it is true or not—a stock or a market can go up, until reality sets in and investors realize that the emperor has no clothes. Here is a typical cycle: A particular stock (or cluster of stocks) will appear on screens as superficially attractive, so some active money will buy in, causing its price to rise. If some persistence develops, momentum will kick in, and quant strategies will put money to work. The stock will soon attract the trend-following crowd, who add their weight to the scale, thereby perpetuating the illusion that the "sham" strategy is working. If there is a seductive story line and some heady growth rates to boot, growth investors will jump in. If the story line is broad enough to package as a theme such as "a super-cycle in commodities" or "cloud computing" or "internet of things," thematic investors, smart beta, and the rest will join the party. By this time, the bandwagon of participants has turned the strategy into a money-spinning formula that everyone wants, no questions asked. The price of the stock keeps rising. Passive will throw even more money in at any price, because its job is not to ask but to invest.

Note that nobody in this gravy train questions whether their activity results in price *discovery* or price *distortion*. Is the stock trading above, at, or below its intrinsic value? Everyone blithely skips that part. Quant doesn't calculate it ("algorithms compute relative value not intrinsic value"), trend followers don't care about it ("don't let facts get in the way of a good momentum story"), growth investors rationalize it ("the high growth assumptions justify it"), and passive ignores it ("theirs not to question why, theirs but to do or die").

By this time, so many participants have piled onto the same stock or group of stocks or sector or theme that it becomes a very crowded trade, with few if any contrarian views to supply a counterbalance. Crowded trades are a form of complacency and herding, which are anathema to the market's goal of fair-price discovery. The market notices this lack of diversity and smacks it with a reality check. It starts testing the crowd with some mood swings or volatility, which quickly rattles the weakest players. Momentum starts to reverse course, and the trade begins to unravel. First the trend followers bail, then the quants exit, soon growth investors take cover, and finally passive investors, the last ones out, lose their shirt trying to get out of positions where there are few takers.

Do Not Fall for the Slogans, Scrutinize the Substance: Real or Fake?

You hear so many pitches backed by compelling data and catchy slogans, it can be confusing to figure out what is real and what is fake. Too many investment-management firms have found it more lucrative to become good asset *gatherers* than good asset *managers*. In their quest for gathering assets, as a marketing ploy, they spew out "gimmicky" strategies as "genuine" investment strategies.

You (or your investment adviser) must learn to recognize the difference. If the goal of the strategy is to offer, say, low volatility or autonomous driving exposure, this is all fine, so long as you understand what is happening. All these offerings in my view are asset-gathering strategies, not investment strategies. They are designed for what *investors* want, not what *markets* need. As an investor you might think, well, what is wrong with that—as long as my wants are met, why should I care about the market's needs? The problem is that what markets do not need, they will not reward. If your wants do not align with what markets want, your investment is unlikely to generate appropriate rewards; on the contrary, it could expose you to more costs and risks.

When you unpack the pitch, you will find that gimmicky asset gathering strategies spun as "genuine" investment strategies are usually a solution in search of a problem. Like a pill for an imaginary illness, you are paying for something you think you want but your body does not need.

Let us say you want a makeover or a massage. It makes you feel better, but your body does not need it and is not going to reward you for it. On the other hand, if you give the body what it really needs—exercise—it will reward you for it. Just as makeup does not make you beautiful and a massage does not make your body fit, buying into "sham" asset-gathering strategies offers a superficial, temporary, feel-good boost, not a real improvement to your financial health.

For example, between 2010 and 2013, it became easy to market "low-volatility" strategies because they were pitched as low risk and met investors' desire for stability, after the traumatic market crash of 2008–09. But what happened? Instead of low risk, all they ended up delivering was low returns. They underperformed the broader benchmarks because they owned stocks in the less volatile but more expensive consumer-staple sector (markets penalize overvaluation, or price distortion, with losses or underperformance).

Asset-gathering strategies take advantage of your fears and vulnerabilities and package them as investment strategies that meet your wants. Like a child's security blanket, it feels very soothing, but it is not in your best interest to hold onto. Wean yourself off it and teach yourself to deal with the ups and downs of a genuine investment strategy. "Genuine" investment strategies may lose the battle but tend to win the war while the opposite is generally true of "sham" strategies.

Passive Investing

Passive implies investing in a widely followed benchmark to secure exposure to a country, sector, theme, region, and/or factor. Typical examples are the S&P 500, the Nikkei 300, or the FTSE Global 100. These tend to be market-capitalization weighted (meaning that the composite companies tend to be large ones), and their constituents change relatively infrequently.

Because far less effort is required to construct and maintain a benchmark, it can be offered at lower cost compared to actively managed strategies, which entail a great deal of effort and higher costs. Passive indices tend to focus on factors such as size, free float, traded liquidity, broad representation, and the like. Given their desire for infrequent change, they tend *not* to account for fundamental attributes that fluctuate, such as dividend yields or debt-service ratios. Passive is more concerned about breadth and depth of market exposure and less focused on valuation or balance-sheet metrics.

The passive approach appeals to those who do not mind letting others decide which stocks to invest in and getting broad instead of curated market exposure, in exchange for low fees.

Passive = Prisoner's Dilemma

Passive investing is a prisoner's dilemma. A paradox in optimal decision-making, the prisoner's dilemma describes a circumstance in which two otherwise rational people act in their own self-interest and end up worse off than if they had cooperated.[2] Both sides start with a logical argument: if markets are efficient, it makes sense to access them at low cost. But passive investors operate by riding on the coattails of active investors, who perform the arduous task of assessing fair prices. If others follow the same logic, over time markets become inefficient, an inferior outcome for everyone.

In a market dominated by passive investors, investing becomes reflexive, driven by *flows* instead of *fundamentals*. Without the

---

2. Why is it called the prisoner's dilemma? The basic concept was first delineated in 1950 by two mathematicians. Soon after, a Princeton math professor named Albert Tucker created a famously memorable scenario that makes the idea crystal clear. The scenario goes like this: Barry and Frank, arrested for breaking into a warehouse, are being interrogated in separate rooms. Both are offered the same two choices: If you confess that the other guy did it, he'll go to jail and you can go free. But if both keep quiet, both get a reduced charge and considerably less jail time. Self-interest would have Barry and Frank taking the first choice—but then which one gets to go free? The only way *both* guys get the best deal (the least jail time) is if each one trusts the other to think cooperatively.

counterbalance of active, passive tends to become a victim of its own success: more money managed passively means more price distortion—which the market penalizes with losses. The Achilles heel of passive is that, like undifferentiated active, it does not further the market's endgame of fair-price discovery. In fact, passive gets a free ride off the work of correct, contrarian active investors. And just as markets do not reward reinventing the wheel (undifferentiated or incorrect active investing), they do not reward free riding (passive) either!

The Passive Bandwagon: Panacea or Problem?

Keep in mind that for the bulk of the assets under management, passive does not actually transact in the securities it owns, it simply marks them to market. In a period of increasing inflows, managers of passive funds bid up prices without regard to whether they are overpaying. If these funds were to face large redemptions and out-flows (which as of December 2018 has not happened in a decade), it would find few, if any, active buyers because the latter have dramat-ically shrunk in size. The larger the gap between the market price and the fair value, the greater the loss passive will have to incur to find a natural active buyer to take the other side of the trade.

In fact, this is exactly what happened in the late 1990s, when clients berated their active managers for their underper-formance against the Nasdaq for several years in a row. As the years rolled by and active managers continued to underperform in a strong up market, investors did what they often do—top ticked a trend (bought at the highs). In 1999–2000, many cli-ents withdrew money from their active managers and plowed it into passive by investing in vehicles such as the QQQs (an ETF which mimicked the movements of the Nasdaq 100), which had doubled. That decision came back to bite when the mar-ket momentum brutally reversed and popular indices such as

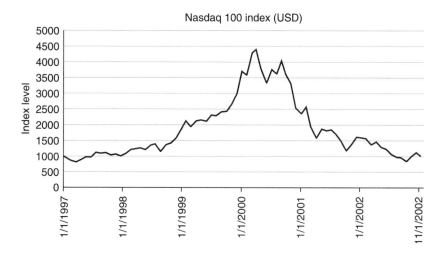

FIGURE 4.2 Index Performance: Nasdaq 100, 1/1/1997–11/1/2002

the Nasdaq 100 fell from a peak of 4,500 in March 2000 to a trough of below 1,000 in late 2002, causing a whopping loss of 78 percent; see figure 4.2.

To put this arithmetic in dollars and cents, if you had put a million dollars in the QQQ ETF in early 2000, three years later you would have lost $780,000, and your nest egg would have shrunk to $220,000. To add insult to injury, in the aftermath of the tech wreck, most active managers handsomely beat the benchmarks and regained the upper hand in both performance and inflows. For instance, if you had invested that same money in U.S. large-cap-blend actively managed strategies,[3] you would be down only

---

3. See Hartford Funds, "The Cyclical Nature of Active and Passive Investing," https://www.hartfordfunds.com/dam/en/docs/pub/whitepapers/WP287.pdf. Skeptics might refute this example as comparing two different benchmarks. I disagree. Active managers deliberately avoided expensive tech stocks that dominated the Nasdaq 100 Index and actively invested in other sectors of the U.S. market within their broader U.S. large-cap-blend mandates; so the comparisons and conclusions are valid from that standpoint.

about 27.2 percent, and your portfolio would be worth $728,000. That is a difference of half a million dollars!

What the Wise Do in the Beginning, Fools Do in the End

It should be clear by now that passive can only deliver on its promise of positive returns at low cost when active predominates and is able to do its job of calibrating fair prices. Of late, however, the opposite is happening—passive is dominating. With that dominance comes the risk of owning overvalued stocks and contributing to price distortion and market inefficiency. I suspect a déjà vu of the Nasdaq 2000–2002 crash in milder form is in the cards. Investors are confusing early success with lasting success, and coincidental success with inevitable success.

The early bird in passive caught the fish, but that attracted too many birds all going after a finite number of fish. These latecomers are unlikely to repeat that early success. When too much money chases too few goods, it bids prices up simply through technical demand/supply imbalances, not fundamental factors. When markets experience an extended or pronounced correction, investors with lemming-like blind faith in passive could be exposed to three painful lessons:

1. Markets do not reward free riding.
2. Markets penalize price distortion.
3. Lemmings tend to reach their demise instead of their destination.

Active: Pronouncement of Dead Man Walking Is Dead Wrong

It is a perennial debate: Should we take the safe route and stick with investments that mirror the stock market itself, relying on standard indexes like the S&P 500? Or do we attempt to do better than the market, using fundamental research to help us find mispriced stocks? The first approach is called passive; the second, active. I am an active manager—something that is not in vogue of late.

Prevailing wisdom would have you believe that active investing has an inferior track record and poor reputation; it is simply not possible, goes the claim, to beat the market. I beg to differ. Active investing, practiced correctly, can deliver outperformance. Not only can it do so, but it has already done so.

A paper published in the *Financial Analysts Journal* in 2017 concludes that there is *no* evidence of underperformance among a group of funds with a high active share[4] (those whose holdings differ substantially from their benchmark). Indeed, those who are also patient (with holding durations of more than two years) have outperformed, on average, by more than 2 percent per year. Earlier studies showed similar results.[5]

It is clear that the headline drumbeat of underperformance by active is misleading as the devil is in the details. A closer

---

4. Active share is a measure of the percentage of stock holdings in a manager's portfolio that differ from the benchmark index. Studies have shown it is a key predictor of a manager's performance potential. The larger that share, the greater the differentiation. Below 60 percent is considered no differentiation, or "closet indexers"; between 60 and 80 percent is considered mild differentiation, or "pseudo" active; and over 80 percent is viewed as very different from the benchmark, or "truly" active. Throughout my investment career, the active share of portfolios I managed has typically exceeded 80 percent, which is why I view myself as a truly active manager and non-consensus investing as a truly actively managed investment approach.

5. Martijn Cremers, "Active Share and the Three Pillars of Active Management: Skill, Conviction and Opportunity," *Financial Analysts Journal* 73, no. 2 (2017): 61–79; Martijn Cremers and Ankur Pareek, "Patient Capital Outperformance: The Investment Skill of High Active Share Managers Who Trade Infrequently," *Journal of Financial Economics* 122 (2016): 288–306; and Antti Petajisto, "Active Share and Mutual Fund Performance," *Financial Analysts Journal* 69, no. 4 (2013): 73–93.

examination of these studies reveals that the biggest underperformers were those who *claimed* to be managing actively but were not. The underperformers fell into two categories: *closet indexers* (benchmark huggers who called themselves active but were not) and *pseudo* active (those with a low active share between 60 and 80 percent who pretended to be active but were not). It was these two types of *faux* active practitioners who diluted the overall performance record of all active managers. The same studies showed that *truly* active managers (those with an active share over 80) beat their peers and passive by 2.41 percent per annum on a gross basis. (Obviously, fees would reduce this, but it is uncommon for the fees of an active manager to exceed say 1 percent, so even after deducting such a fee, the net performance would exceed the relevant benchmark's returns.) When you look underneath the covers, there is a very compelling difference and argument in favor of *truly* active and against *pseudo* or *closet* active, not all active.

The results found by these studies fit the ideas in this chapter. Truly active managers contribute to fair-price discovery and deserve to get rewarded by markets with excess returns—and they have been. Those who did not manage actively (but marketed themselves as if they were), as well as those who managed naïvely with little differentiation or skill, were destined to fail—and did.

Markets Do Not Care for Your Wants, They Care for Their Needs

Remember that markets rule and referee, while investors merely express their views (with their money). If you indulge in your wants at the expense of the market's, you are on the losing side and get penalized. If you serve the market's needs, you are on the winning side and get rewarded. The smart move is to align yourself with what the market needs—an investment approach that leads to fair-price discovery and reduces price distortions. This is exactly what non-consensus investing strives to do, and in performing this double duty, it gets a shot at being doubly rewarded with above average returns. I call these returns "upset victories" in investing. They are the topic of the next chapter.

Top Takeaways

1. Investing is unlike any other field: not only are the rules of engagement *different*, they are *asymmetric*. If your views are consensus, you may not score any points for being correct, but you will incur penalty points for being incorrect.
2. Markets reward differentiated research that not only proves you are right but also proves the consensus wrong.
3. Markets reward efforts that lead to fair-price discovery and penalize those that lead to price distortion. Markets do not reward free riding nor price affirmation, which is the investment equivalent of reinventing the wheel.
4. Strategies that do not contribute to fair-price discovery are sham strategies, not investment strategies. Asset-gathering strategies serve the false wants of investors, not the true needs of markets. Markets do not reward what they do not need.
5. Non-consensus investing aligns itself with what the market wants and incentivizes: diversity of views contributing to fair-price discovery and less price distortion. For performing this double duty, non-consensus investing gets a shot at being doubly rewarded.
6. Passive is a prisoner's dilemma. When everyone goes for it, all are worse off, not better off.

7. Studies show that truly active managers with a high active share have outperformed their peers and passive indices, even after fees and expenses. Non-consensus investing is a truly active way of investing, designed to beat a benchmark, not match it.

5

Score Upset Victories

Investing is a pari-mutuel sport in which you are betting against other people, because every share you buy is being sold to you by someone else. If you place the same bet on that share as everyone else, you may not win money even if you backed the right outcome because the price you must pay to engage in that trade already reflects the prevailing odds. Only the bookie makes money, not the bettor.

In investing, it is not enough to be correct. Your correct call must also be unexpected and not built into the prevailing stock price. Correct, non-consensus calls yield upset victories which make you money. In this chapter, I provide case studies of real-life upset victories to show you the process in action.

Getting the Most Bang for Your Research Buck

Many have called investing "the loser's game" because the odds of being incorrect are high, and so are the penalties. Losses can pile up fast. This raises the question, why bother if it's so hard? Because if you're right, you can make a lot of money.

The higher the barriers to success, the greater the payoff for those who cross them and succeed. It's rather like a lottery whose prize money keeps getting larger: the one who eventually wins, wins big. The more money thrown into the investment pot by those following the crowd (the fair-price *distorters*), the more money there is for the few contrarians (the fair-price *discoverers*) to win. This explains why the payoffs for being correct *and* contrarian can be so lucrative: not only is the pie growing larger, but there are fewer people who can claim a piece.

In the previous chapter, I outlined the essence of non-consensus investing: it is not enough to be correct, you must also prove the consensus wrong. When you do, you will have scored an upset victory. Anyone who follows a sport or an election knows how exciting that can be. For investors, upset victories are not only the most thrilling to watch, they are also the most lucrative, as they yield the most bang for one's research buck.

> **"Upset victories are not only the most thrilling to watch, they are also the most lucrative. Asymmetric risk-reward tips the scales in favor of lonely trades and against crowded trades."**

Before I go further, a word of caution is in order. For convenience, throughout this chapter (and the book), I use sports and gambling analogies, with words such as "lotteries," "bets," and "prize money," to explain certain concepts. However, I want to make it clear that investing is not about gambling or betting or playing games, but about conducting serious, differentiated research which uncovers information that proves both correct and non-consensus.

As the Odds Change, the Payoffs Change

Investing is a pari-mutuel endeavor, where you are betting against other people, since every share you buy is being sold to you by someone else. Unlike gambling, where the odds of winning and losing are preset by the casino and no gambler's bets can alter those predetermined odds, in investing, each investor's decision alters the preexisting odds. And as the odds change, the payoffs change. Of course, investing is not a zero-sum game, but one in which everyone can win something. However, those who score upset victories win way more, and that makes all the difference, because the goal of an active investor is to beat the market, not just match it.

Think about a football match. Let us say you bet that Team A is going to win because that's what everyone says. Sure enough, Team A wins. This is great—you were correct! What is the prize for being correct? Zero. Because to place the bet you had to pay the bookie an amount that reflected those high odds. Your expectation matched everyone else's and was baked into the cost of placing the bet.

Now, what if you thought Team B was stronger, even though few agreed, and bet against the odds? And what if Team B pulled off a big upset? You can jump for joy because you just made a lot of money. Replace "team" with "stock" and "win" with "business success" and you will see how the pari-mutuel analogy applies to investing.

Suppose that you, like everybody else, thought ABC was a great company and would make $10 in earnings and grow at 10 percent a year for several years. Now let us say that happens. ABC reports $10 in earnings and guides to a future increase of 10 percent as part of a three-year strategic plan. Hey, you were right! What is the prize for being right? Nothing. You go home empty-handed because:

1. To place the bet, you had to pay the seller an amount that reflected those high odds. That is, to buy the stock, you had to pay the high price the stock market demanded.
2. Your view was also the consensus view, and the odds (the stock price) already reflected that. There is no prize for such a copycat call. The stock will not go up when it reports the earnings that everyone expected. So *your view is right, but nobody gets proven wrong.*
3. Your victory proves pyrrhic, earning you bragging rights (you can make noise) but not bounty rights (you did not make money). The cost to place the bet is so high that even if your research is correct, you do not win much money.

To make matters worse, the money invested in ABC stock ties up investment dollars that could have been deployed more profitably elsewhere—an opportunity cost, not an opportunity.

Now let us say you bought XYZ stock, even though the consensus had a bleak view of its earnings prospects. Your independent, fundamental research told you that XYZ's earnings would not only not decline but in fact would increase for many years into the future. If you are right, you will earn a lot of money for being both correct and contrarian. Here is why:

1. To place the bet, you had to pay the seller an amount that reflected those low odds. Because the consensus had underestimated its real value, the market set a low price. You picked it up at a large discount.
2. Your view was contrarian. Not only were you right, but you simultaneously proved others wrong, allowing you to pocket the difference between the two views priced into the stock.
3. You scored an upset victory. As XYZ's stock price appreciates to reflect its higher intrinsic value, the money you invested generates a good profit. This is none other than the market rewarding you for your act of restoring efficiency: you helped an undervalued security reach its fair value.

In summary, to make profitable investments, you must disagree with the consensus view on the underlying quality of a business and the value spread implied in its stock price. If you own what everyone else does (crowded trades), the odds of success are not only priced in but most likely *overpriced* in. This is generally a recipe for losing money, not making it. However, if on a systematic basis you conclude that the stock price is not pricing in those odds correctly, and you take the other side of the trade, you can make a lot of money.

Crowded Versus Lonely Trades: Asymmetric Risk Reward Potential

The past decade has been an especially difficult period for contrarian investors like me, as the opposite approach—momentum investing—seems to have worked best in beating the market. When a style is working, everyone latches onto it and few dare to question it. Before you know it, a *consensus* trade becomes a *crowded* one. Crowded trades are also referred to as bubbles, manias, or frenzies. (I sometimes call them obsessions or fixations.) Of late, betting on the momentum factor has become a very crowded trade. Momentum and crowded trades are anathema to my investment approach.

Here are a few examples of crowded trades I avoided. I have mentioned this before but it bears repeating: I use my own experiences as examples to best illustrate how I practice what I preach and because concrete anecdotes help you to better understand the real-world application of theoretical concepts. However, keep in mind that all investment theses have a finite shelf life and my views presented here may not be current nor complete nor should their accuracy or performance be extrapolated into the future.

Health-Care Boom, 1994–1999

I avoided owning health-care stocks, even though most industry observers and market participants predicted enormous growth for the sector. On the face of it, the thesis appeared to be on solid ground: baby boomers in the United States were aging, and disease incidence was rising elsewhere. Surely drug companies would

FIGURE 5.1 Share price performance: Pfizer, 1/31/1994–12/31/2018

do well. Who could argue with that? Well, the facts caught up with the fiction. Even though volumes went up as demand grew, drug prices collapsed as patented drugs went generic and new drug pipelines disappointed. Pfizer's stock exemplified this trajectory (figure 5.1). It rose tenfold from around $4 in 1994 to $45 in 1999. A decade later, the boom had turned into a bust, and the stock plummeted to $13. It has since recovered to $45 but that is a pyrrhic victory and a large opportunity cost for anyone who held the stock for twenty years (1999 to 2018); they experienced no returns but a lot of risk (and aggravation). Over that same time frame, the S&P 500 Index has roughly doubled in price.

TMT (Tech, Media, and Telecom) Mania, 1996–2000

I tried to make sense of the investment case offered up by Wall Street, but the arguments were so specious, I could not believe anybody would make them, let alone buy them. Proponents of these crowded trades were like magicians trying to redirect our attention to red herrings:

- If the companies did not generate *free cash flows*, we were told to look at *earnings*.
- If they did not make any *earnings*, we were redirected to *revenues*; earnings would come later.
- If there wasn't much in the way of *revenues*, we were told to look at *eyeballs*; it was all about user engagement.
- If there weren't enough *eyeballs*, we were redirected to the founder's *vision*; the eyeballs would follow.

The arguments boiled down to buying *concepts* instead of *companies*. It felt surreal because it was. Eventually investors began to realize that the emperor had no clothes, and the Nasdaq (which was heavily weighted in TMT stocks) crashed, losing 78 percent of its peak value. What took five years to make took less than three years to lose (most of it anyway). What is worse, many of the concept stocks in the Nasdaq went out of business, causing permanent losses. In investing, it is not what you *make* but what you *keep* that matters. Your checks will bounce if you write them based on what your portfolio used to be valued at its peak, but is no longer worth that high-water mark.

Real Estate and Banking Bubble, 2003–2007

I had witnessed many real estate and banking bubbles in countries as pristine as Switzerland and as dynamic as Hong Kong in the 1980s and '90s. Because of that experience, I was certain I was seeing signs of a financial bubble in America. Incidentally, this speaks to the power of global research: when you cover fifty countries around the world, as I do, you see fifty times as much. So even when pundits such as Alan Greenspan and Ben Bernanke debunked the notion of a nationwide housing crisis, I took the opposite path, selling many of my financial stocks in 2006. Two years later, the financial crisis of 2008 sent markets into unprecedented turmoil. Many financial institutions went under or had to be rescued at taxpayer expense. As companies such as Bear Stearns, Lehman Brothers, Fannie Mae, and Countrywide Mortgages either went bankrupt or were acquired at throwaway prices, investors holding those shares lost 90 or even 100 percent.

The Obsession with Gold, 2009–2012

On the heels of the 2008 financial crisis, investors scurried away from equities into the perceived safe haven of gold. The price shot up from around $900 to $1,800 between 2009 and 2012, only to collapse to about $1,200 in 2018. I avoided the crowded trade of buying gold and instead bought equities. The contrarian call proved its mettle as a popular gold sector ETF increased in value by only 33 percent, while the S&P 500 went up about 300 percent—a ninefold difference in performance.

The Super-Cycle in Commodities, 2003–2007

Commodity prices, from oil to copper, shot up as unexpected demand from China caused supply shortages. When supply came on stream (as it inevitably does) and demand cooled off, prices fell, causing commodity stocks to collapse. High flyers like OGX (an oil and gas company) went bankrupt. Crowded bets on Noble Group (a commodities trading company) in Singapore got eviscerated (figure 5.2). The stock had soared from S$2 to S$18 from 2003 through 2008; in 2018, it was trading below a buck. I had avoided owning these soaring stocks. Sure, I missed out on their

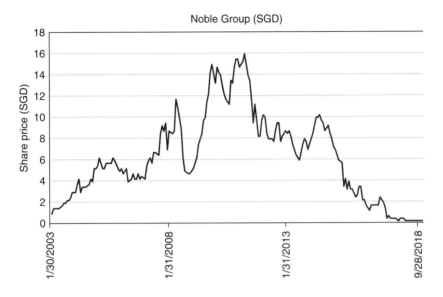

FIGURE 5.2 Share price performance: Noble Group, 1/30/2003–12/31/2018

gains during the good times, but I also spared myself from the crushing losses that ensued.

They say you can tell the experts are wrong when they unanimously agree on something. In all the preceding examples, the crowds believed their investment theses to be foolproof bets resting on solid ground—until they were not. In my experience, at best, crowded trades won't make you much money, but at worst you could end up losing a lot of it (if not initially then eventually). On the other hand, at its best, the lonely trade can often help you score big, but if it doesn't work out, you won't lose much money either. This asymmetric risk/reward tips the scales in favor of lonely trades and against crowded trades. This is where correct fundamental research comes into the picture. If the correct research is also non-consensus, you have all the makings of an upset victory.

Non-Consensus Right = Might

With apologies to Archimedes, I believe that non-consensus invest-ing is the small but mighty lever that can upend the prevailing wisdom of the investment world and potentially generate outsize payoffs. The following example will illustrate.

Between 2012 and 2018, my unconventional view of undervalu-ation in what I called "enterprise staple" stocks such as Microsoft versus overvaluation of "consumer staple" stocks such as Procter & Gamble (P&G) allowed me to score an upset victory. The pre-vailing view was that consumer staples were franchises with stable and recurring revenues and should therefore trade at a rich pre-mium for such attractive attributes. But I realized that software had also become a staple, in the corporate if not consumer world, but the stock market did not see enterprise software companies such as Microsoft through that lens. This variant view enabled me to own it well before the construct became mainstream. Figure 5.3 shows the enormous difference in absolute and relative returns

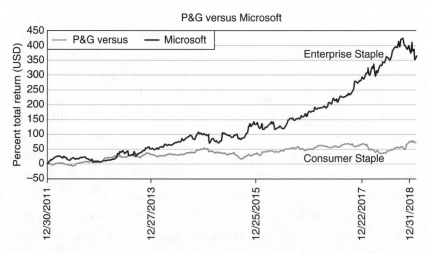

FIGURE 5.3 Relative performance: P&G versus Microsoft, 12/30/2011–12/31 /2018

that a correct, non-consensus call can produce. That said, under normal market conditions, it is highly exceptional to identify such large mismatches in one's view versus what's priced in by the consensus. Microsoft is among the handful of rare stocks where I have experienced the kind of outsized annualized gains shown here. So don't count on hitting it out of the ballpark too often. Most (annualized) investment payoffs are about hitting singles or doubles and, more importantly, not getting struck out.

The bottom line is that betting on the underdog can improve the odds of making a lot of money, while betting on everyone's favorite increases the odds of losing it. (A prerequisite is that your research on the underdog must be correct.) The point of sharing these real-life examples was not to cherry-pick my best ideas but to demonstrate how it is possible to make a lot of money with less risk if you can uncover with *foresight* what the rest of the world sees in *hindsight*. I cover how to do such differentiated research in chapter 8, "Ditch the Database, Embrace the Search Engine."

In this chapter we learned how it is possible to secure large returns via upset victories if our answers (aka research) are both correct and non-consensus. The next chapter will focus on the flip side: why it is important to avoid incorrect answers. They detract from efficient price discovery, so markets penalize them with losses. The more incorrect they are, the greater the contribution to market distortion and the greater the losses. Losses hurt overall returns more than gains help. Read ahead to understand how and why.

Top Takeaways

1. Investing is a pari-mutuel endeavor in which people bet against other people and, in the process, dynamically alter the odds and the payoffs.

2. Investing is not a zero-sum game; everyone can win something. But those who score upset victories win way more, and that makes all the difference, because an active investor's goal is to do *better* than the benchmark, not just match it.

3. If you place the same bet as everyone else, you may not win money even if you backed the right outcome, because the price you must pay to engage in that trade already reflects the prevailing odds. Only the bookie makes money, not the bettor. That is, the consensus view is already priced into the stock.

4. If you have a consensus view and own what everyone else does, chances are that the odds of success are not only priced in but *overpriced* in, which is symptomatic of a crowded trade. This is generally a recipe for losing money, not making it.

5. Investing is about getting bounty rights (making money), not bragging rights (making noise), by scoring upset victories. If your correct views are consensus, you end up with pyrrhic victories that boost your ego but not your nest egg.

6

Do No Harm

In investing, you win more by losing less. Since you always lose money from a higher number but make money on a lower number, avoiding losers and losses is more important than picking winners.

This chapter explains why you should pay at least as much attention, if not more, to risk management (how much you will lose) instead of just thinking about return management (how much you will make).

Repackaging risk, or swapping one kind of risk for another, is not reducing risk. Failure to think about the various types of risks is the bigger challenge, not failure to find.

Avoiding Losers Is More Important Than Picking Winners

Most people believe that if you have the moxie and the mind-set to spot the hot dot or the hot stock, you are on your road to riches. This notion—that successful investing boils down to picking the winners—is so widely accepted and so rarely questioned that it has become the sine qua non of how the "smart" money invests in markets.

It sounds like a great concept—if only it were true!

Let us say you have $100 and make a bad investment in a risky stock that loses you 50 percent. You now have only $50. You need your $50 to double (go up by 100 percent) simply to break even. It is tough to find investments with 100 percent upside, let alone face the added insult that even after you miraculously find such a great investment opportunity, you end up only where you started! On the other hand, let us say you lose only 20 percent on your

$100 investment, so your principal declines to $80. Now when you find that 100 percent upside investment opportunity, your $80 becomes $160, giving you 60 percent capital appreciation.

You always lose money from a higher number but gain money from a lower number, which is why incurring heavy losses proves more damaging than missing some gains. Investors are better off researching potential for failure and avoiding losers than chasing success stories and picking the winners. The main reason to invest in equities is to compound capital, and losing money is the albatross. See table 6.1 for gains you must make to cover losses you incur.

> **"You always lose money from a higher number
> but gain money from a lower number."**

To demonstrate how this plays out over a full market cycle (straddling both bull and bear markets), table 6.1 shows a hypothetical performance history over an arbitrary ten-year market cycle which includes both bull and bear markets, from say 2001 to 2010. I want to underscore, this table should be viewed as an illustrative, arithmetical example of how an actively managed portfolio that pays attention to risk (hereafter referred to as "hypothetical risk-aware active portfolio" or "HRAAP") ultimately results in higher returns. This harkens back to the point I made in chapter 2, "'And' Not 'Or,'" on the paradox of investing where reducing risk is critical to enhancing returns. It is a counterintuitive concept, so it is best to see how this plays out via a case study.

Now, as we shall see later in this chapter, risk comes in many forms and can be described or defined in many ways, but for purposes of this thought experiment, I want you to think of risk as losing money and returns as making money. Also, assume that the performance numbers shown for this hypothetical risk-aware active portfolio are net of all fees and expenses. Furthermore, note that the benchmark's performance is shown for comparison purposes as one cannot actually invest in it. Last but not least, you should

Table 6.1

Illustrative performance trajectory of a hypothetical risk-aware active strategy over an arbitrary ten-year period from 2001 to 2010

| Year | Performance in % | | Performance in $ | |
	Hypothetical Risk-Aware Active Portfolio (HRAAP)	Hypothetical Benchmark	Growth of $100 (HRAAP)	Growth of $100 (Benchmark)
2001	–8.9%	–17.5%	$91	$83
2002	–5.2%	–15.9%	$86	$69
2003	33.3%	38.6%	$115	$96
2004	16.7%	20.2%	$134	$116
2005	12.9%	13.5%	$152	$131
2006	32.9%	26.3%	$202	$166
2007	5.7%	11.2%	$213	$184
2008	–23.4%	–45.8%	$163	$100
2009	23.5%	25.0%	$202	$125
2010	7.1%	18.8%	$216	$148
CAGR	8.01%	4.01%		
Annualized outperformance	4.0%			

Note: Past performance does not guarantee future results

not think of this table as some sort of proof statement that all risk-aware active portfolios will outperform a benchmark (there are no such guaranteed outcomes in the world of investing). It is merely to illustrate the mathematics of losses and gains and showcase the importance of risk management versus return management.

The second and third columns in Table 6.1 show the *percentage* gain or loss of the hypothetical risk-aware active portfolio and the benchmark, respectively. The fourth and fifth columns capture the moves in *absolute* dollar terms (often referred to as "growth of

$100"). The key is to observe how the *relative percentage* performance versus *absolute dollar* performance manifests itself, year by year and then cumulatively.

Notice how in 2001 and 2002, by losing far less than the benchmark, the hypothetical risk-aware active portfolio secured a large lead, only correcting to $86 while the benchmark plunged to $69. Then in 2003, despite underperforming by over 5 percent when markets rallied 39 percent, the HRAAP was worth $115 (column 4), delivering 15 percent capital appreciation while the benchmark was still not breaking even at $96 (column 5). This illustrates how losing less allows you to win more and why you should pay at least equal attention to risk management—if not more.

This is how the paradox plays out and why *reducing risk helps to enhance returns*, instead of undermining them. You may be familiar with the old adage, a dollar saved is indeed a dollar earned. Furthermore, note that even at the peak of the bull market in 2007, the HRAAP was ahead at $213 versus the benchmark's $184. This illustrates that *attention to risk management does not come at the expense of return management.* Most investors pay more attention to returns than risk, while my non-consensus investment approach argues for the opposite: pay more attention to risks than returns. Note how by prioritizing risks (losing less) over returns (making more), the hypothetical risk-aware active portfolio performed double duty by delivering *both*: lower risks (lower capital losses in bear markets) *and* higher returns (more capital gains over the full market cycle). This is how the counter-intuitive principles underpinning non-consensus investing enable it to deliver the "and" proposition instead of settling for "or," as described in chapter 2.

Another point to note is that in 2008, when the markets crashed 46 percent, the hypothetical risk-aware active portfolio declined far less that year, and experienced 65 percent cumulative capital appreciation, compounding to $163 while the benchmark just broke even at $100. This is the power of active management: *if you deviate a lot from the benchmark, you can also experience returns that are quite different from it.* Of course, different performance cuts both ways—underperformance or outperformance. A sound investment process can help to improve the odds of the latter versus the former.

Frequency Versus Severity

Another interesting thing to call out in the performance table above is that even though the hypothetical risk-aware active portfolio outperformed in only four out of the ten years (frequency), three out of those four years were mega bear markets (severity). The significant point is this: Losing less during those big market corrections enabled the HRAAP to grow from a higher base in the next upcycle and develop a large lead over the benchmark, in both relative and absolute terms. Cumulatively, the annualized 4 percent outperformance over ten years means a million-dollar invested in the HRAAP would have appreciated to $2.16 million, compared to $1.48 million if invested passively in an index fund that mirrors the benchmark.

This is why I recommend adopting an unconventional approach of considering the risks of an investment idea first and returns thereafter: it saves you both money *and* effort. Here is how. Avoiding or abating the risk of large losses upfront means you save your hard-earned money *and* you do not need to hit a lot of home runs. Because the losses are small, you can easily offset them by hitting good singles. Not only is that easier, it also keeps you out of trouble: you don't have to take unnecessary risks.

Indeed, the deeper the hole gunslingers dig themselves into, the more desperately they need to chase large moneymaking ideas, which often means taking on more risk, trapping them in a vicious cycle.[1] As we all know, large moneymaking ideas are hard to come by. By not needing large upside to begin with, you have improved the odds of finding such winners. Ergo, weeding out risk upfront saves you both money *and* effort.

From 2012 through 2014, by *not* owning risky or richly valued oil stocks, I avoided the blowups that crippled that sector in 2014–2016, when oil prices crashed. So, despite not owning high-flying social media and internet-related stocks, my performance did not suffer. This is because my portfolios did not need hefty returns from the winners (social media and internet-related stocks) to offset large losses as I had avoided the big losers (risky oil stocks) in the first place.

Out of Sight, Out of Mind:
Exposure Versus Experience

Ironically, despite its importance, few investors proactively pay attention to risk management. Those who do often only pay lip service. Worst of all, there are many who consciously take on more risk instead of reducing it. Why is this? Why do so many work against their best interest?

They do so because risk is invisible and intangible—a silent killer, rather like high blood pressure. We all know that high blood pressure works in stealth mode inside the body with few visible external signs. But left unattended, it eventually reveals itself in spectacular form as a massive heart attack or stroke. The terrible twist is that such a tragedy can usually be avoided, as there are ample ways to manage the disease with medications and lifestyle changes. Likewise, while investment risk is

---

1. In the sometimes colorful language of investing, a gunslinger is a money manager who is willing to take big risks to increase the potential return on investments—perhaps not quite as romantic as Wyatt Earp, but just as dangerous.

not always visible, we can proactively identify and manage it to avoid its worst effects.

Sticking with the analogy, we know that not only can high blood pressure be genetically inherited, it can also be self-inflicted via poor lifestyle choices. In the same way, not only is risk inherent in business and investing, it can also be self-inflicted by poor financial and strategic choices. The positive aspect to both chronic conditions is that we can overcome them with a sound regimen.

It is tempting to think that you can assess risk with a simple checklist. Unfortunately, it's not that easy. For one thing, risk comes in many forms: financial-leverage risk, corporate-governance risk, currency-devaluation risk, regulatory risks, low-barriers-to-entry risk, and on and on. For another, risk is often hidden from plain sight or comes in a disguise, not revealing its true character or intensity until it is too late.

But where to look? It's obviously easier to look for risks that have materialized in the past, so you can benefit from experience. For example, think about investing in bank stocks during a recession. That might involve estimating loan-underwriting risk, but you would have ample statistical data on default rates to help you handicap future expected losses. You would be benefiting from underwriting experiences of the past. However, there is another, more sinister type of risk you should be on the lookout for, and it can be vastly different from risk *experience*. I'm talking about risk *exposure*.

Exposure is a risk that has not yet materialized, which makes it all the easier to overlook. However, this is exactly the kind of risk that can come back to haunt you with devastating consequences. The common insight applies here: absence of evidence is not evidence of absence. Just because you do not see the evidence of risk, does not mean it does not exist. If you did not wear your seat belt and did not have an accident for five years in a row, it does not mean that you were not taking a risk with your life. You *exposed* yourself to the risk of a severe or fatal injury all along; you just didn't *experience* the consequences of it.

Bear Markets Reveal the Power and Payoff of Risk Management; Bull Markets Do the Opposite

In bull markets, where the focus is on returns, there is a greater tendency to become complacent about risk. This is dangerous. At precisely the time when investors should be paying more attention to risk, they pay less.

It is unfortunately fairly typical for gunslinging money managers who outperform to earn glowing accolades in the media, more business from their clients, and larger bonuses from their employers, while risk-conscious managers who underperform are criticized or canned. Faced with such skewed incentives, it should not surprise anybody that few money managers pay attention to risk. This feeds a self-fulfilling cycle of ignoring risks which multiply unabated and finally blow up in our faces (as we all confronted in 2008). Only then does the payoff appear for the risk-conscious manager, who suffers the pain of underperformance in the *present* while the benefits of risk management arise in the *future*.

Risk Measurement ≠ Risk Management

Although it is crucial to measure risk, do not focus unduly on the *numbers* at the expense of the *narrative*. No amount of quantitative measurement will give you a full picture of risk management; you must judge facts and data in context. Indeed, many risks cannot be measured mechanistically or statistically. Remember, risk is an exposure, not only an experience. You cannot really measure what you have not experienced.

In fact, many managers who claim to measure risk by running risk optimizers and risk reports are taking false comfort because they are relying on current or historical data. Risk management is forward, not backward, looking. In a sense, you need to apply both science and art to understand risk experience and exposure. You will fall short if you rely solely on formulas, checklists, or risk reports. Worst of all, running such reports will engender a false sense of security, deluding you into thinking you are proactively managing risk when in fact you are just as likely to get blindsided by risk as someone who does not run such reports.

"You cannot really measure what you have not experienced."

In my view, this is exactly what happened in the years leading up to the financial crisis of 2008. It is not that regulators, central bankers, management teams, rating agencies, and money managers were not looking at risk reports on the banking sector. The problem is that they were looking at misleading metrics such as value at risk, or VAR.[2] The formula for calculating VAR relies on measuring volatility *experienced*, which was of little help in 2008 because the securities were often new and had limited trading history (data). Therefore, to understand risk *exposure*, investors needed to use judgment, not statistics. If they had, they would have realized that the facts, taken out of context, were misleading. They would have seen that during a persistent bull market with an upward trending bias, volatility was likely

---

2. VAR, value at risk, is commonly used in the banking industry to measure the risk of loss on investments. It estimates how much a set of investments might lose (with a given probability), under normal market conditions, in a set time period such as a day or a month.

to be understated, and thus would give a skewed sense of risk exposure.

Before all this, in 2006–2007, instead of relying just on VAR, I researched a whole range of risk factors and exposures in the banking sector and foresaw the high-risk exposures such as asset/liability mismatch risk, maturity-mismatch risk, wholesale-funding risk, counterparty-risk, and so on, that had eluded many. You do not need to understand the definition or details of these risks to appreciate the point that *risk is not one-dimensional* and cannot be properly identified unless analyzed from all vantage points. I supplemented these *quantitative* analytics with *qualitative* assessments. For instance, I examined corporate-governance incentives of CEOs and found that their compensation packages often incentivized them to expand their banks and maximize short-term returns rather than walk away from risky assets. Thanks to such a holistic assessment of risk, I proactively reduced my exposure to bank stocks and was able to better protect my clients during the financial crisis of 2008.

But even though what I did was right, it was not easy. My proactive risk management helped me to outperform in 2008, but it had caused me to underperform in 2007. I had been put on watch lists in 2007, which is institutional code for "If you don't fix this soon, you will be fired." The irony is that although I was looking out for my clients (by paying attention to *risk*), they thought I wasn't (because they were looking at my *returns*). My word of advice to all those who may find themselves in this unfair predicament: Think of professional money management as good parenting. Your kids will undoubtedly resent you when you deny them their mac and cheese in favor of veggies, even though you are acting in their best interest. Like a good parent, keep fighting the good fight. The resentment eventually turns into gratitude and the critique into compliments.

Measuring the Wrong Thing Is the
Biggest Risk You Can Take

Many people in the investment world rely on statistics to measure returns and risks, but they don't always measure the right things. One statistic that is often used—frankly misused—is beta, which is defined as the ratio of a stock's or portfolio's volatility to the volatility of the market as a whole.

It works this way: A beta of, say, 0.8 or 1.2 means that if past relationships hold, the price of a security is likely to move up or down in that proportion to the market benchmark. A beta below 1 suggests it will move with less amplitude, and vice versa. But risk is not a proportionate or relative move; it is an absolute and permanent impairment of capital. Just because something has a smaller or larger amplitude does not make it risky per se.

This is a case of confusing volatility with risk. As we saw in chapter 3, they are not the same thing. Think of stock-price volatility as the minor heart-rate fluctuations that we routinely experience when we move from resting to walking to running. They are not significant, and you can usually ignore them. On the other hand, chronically high blood pressure, for which you may see no obvious outward signs of fluctuation, is a huge risk. You would find it absurd if your doctor measured your heart rate all day long and completely ignored measuring your blood pressure. But this is exactly the absurdity we indulge in when we focus on beta or volatility instead of risk. Unfortunately, because we cannot easily measure or visualize risk before it happens, while measures such as historical beta, volatility, or tracking error are precise and tangible, people fall into the trap of measuring something that does not matter because they can, not because they should. Measuring risk is *right but not easy*; measuring beta and volatility is *easy but not right*.

Another measure of risk used by investors is tracking error, a number that expresses how closely a portfolio follows the index to which it is benchmarked. I view it as a misleading metric because it ignores a critical point: *why* is that manager tracking far from the benchmark? If it is to avoid permanent impairment of capital (which is the definition of risk), then a high tracking error is a good thing (because it reduces risk). Too often, though, the marketplace views a high number as *increasing* risk. Adding the insinuating word "error" is the culprit. Just as not all cholesterol is bad for you, not all deviations from the benchmark are bad.

Swapping Risk Instead of Reducing It

As if ignoring or mistaking risk were not bad enough, another trap that even some well-informed investors fall into is to *swap* risk instead of *reducing* it. It is among the most dangerous forms of risk-taking because you do not even know that you are exposed to it.

I recall researching Aggreko, a global company headquartered in the UK that rents portable power-generation equipment to countries and companies experiencing power outages or shortages. I was quizzing a member of the management team on their risk-management strategy, especially in emerging markets such as Latin America, where the risk of currency devaluation is high. He explained that they had proactively addressed this risk by structuring all their Latin American contracts and payments in U.S. dollars, so it was the customer, not Aggreko, that assumed the currency-devaluation risk. To any "check the box" type of investor, this response would have been satisfactory. But I have learned from experience to assess the larger context, and my contrarian conclusion was that the company remained exposed to a lot of risk, except it was not *currency* risk but *counterparty* risk instead. (Counterparty risk is the risk to each party of a contract that the other side will not live up to its contractual obligations.) Here is why.

When a currency devalues, unless the customers have dollar revenues to pay off dollar-denominated liabilities, they will end up defaulting on that obligation. While Aggreko was being truthful about its arrangement, it was nonetheless a misleading and myopic form of risk management because all they had done was *swap* risk, not *reduce* it. Sure enough, several years later in 2012, Aggreko stock took a big hit when many Latin American customers defaulted on their payments and the company had to write off a large chunk of their accounts receivable as bad debts.

A well-meaning but equally damaging form of swapping risk comes from the recent obsession with owning stability at any cost and avoiding volatility at any cost. Of late, this has manifested itself in stocks of consumer staples becoming quite expensive because, in their rush to avoid earnings volatility, investors were willing to pay more for stocks that *felt* stable. They swapped earnings-volatility risk for stock-valuation risk. Risk is risk, no matter what label it wears. The goal of risk management is not to swap one form of risk for another, but to reduce or get rid of it, or at least get paid for it and not pay for it.

Doubling Up on Risk Instead of Reducing It

Once upon a time, activists (people who attempt to use their rights as shareholders of a publicly traded corporation to bring about change within or for the corporation) focused on highly mismanaged or undermanaged companies. Of late, however, it is astounding to see the list of companies that have attracted activist attention: companies like Apple, Nestle, and Fanuc, a veritable who's who of their respective countries. What is more worrisome is that instead of focusing on fundamental improvements in corporate strategy or execution, many activists now overwhelmingly focus on what they call "maximizing capital structure." It's nothing but a euphemism for leveraging up the balance sheet to fund share buybacks.

Rampant short-termism and the rising threat of shareholder activism have put many CEOs and boards on notice. They feel compelled to engage in short-term quick fixes even at the expense of the long-term health of the company. It has bizarrely become both a badge of honor and a form of blackmail for boards to bless share buybacks at any cost, under the pretext that if they do not do so proactively, an activist investor will force them to do so anyway, often by removing them from their coveted seats.

Expensive share buybacks funded with "cheap" debt are nothing but a form of doubling down on risk. Not only are you taking valuation risk on your overvalued shares, you are adding financial-leverage risk onto your balance sheet. Many investors encourage companies to buy back their shares in bull markets only to cut those programs in bear markets, when they should be doing the opposite. Buybacks serve the interests of short-term traders by temporarily boosting the share price but hurt the long-term investors who are left holding the bag when the business cycle turns for the worse. Sadly, this is what played out at GE in 2018. The once iconic blue chip went into a free fall after squandering precious capital in buying back shares in prior years when it should have used that capital to strengthen its balance sheet, reduce its underfunded pensions, and invest in its business. Long-term stock-price performance arises from value creation in the underlying business, not from tinkering with the capital structure via financial engineering.

To add insult to injury, the companies and money managers who have the guts and grit to stay out of this fray find themselves in the unfortunate predicament of having to apologize for their conservative risk management. Cash has become a four-letter word, while debt is not. It has become fashionable to ridicule companies holding cash (which is nothing but a form of risk management), while taking on debt is encouraged.

I view a net-cash balance sheet as a sign of strength, not weakness. In an uncertain world, cash is king. It enables companies to take advantage of opportunities or combat threats. Of course, we should not take any precept or principle to an extreme. I am not for management teams hoarding excessive cash, and obviously deciding what level is excessive is a judgment call. But I would rather the board and long-term shareholders make that decision than short-term traders or fly-by-night activists.

I find an acute form of double-barreled foolishness in the private equity markets (meaning investments in equities that are not listed on a stock exchange and are unavailable to the public at large). Many private equity investors are turbocharging their risk (although they flatteringly refer to it as enhancing their returns) by loading up on leverage to boost returns. A little leverage for a short period of time can be useful, but a lot of leverage is dangerous and can wipe you out.

When a private equity fund's portfolio holding loads up on debt, recognize it for the risk that it is: it could unravel during less sanguine times and negate any returns you hoped to make. In 2007, a consortium led by Kohlberg Kravis Roberts & Co., Texas Pacific Group, and Goldman Sachs acquired the largest electricity utility in Texas, then known as TXU, for $48 billion. Then they loaded it with about $40 billion of debt. A short seven years later, in its new incarnation as Energy Future Holdings, the company filed for Chapter 11 bankruptcy—one of the ten biggest nonfinancial bankruptcies in history! While the private equity managers managed to earn more than $560 million in fees from the transaction, many investors lost billions of dollars on the deal. This goes to show how excessive debt can wreak havoc even in a presumably stable, low-risk business such as a utility and trip up even the savviest investors.

Private equity funds going on a debt binge in their portfolio holdings is a contemporary twist on an old trick played by conglomerates on unsuspecting investors in the 1980s and 1990s. Back then, conglomerates loaded up their subsidiaries with debt while the holding company's balance sheet appeared pristine because debt was not consolidated upstream. Many family-owned conglomerates in Asia engaged in this accounting maneuver in the 1990s and ended up defaulting on or restructuring their debt. This hurt their creditors and investors as well as the financial system at large, culminating in the Asian crisis of 1998. Think of a private equity fund as a conglomerate that owns multiple businesses. The fund may not appear to be leveraged, but the underlying holdings are, exposing you to more risk than you realize. The *Financial Times* shed light on this practice in an article titled "Private Equity's Love Affair with Leverage" (October 25, 2009). The article referenced a study conducted by Boston Consulting Group which concluded that, after fees and adjustments for risk, private equity funds do not outperform public equity markets. This is a doubly dismal outcome: private equity is an illiquid asset class and needs to compensate for that illiquidity with higher returns.

Debt and bear markets are a disastrous combination, as many consumers found out when house prices crashed in 2008. Everyone who had taken, given, or invested in mortgage debt had assumed the house was worth X, then found themselves in trouble when it suddenly became worth far less. But the debt owed stayed the same as before, causing many homeowners to face foreclosure.

Despite clear evidence of the risks arising from excessive leverage, we still hear the argument that debt is inexpensive and surely taking advantage of cheap money is smart. But no matter how cheap it appears to be from the standpoint of interest cost, debt comes with a deadline. It must be repaid in full someday, and that day may come sooner than you plan for.

This is what some adventurous traders and foolhardy companies found out when the Swiss National Bank (SNB) stunned markets on Thursday, January 15, 2015, by scrapping its three-year-old peg of 1.20 Swiss francs per euro. In a chaotic few minutes after the central bank's announcement, the Swiss franc soared by around 30 percent in value against the euro.

As the currency continued to oscillate wildly, many traders were suddenly faced with margin calls (requirement to repay debt immediately by selling the collateral backing it). As the collateral value of their underlying assets plunged but the margin debt stayed fixed, these traders watched their net worth get wiped out. They went bankrupt within hours. Not only did those traders lose all their money, but several of the foreign exchange trading platforms that had hosted them were also wiped out, which in turn caused their counterparties to book losses as they suffered collateral damage. It was like watching dominoes fall in rapid succession, except it was happening to real people and institutions.

The world's third largest retail foreign exchange broker, FXCM, had to get a $300 million bailout after taking huge losses. Its shares plunged more than 70 percent in after-hours trading on Friday, January 16, 2015. Still, FXCM fared better than its competitor Alpari, a UK-based foreign exchange broker, which entered insolvency.

It took mere hours to annihilate what had taken years to build. The traders and foreign-exchange-trading platform companies learned a costly lesson: Debt is a double-edged sword; it can amp up your returns in the good times but wipe you out during the tough times. Such binary outcomes make a highly indebted company very speculative. My advice: avoid it.

A similar doubling-up on risk plays out in the corporate world, where management teams often justify expensive acquisitions on strategic grounds of speed to market or amplifying the growth rate. Studies repeatedly show that most acquisitions do not create value, yet that has not prevented companies from arguing they will be the exception that defies the rule. During the heyday of emerging markets between 2001 and 2011, many companies and investors alike chased the heady growth rates of emerging markets and justified egregious acquisitions as the new "must have" beachhead asset. Even the conservative German company Beiersdorf (the maker of Nivea-branded skin-care products) fell for this "growth at any price" trap and paid close to half a billion dollars for an expensive Chinese hair-care acquisition, only to write it off a few years later.

Acquisition risk is a special form of denial in which inferior risk management is indulged in the name of superior return management. Invariably, management teams and investors justify their expensive forays with arguments of faster growth and immediate profit accretion. The downside emerges much later, when accounting regulations force them to confess to their mistakes by impairing the value of the asset. Once again, focusing on short-term gain and ignoring long-term pain proves to be a losing investment strategy in the fullness of time. Overpaying for an asset in the name of strategy is simply obfuscating the valuation risk.

Another form of doubling up on risks comes when a company with operating leverage takes on financial leverage. That is a deadly cocktail in times of adversity. Many financially leveraged energy companies went bankrupt when oil prices crashed unexpectedly in 2014 because their bonds and shares plunged simultaneously as investors priced in both bond default and equity-dilution risk. At exactly the time that the company needed to raise money to get through the downturn, both equity and debt markets closed their doors because of this layering of risk upon risk.

Risk is absolute, not just relative. A lot of small risks with low probabilities can add up to a gigantic fat-tail risk. Layering risk upon risk ensures multiple ways to lose, instead of multiple ways to win. Doubling up on risk means that a humdrum downturn can explode into a full-blown crisis. Do not put yourself in such a vulnerable position in the first place.

Risk Management Is About Assessing Risk, Not Avoiding It

Risk is omnipresent. There is no denying it or avoiding it. Your only choice is to find it and deal with it. Equity investors need to be especially vigilant about risks because they are the risk-bearers of first resort. Risk management is not an attempt to eliminate all risks (that is impossible) but to distinguish between those risks that are minor—in which case the equity is worth buying at a good price—or major, meaning you should steer clear at any price.

If the risks in the business are outsize, unquantifiable, or of a binary/speculative nature, stay away. Do not own the stock at any time or any price. This is an absolute standard, not mitigated by a low or falling price. Warren Buffett put it best in his 1996 annual letter to shareholders: "If you wouldn't own the business for ten years, don't even think of owning it for ten minutes."

If, on the other hand, the risk is small and manageable, that's the time to adopt an engagement policy and assume the risk when you are paid for it, in the form of an attractively discounted price. Markets are often efficient or ebullient and may not pay you to take the risks. But I have found that if one waits patiently for something, somewhere in the world, to go wrong, it usually does. In the real world, even high-quality, low-risk businesses can face air pockets in earnings, missteps in execution, or any number of externalities that might cause temporary weakness. If that makes their stocks experience a swoon, you should scoop them up as investment bargains.

In other words, when markets pay you to assume the risks of a high-quality business, you should bear them. When markets do not pay you, you can sit back and wait for a setback in the business or pullback in the share price. Let the opportunity come to you, and only engage when the risk/reward balance becomes attractive. Thus, *risk management is not only about risk reduction but also about return enhancement.* You can take advantage of risk to generate returns if a stock is mispriced.

Obviously, if the litmus test of whether to own or avoid a business is its innate quality, you need to know how to evaluate that. That is the topic of the next chapter. Here I want to focus on how to identify and manage risk. This brings us one more important risk we must consider: the risk of making a mistake.

Despite all our training, good intent, and best efforts, we are human beings and not immune from mistakes. Investment mistakes are inevitable, but you can still have solid returns. The way to do that is by insisting on a margin of safety.

Margin of Safety = Heads I Win, Tails I Do Not Lose

Investors can reduce the risk of large losses by insisting on a large value spread between the price of a stock and its intrinsic value. That difference is your margin of safety. If you buy an asset at a steep discount to its underlying value, the odds of a permanent loss of capital are low, protecting you from risk. The greater the discount, the larger the margin of safety, and thus the better the risk-reward of the investment opportunity.

Let us say you have estimated the intrinsic worth of a company as $100 per share, but it is trading at $80. This means that the stock is at a $20 discount to its intrinsic worth. If that $80 stock then falls to $50, an exceptional investment opportunity appears. If your assessment of the business as being intrinsically worth $100 does not change, the fluctuation in the share price is giving you an amazing opportunity.

It is important to recognize what has happened to both the upside potential and the downside risk. Risk is reduced because the share price has gone well below the intrinsic value. At $80 converging to $100, you will generate a 25 percent profit on the investment. At $50, you will make 100 percent. That's the magic of the discount: as the price falls well below intrinsic value, the downside is limited *and* the upside has increased.

That said, securing a margin of safety is not an absolute fail-safe. It improves the odds of a good payoff but does not make you impervious to a loss. No matter how well you research an investment proposition, you will get some wrong. Investing is not about making no mistakes; it is about keeping the costs of the mistakes low enough that you can recover from them and not ruin all the excellent work done on other investment decisions. Differently put, having a margin of safety reduces the scope for a *mistake* to turn into a *mishap*.

A margin of safety is also about making sure markets pay you for the unexpected to happen, rather than just focusing on what you must pay for the expected. Benjamin Graham, the father of value investing, explained that the function of the margin of safety is to render unnecessary an accurate estimate of the future. This means that with a margin of safety, even if the future does not pan out as you forecasted, your losses are low. With a margin of safety, your nest egg suffers less, and often it is only your ego that gets bruised.

Proactive risk management demands that you consider what can go wrong and quantify the downside scenarios instead of banking on the upside potential and what can go right. By buying stocks when bad news is priced in but good news is not, you create an additional margin of safety. The stock may not go up, but it doesn't go down much either: *heads you win, tails you don't lose*. Thus, risk proves to be an opportunity cost, not an actual cost. It is underperformance compared to expectation (annoying but not critical), not permanent impairment of capital (damaging to your financial well-being).

Error of Omission: You Snooze, You Lose

Part of astute risk management is to not be afraid, because excessive fear can cause you to miss out on opportunities. I call this risk an error of omission, and I too have fallen into this trap.

I made this mistake a decade ago, when I passed up on owning Interactive Brokers, a leading low-cost platform to trade equities, especially international ones. It is the largest electronic stock brokerage firm in the United States, by number of daily average revenue trades, and the leading foreign-exchange broker (firms that facilitate trade in foreign currencies). It is also very well capitalized;

its equity capital exceeds $6 billion. Management and employees own more than 84 percent of the company, so they have ample skin in the game and are as exposed to the downside as they are to the upside. This ensures that they will run their business conservatively and explains why they hold no material positions in exotic, high-risk securities such as CDOs (collateralized debt obligations), MBSs (mortgage-backed securities), or CDSs (credit default swaps), or unlisted securities or derivatives. The gross amount of their portfolio of debt securities, with the exception of U.S. government debt securities, is less than 10 percent of their equity capital. Rated "the low cost online broker" for *eighteen years in a row* by Barron's, they offer low-cost access to invest in stocks, options, futures, foreign exchange, and fixed income on more than 120 global exchanges in the world. Their low-cost position is derived from their home-grown proprietary online trading technology, built over the past forty years, which enables them to provide competitive pricing, high speed, diversity of global products, and advanced trading tools. Their low-cost position is also a function of their assiduous focus on simplicity and frugality. In my opinion, they are the Costco of the brokerage world—high quality and unbeatable prices.

While I recognized the quality of the franchise, I was worried about the low free float of 16 percent and limited trading liquidity in the stock. This was flawed thinking on my part. As a long-term patient investor, I could afford to take the risk of lack of liquidity. In addition, I could have managed the risk by limiting my position size. This error of omission proved costly; the stock quintupled, from around $15 in 2008–2009 to $80 by mid-2018.

Conclusion: Seek and Ye Shall Find (and Get Paid)

In life, we don't give up striving for success because some struggles or sacrifices come with it. We figure out how to manage and overcome them, so they do not overwhelm us. Similarly, in investing, you must not give up the pursuit of any return just because it comes with some risk. Instead, you learn to identify risk, manage it proactively and prudently, and insist on getting paid for it.

That said, I know it is not easy. In the real world, businesses and stocks do not come with black-and-white risk labels attached to them; they come in many shades of gray. It takes a great deal of due diligence and acumen to figure out the risk and reward of an investment opportunity and decide whether you should engage or walk away. In markets, such truth may reveal itself in years and decades, not days or weeks. During that time, a great deal of risk may exist without your realizing it.

When the risks of an investment are not obvious, but the returns are, this does not mean risks are nonexistent. They are just not in plain view or have not materialized yet. I refer to this out-of-sight-out-of-mind risk as a *blind spot*. Risk management requires a contrarian bent of mind. It means that you must pro-actively seek out bad news and figure out what can go wrong, and you must do it *before* the horse leaves the barn. Nonetheless, many investors behave like daredevils, hoping for the best instead of preparing for the worst, as if some magical risk alert will go off a minute before midnight so they can wait to deal with it then. Think of risk management as an insurance policy: you need to buy it before the accident or catastrophe occurs, not after.

Risk is a virus that can mutate unpredictably, not a bacterial cell that multiplies predictably. Your doctor would not confuse a bacterial infection with a viral one, and neither should you. Like a potentially deadly virus that keeps morphing, risk requires you to be constantly vigilant and stay a step ahead. This requires judgment, foresight, and multidimensional approaches, not reliance on rote checklists or static metrics. Managing risk is an ongoing process, not a one-and-done task.

While identifying and managing risk may appear daunting at first, it is not that hard to find if you know what you are looking for and how to look for it. But if you do not look, you will not find, even if it is staring right back at you. In fact, failure to think about the diverse types of risks is the bigger challenge, not failure to find.

Remember: Being risk *aware* does not mean you should be risk *averse*. You must strike the right balance between worrying about losing money (my definition of risk) and worrying about missed opportunity (to make money). One way to clarify this is to remember that risk and uncertainty are not the same thing. In his 1921 book, *Risk, Uncertainty, and Profit*, Frank Knight, an economist, formalized a distinction between the two. He understood that an ever-changing world brings new opportunities for businesses to make profits, but also means we have imperfect knowledge of future events. Risk, according to Knight, applies to situations in which we do not know the outcome but can accurately measure the odds. Uncertainty, on the other hand, applies to situations in which we cannot know all the necessary information to set accurate odds in the first place.

"Being risk aware does not mean you should be risk averse."

Fundamental research is about figuring out what you know and do not know or cannot know, to separate risk from uncertainty. This chapter has given you cues and clues to sharpen your antennae on risk. However, if you do not know how to tune into risk, or do not want to, that's fine. Outsource it. You do this in many aspects of your life, by finding the best doctor to avoid the risk of dying from some disease or the best lawyer to avoid the risk of losing a lawsuit. Apply the same logic in investing. Find the money managers or financial advisers who know how to manage the risks of your investment portfolio, not just its returns. As Peter Bernstein, the guru on risk management, rightly noted: "Risk is a choice, not a fate."

Top Takeaways

1. You always lose money downward from a bigger number and gain money upward from a lower number. This explains why avoiding losers is more important than picking winners.
2. Risk experience can be vastly different from risk exposure. The former may understate the latter, resulting in more risk than you bargained for.
3. Swapping risk is not reducing risk. Risk comes in many disguises. By unduly focusing on one form of risk that is top of mind, you may be ignoring another form of risk that has not yet reared its ugly head.
4. Investors often benefit from risk management in the future, but they always experience the costs in the present. Rewarding risk takers at the expense of risk managers incentivizes wrong behaviors: trying to win the battle instead of the war.
5. Risk is omnipresent. Instead of trying to avoid it or ignore it, manage it, and insist on getting paid for it. Always strive for a margin of safety in investments; it ensures a mistake does not turn into a mishap.
6. Being risk aware does not mean you should be risk averse. You must strike the right balance between worrying about losing money (risk) and worrying about missing the opportunity to make money (returns). When you are paid to take risks, you should take them.
7. Do not mistake risk measurement as risk management.
8. Risk is a choice, not a fate.

7

False Positives and Negatives

The cardinal mistake in investing is to lose a lot of money. Obviously, nobody loses money willingly, so what is the X factor that trips them up? Quality—or, more specifically, misunderstanding quality. This chapter outlines the counterintuitive framework you need to assess quality correctly.

The contrarian pays more attention to researching what can go wrong than what can go right. This chapter shows how to look out for fads and frauds, which are nothing other than failures masquerading as successes. BlackBerry is presented as a case study of a fad masquerading as a franchise. Could Apple be next?

The X Factor: Quality

Just as prevention is better than a cure, avoiding mistakes is smarter than having to fix them. In investing, the cardinal mistake is to lose a lot of money. Obviously, nobody loses money willingly or knowingly, so the question is: What causes people to lose money unexpectedly and unwittingly?

The answer is quality—or, more specifically, a misconception of quality.

Identifying quality is more complex and nuanced than most people realize. In fact, the financial crisis of 2008 was nothing but a series of revelations that quality had been massively misjudged—by bond and equity markets, by investors, by management teams, by regulators, and by rating agencies. Institutions and instruments previously rated AAA fell like dominoes because perceptions of quality did not match the revealed reality.

The fact that so many smart people got it wrong should tell you that distinguishing genuine quality from deceptive quality is not as straightforward as it seems. Partly this is because conventional wisdom, which works so well in life, works very poorly in investing. In your day-to-day choices, it is perfectly reasonable to extrapolate your past performance into the future. Not so in investing. Even though a stock may have gone up in the past few years, that does not mean it will perform well in years to come. Sony was once the Apple of Japan, flying high on a string of global hits with the Walkman and the Discman. But change, competition, and complacency ensure that the apple carts of winners and losers often get upset, upended, or even swapped around.

To make matters worse, conventional thinking not only fails to diagnose quality, it often leads you to *misdiagnose* it, giving you the equivalent of a false positive or a false negative medical test result. In the investment world, making decisions based on misleading assumptions or wrong answers can put you in serious jeopardy. Not only will you not make money, you will lose it, and potentially lots of it. On the other hand, correctly understanding quality yields tremendous bang for the buck. It not only helps you avoid losers; it also helps you pick winners.

If the quality of the underlying business is better than commonly understood, chances are the stock is mispriced and undervalued. Arbitraging the difference between the two is either your gain (if you correctly understood the quality attributes) or your loss (if you misunderstood them). Therein lies the trick and the treat: If you get it right (and prove others wrong), you win; get it wrong, and you lose.

Yet, even though understanding quality is so critical, few people get it right. People who think they just know quality when they see it usually don't. This is because quality is made up of many interlocking parts. It's far too complex for simple formulas or checklists. The biggest challenge in investing is that low quality often masquerades as high quality, and vice versa. In the following pages, I will show you how to avoid falling into the trap of conventional thinking, which confuses low quality with high quality, and embrace the power of counterintuitive thinking, which correctly distinguishes between the two.

Signposts or Red Herrings?

We humans are reductionist by nature. We gravitate toward simplicity, sometimes at great cost. So when we think about quality, we automatically associate it with familiar rubrics—a brand, a competitive advantage, a captive client base, or a dominant market position. Or we tell ourselves that quality shows itself as pricing power or high profit margins. On the face of it, these depictions seem correct. What can possibly be wrong with it?

How about everything?

Indeed, these classic buzzwords of quality are some of the false positives I cautioned you about. To think like a contrarian, you need to examine the counterfactual. Ask yourself this: If brand signifies quality, why did the stocks of iconic brands such as Macy's, Sears, and Marks and Spencer get pummeled in the markets?

If pricing power is a litmus test of quality, should you own the (loss-making) U.S. Postal Service because they have always raised stamp prices and never once lowered them?

How about owning the telecom companies that had such dominant market share that they had to be broken up? Does anybody even remember what happened to the Baby Bells? Where did their dominance go?

You get the drift. Many of the traditional gauges of quality can be head fakes. So how do you go about separating the reality from the red herrings, the crucial from the superficial? For that, we need to turn to some case studies that will help rewire your brain to a different, more non-consensus way of thinking.

Frothy Skim Milk Versus Cream:
A Case of Quality That Was Not

Do you remember the company that made BlackBerry phones? Research in Motion (RIM) was its name (since changed to BlackBerry Ltd.), and back in the early 1990s, this company epitomized quality.

In those pre-smartphone days, the 2G cellular network was optimized to carry voice, not data, so the network would get clogged with calls competing with texts or emails, and calls would drop. But RIM had an edge over its competitors: they had figured out a way to compress the data in such a way that BlackBerry phones could efficiently transmit it without unduly congesting the network, thereby avoiding dropped calls. RIM's proprietary technology not only compressed data, it also encrypted it, which made it safe to use by both enterprises and government agencies. BlackBerry naturally became the go-to device for these organizations, and soon made its way into the consumer mass market.

To anyone looking at the financial metrics, the company was on fire, with high growth and high returns. You are probably familiar with Porter's Five Forces: industry rivalry, threat of new entrants, threat of substitutes, bargaining power of suppliers, and the power of customers.[1] RIM could have been a mascot for Professor Porter; it checked all the boxes.

- It had a dominant product and very few rivals.
- Thanks to its proprietary encryption and compression technology, there were no threats of substitutes.

---

1. The Five Forces framework was created by Harvard Business School professor Michael Porter to analyze an industry's attractiveness and potential profitability. Since its publication in his book *Competitive Strategy: Techniques for Analyzing Industries and Competitors* (New York: Simon and Schuster, 1980), it has become one of the most popular and highly regarded business strategy tools.

- Its utility and uniqueness resulted in a strong bargaining position with its suppliers and customers.
- It was able to charge premium prices for its services and devices.

Because of all that, RIM enjoyed spectacular earnings growth and a stock price that soared from a low of $1.42 on October 10, 2002, to a high of $145 on June 20, 2008—a gain of roughly 100 times in less than six years!

If that was not a quality business, what was?

Yet RIM turned out to be the biggest booby trap of all: a low-quality company masquerading as high-quality. And it fooled a lot of investors. Neither RIM's brand nor its competitive advantages helped it withstand the onslaught of something so simple and inevitable that anyone could have seen it coming—the force of change.

With the arrival of 3G and 4G cellular networks, which were optimized to transmit data more efficiently than the older 2G network, RIM did not lose its moat—its moat became irrelevant, and the company became marginalized in the marketplace. Its quality, once priced as a lasting franchise, was revealed to be a passing fad.

If you misdiagnosed RIM's true quality—and many did—you lost a lot of money. From its peak in June 2008 through June 2017, the $100 stock had fallen to $10. To break even from such a losing investment, you would need another investment idea that would go up a whopping 900 percent. That is a very tall order. Better to not lose 90 percent in the first place. This explains why avoiding losers should be the primary aim, not an afterthought (as we learned in chapter 6: do no harm).

Why didn't anyone see beyond RIM's financial metrics? Because as conventional thinkers people are accustomed to judging quality by tangible measures like profit margins and earnings growth, or by intangibles such as a brand. But neither of these was a litmus test of enduring quality. To understand quality, we must look beyond the horizon and around the bend, because quality isn't a simple label but a latticework of interlocking attributes.

Your Secret Weapon in the Quest for Quality: Ask "Why," Not "What"

If you judged RIM by numbers alone, it looked fantastic. But the moment you broadened your perspective, what appeared to be surefire quality started to look vulnerable. That is what happens when investors are too easily satisfied with understanding the "*what*" instead of going deeper into the "why." The question is not "*What* is their market share?" but "*Why* do they have that market share?" Not "*What* is the profit margin?" but "*Why* do they have that profit margin?" "Why" provides the missing link that goes past the symptom to the source.

Taking a page from Socrates, I have developed a mantra of five whys: *Why after why after why after why after why.* This relentless line of inquiry enables me—and you—to conduct a root-cause analysis to correctly distinguish between high and low quality. It goes like this:

1. *Why did the BlackBerry succeed?* It could compress data into compact packets. This technological capability was highly desirable when consumers started to switch from plain text messaging to longer emails, causing congestion in a 2G network designed to carry voice, not data.
2. *Why would their success last?* It would not. The next-generation networks (3G, 4G, 5G, etc.) were better optimized to carry data and not just voice.
3. *Why would their product remain competitively advantaged and differentiated?* It would not. The cellular network, not the (BlackBerry) device, would solve the problem of congestion.

4. *Why would they make superior revenues, margins, and returns in the future?* Contrary to consensus expectations, they were likely to experience a collapse of market share, revenues, and profits as their core technological advantage and differentiation became irrelevant.

5. *Why would the stock go up?* It wouldn't. In fact, it would go down as telecom companies deployed next-generation (3G, 4G, 5G) networks and the company started to lose market share and miss earnings expectations. Investors would figure out that BlackBerry's best days were behind them.

By asking the right questions, I uncovered a bleak future. Other investors extrapolated a bright future because they focused on the *financial model* (which looked great at the time) but neglected the emerging threat to the *business model*.

This case study underscores how conventional wisdom does not prepare you for inflection points—game-changing developments where the future may be dramatically different from the past. This is what makes investing such a tough puzzle: it is challenging to fathom and forecast change or anticipate winners turning into losers. Mastering it requires rewiring the way you think and how you interpret and react to information. If you do not proactively find the blind spots in your research, you do not even know what is about to hit you. In investing, *what you do not know is often more important than what you do.*

Understanding the ins and outs of an industry and keeping tabs on where it is headed is a good starting point to reduce the risk of being blind-sided. This can then be extended to understanding the food chain and value chain of various players in that industry. Last but not least, you need to develop a good appreciation of every player's capabilities, competitive positioning, and business strategy. Management quality and track record also need to be judged. Beyond that, risk factors and growth prospects need to be carefully evaluated and quantified. If all this sounds like a lot of work to vet a single investment idea—it is! But those who can garner the necessary knowledge and apply it can profit from those who can't.

The BlackBerry case study also epitomizes another lesson. Many value investors bought RIM's stock on the way down, believing it to be cheap (underpriced) based on financial metrics and multiples. They repeated this mistake when they bought bank stocks as they were falling in 2008, using the same circular logic of cheapness. Historical financial numbers or naïve valuation metrics such as low price-to-book or price-to-earnings ratios will not tell you that the quality of the underlying business is about to deteriorate. *Non-consensus investing is about buying quality when it goes on sale, not buying junk at clearance prices.*

This is what makes non-consensus investing quite different from rote approaches to value investing. Non-consensus investors care about what they are *getting* (the quality of the underlying business), not just what they are *paying* (the headline valuation metric). Other types of value investors care predominantly about what they are paying, not about what they are getting—which is why they often end up owning a value trap rather than a value bargain. Knowing how to correctly distinguish quality from junk is a prerequisite to generating higher returns with lower risk—which is a central aspiration of non-consensus investing.

This next section will debunk many of the conventional criteria that are commonly used to assess quality and give you the contrarian but correct ways of thinking about it. I have peppered the section with actual case studies, so you can see real-life applications of this concept. It is worth reiterating that all stock examples or theses expressed are meant to be illustrations, not recommendations.

Table 7.1

Familiar but flawed	Real and reliable
Indicators of low quality	**Indicators of high quality**
Competitive advantage	Darwinian[1] advantage
Leading market share	Growing market share
Pricing power	Price disrupter
Captive customers	Loyal customers
Brand	Value proposition
Results	Process
Buzz model	Business model
Luck	Skill
Patents	Know-how
High tech	Proprietary tech

[1]Charles Darwin, was an English naturalist, geologist, and biologist. He is best known for his contributions to the science of evolution which he argued resulted from a process of natural selection through adaptation or more colloqially known as "survival of the fittest". He published his findings in 1859 in the now-classic book On the Origin of Species which was translated into many languages. During his lifetime, the book become a staple scientific text but also resonated with people from all walks of life, becoming a key fixture of popular culture.

Ten Myths and Truths About Quality

Let's start with a summary chart, table 7.1. On the left are ten familiar but flawed indicators of quality. These overused, empty buzzwords are red herrings leading you astray. On the right is a corresponding list of real and reliable ways to gauge genuine quality. We will look at each one in depth.

Competitive Advantage Is Overrated

In fact, "competitive advantage" is a misnomer. To be a high-quality business, it is not enough to beat the competition today;

you must also remain competitive and relevant tomorrow. That requires a Darwinian advantage.

You know the phrase "survival of the fittest." What Charles Darwin meant was not that the strongest or smartest of the species survive, which is how most people interpret it. It is those who are most capable of *adapting to their environments over time* who gain the upper hand. The same is true of a business. A so-called competitive advantage will take you only so far. To succeed, you cannot have just one ace up your sleeve; you need many intertwined capabilities. That is your Darwinian advantage.

Take Kodak and Fuji, for example (figure 7.1). They were rivals for years. Kodak had the advantage in the world of analog film, but as digital technology disrupted the film business, the company

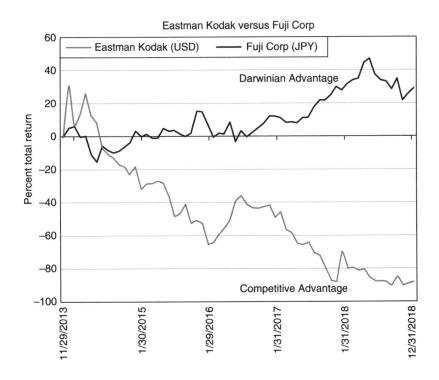

FIGURE 7.1 Relative Performance: Eastman Kodak versus Fuji Corp., 11/29 /2013–12/31/2018

failed to evolve. Like Kodak, Fuji faced the same existential head-winds as its analog film business also faced digital threats. But unlike Kodak, Fuji adapted and built evolutionary advantage by applying its knowledge of chemistry and film coatings to new applications and end markets. Today, Fuji is thriving, with multiple streams of earnings ranging from high-tech copier toner to film coatings for LCD panels used in TVs.

In building evolutionary advantage by adapting to a new world, Fuji rose to new heights while Kodak self-destructed by depending on its limited, point-in-time competitive advantage. Darwinian advantage yields *lasting* quality; competitive advantage represents *lazy* quality.

People are quick to talk about a company's high profitability as a metric of success. But over time, capitalism dictates that excess profits will get competed away. The longer you can prevent this from happening, by building Darwinian advantages that keep competition at bay, the longer you can earn excess returns. That is *earnings power with staying power*.

> **"Darwinian advantage yields lasting quality;
> competitive advantage represents lazy quality."**

Competitive advantage focuses mostly on barriers to entry, which may prove short lived. Darwinian advantage is about continuously raising the bar not just on barriers to entry but also on barriers to success. It's a process of developing interlocking advantages that are layered on top of one another to provide a wide and long lead over the competition.

Toyota does this by deploying *kaizen*, a system of continuous improvement, on a whole host of fronts, from investing in superior engine technology to implementing just-in-time manufacturing to cross-training workers to developing best-in-class global supply chains and manufacturing footprints to delivering a high-quality yet low-cost, reliable, and durable product to its consumers.

Competitors can try to take on Toyota on any one plank, but to surpass it on all fronts requires heroic resources and capabilities that most companies would be hard pressed to marshal. Better to pick a weaker competitor than to take on the strongest and most adaptable.

The Myth of Market Share

Now let us consider the smoke and mirrors of *leading* market share versus the more powerful indicator of quality: *growing* market share.

Baby Bells in the United States used to enjoy leading market share in the telecommunications industry. But their lead did not last because they took it for granted and failed to invest in next-generation networks to deliver broadband data connectivity and high-speed internet. The cable-TV industry sensed an opportunity and outsmarted the telecom incumbents by investing in a high-speed network that could carry both pay TV and high-speed data/internet. That meant they could add telephone services at low marginal cost. Many Americans now get triple-play services (voice telephony, high-speed broadband, and pay TV) from their local cable-TV company, and the once-dominant telecom companies have been relegated to losing market share instead of expanding it. Not surprisingly, many cable-TV stocks have been star performers while telecom stocks have lagged.

Now, I would not want you to construe this as an invitation to buy any challenger business model that is expanding its market share. This case study is meant to be a reminder of how conventional frameworks that equate high market share with quality is a false positive. Indeed, we appear to be on the cusp of another big shift. The cable-TV business model itself is being upended by new challengers, such as Netflix, that are expanding their market share by offering better value propositions to consumers.

In contrast, cable companies keep raising prices, which sends customers in search of more compelling alternatives such as Hulu or Disney+, a new soon-to-be-launched video streaming subscription service by Disney.

While expanding market share is better than not, it is a means to an end, not an end in itself. Pursuit of market share should not come at the expense of developing strategic advantage and pursuing long-run profits. Markets are dynamic, and winners and losers are continuously shifting. Companies that assiduously focus on offering consumers compelling value propositions get rewarded and win market share, while those that simply make hay while the sun shines ultimately prove to be lazy, not lasting, quality.

The Myths of Pricing Power and Captive Customers

Many people believe that pricing power or captive customers are unambiguous signs of quality. But they may not be.

Recall that legacy airline carriers in many countries had pricing power—not because they ran their business well but because they had a monopolistic hold over prime routes and airport landing slots. They abused that power by keeping prices high. You know what happened next. Upstarts such as Southwest in the United States, Ryanair in Europe, and WestJet in Canada jumped in to develop low-cost airlines and gain customers by lowering fares instead of raising them.

The point to remember is that soaring prices can become a source of vulnerability, rather than a symbol of strength, if consumers balk at the deteriorating value proposition. Case in point: Gillette. For years, it regularly raised prices, seeming immune to the laws of gravity. Then in 2016, it got a rude reality check when consumers began moving in droves to the upstart alternative, Dollar Shave Club. Gillette was forced to lower prices. Quality may not necessarily be defined by who can raise prices but by who can lower them.

Companies that can lower costs and offer more for less may be the success stories of tomorrow. Silicon Valley readily comes to mind here, but there are examples even in the traditional manufacturing sector. This was the case with Rational, a Mittelstand (midsize German company) renowned for making the best industrial-grade convection ovens for the hospitality industry. For decades, despite constant product improvement, it had spurned the easy path of raising prices. By offering such unbeatable value to its customers, it raised the bar for the competition, not its prices. This kept the customers happy and kept the competition at bay. Result? In the decade that ended in May 2018, Rational stock has increased tenfold.

Another marker of quality is repeat purchases by customers. But beware: if the cause of the repeat purchase is lack of choice, this measure becomes meaningless. Remember that many legacy telecom companies took their captive customers for granted and neglected to provide value. They mistook *captive* customers, who had nowhere else to go, for *loyal* customers. The moment those customers got a choice, they shifted their business en masse, exposing the business model for the low quality that it was. Captivity is not loyalty. High-quality businesses are those where customers willingly do business even if they could go elsewhere, because they are getting real value for their money.

Brands May Be Overrated

Businesses spend billions of marketing dollars every year on brand recognition. Unfortunately, the size of marketing spend is no guarantee that the brand will always be on top. No amount of advertising or public relations can rejuvenate a brand when the product itself does not live up to the promise. Look at (figure 7.2). It was once an iconic cosmetic brand and remains well known even today, but that did not protect it from weak consumer demand.

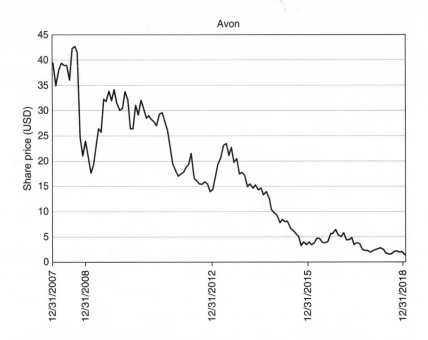

FIGURE 7.2 Share price chart: Avon Products, 12/31/2007–12/31/2018

The businesses suffered, and so did the stock. From December 2007 to December 2018, Avon stock fell more than 90 percent while the S&P 500 has gone up by almost 66 percent over the same time frame.

The worst offenders are those that rely excessively on their brands to do the heavy lifting of increasing revenues. Abercrombie & Fitch thought it could buck the trend by relying on its brand to justify high prices when its peers were offering far more compelling product or value propositions. After consumers gasped from sticker shock, the company debased its signature label by offering widespread discounts and ongoing promotions. The stock collapsed as the halo around the brand evaporated. Abercrombie & Fitch had pricing power—until it did not.

This is why I am not a fan of ascribing value to brands as a special asset on the balance sheet. Not only can they be ephemeral and hard to estimate, this practice may be tantamount to double counting. The value of the brand is implicitly captured in the revenues, earnings, and cash flows of the company, so the contribution is already embedded in the valuation of the firm.

Also note that many consumers are starting to care more about the authenticity and origin of a product than just its brand. The Muji brand (the word translates to "no logo" or "no brand" in Japanese) has become a runaway success worldwide by offering a minimalist design at affordable prices. Muji devotes little money to advertising or traditional marketing, relying instead on word of mouth, a simple shopping experience, and the anti-brand movement. Muji's no-brand strategy also means its products are attractive to customers who prefer unbranded, generic products for aesthetic reasons. Lower branding costs enable lower prices despite the high quality, which in turn results in such a compelling value proposition that customers keep coming back for more. This creates loyalty and provides longevity to a business.

I am not against brands per se but want to point out that what works well in life may not translate well into investing. Familiar household names with strong brands such as Avon and Abercrombie do not necessarily make good investments, while lesser known companies such as Ryohin Keikaku (the company behind the Muji brand) that base their appeal on compelling product attributes may well prove to be the winning ideas.

Over the five years ending in December 2018, Abercrombie stock was down 40 percent and Ryohin Keikaku stock was up more than 130 percent in local currency (figure 7.3).

The trouble with relying on a single metric, even a bedrock attribute such as a brand, is that it makes investors complacent. You may be so in love with the brand that you completely overlook deeper problems, such as deteriorating product quality or changing market trends. Indeed, Kodak still has a brand that

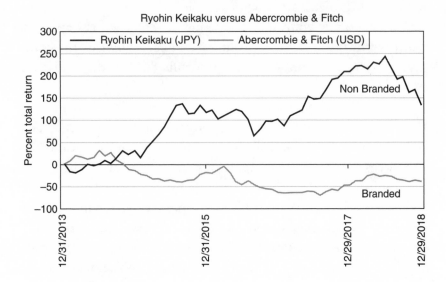

FIGURE 7.3 Relative Performance: Ryohin Keikaku versus Abercrombie & Fitch, 12/31/13–12/31/18

many recognize, but it doesn't help. Even in the company's new incarnation, its stock fell from $25 in 2013 to $9 in June 2017.

Understanding true quality requires one to look at subtleties rather than superficialities. Brands, no matter how vivid or familiar they may seem, are not a free pass that lets you ignore deep, full-fledged research on a business. Nor do they offer some innate immunity from failure or loss. Brands are the cost of doing business. They may raise the stakes for new entrants who can't afford to spend millions on advertising or may buy companies some time and leeway if they face a public relations fiasco, but they are not a magic wand that can ward off all challenges or challengers.[2] The product or service must perform and continue to satisfy customer wants or needs.

---

2. To make this even trickier, today social media and digital marketing are leveling the playing field between the haves and have-nots. Even small budgets go a long way in an online and direct-to-consumer world.

Judge the Decisions, Not Just the Outcomes

Another red herring that keeps investors going in circles is look-ing at the quality of *outcomes* when they should be looking at the quality of the underlying *decisions* a company makes.

Northern Rock, a mortgage lender in the UK (the equivalent of Countrywide in the United States), was considered a blue-chip stock of its time. Back in the mid-2000s, the company was increas-ing its earnings and dividends at a rapid clip. It was everybody's darling, but not mine; I believed it was high risk and low quality. Why? Because it was relying on the cheap but footloose whole-sale market to fund its business instead of building a costlier but stickier deposit franchise. At the time, the wholesale funding mar-ket was flush with cash and eager to lend, but I knew from long experience that it was a fickle funding source and could prove to be the Achilles heel of the business model.

Two years later, management's shortsighted decision, to rely on easy money and not develop a stable deposit funding base, put the company in jeopardy. In 2008, when the wholesale funding markets dried up during the financial crisis, the market was stunned (I was not) that Northern Rock was among the first financial institutions to need a government bailout. Then, when the British government nationalized the company, the stock went to zero and investors lost 100 percent of their money. This is the worst kind of loss for a share-holder because you don't ever get a chance to make it back when the company has gone bankrupt—it is game over (or what I would call "a permanent impairment of capital"). While the going was good, a robust growth rate and a successful financial track record gave the illusion of prosperity at Northern Rock. But if you judged the quality by the decisions the management team made, you knew they were making an extremely poor trade-off between risks and returns.

In stark contrast, consider the decisions made by Toyota, which constantly reinvents itself to survive and prosper in the next century. They do this by reinvesting and reducing risk in the business, even at the expense of current margins and returns. The decision to develop a hybrid engine (powered by both gasoline and a battery) is a good example. Few people realize it today, but this was a tough call for a company that made great gasoline engines. Still, in the long-term interest of consumers and stakeholders, it was the right decision. Indeed, so farsighted was the management team that they were early investors in Tesla, an all-electric car that could be a challenger to its mainstay business.[3] Toyota is open to cannibalizing its core competitive advantage to develop a new one, and by constantly moving the goalposts forward, it creates an increasing lead over its competitors, who will find it difficult if not impossible to catch up. Such well-rounded decision-making of paying as much attention to preempting future threats as to availing itself of current opportunities—is a hallmark of a high-quality business.

The superior quality of decisions provides a company with both strength and strategic optionality that it can draw from in tough times. This explains why Toyota remained resilient in the wake of many recent setbacks, including large product recalls on the back of safety concerns in the United States in 2012, and the disruption of its supply chain because of the tsunami in Japan and flooding in Thailand. Its strong net-cash balance sheet, along with the years of trust and goodwill built with its customers, allowed it to overcome multiple challenges without compromising its long-term future.

However, ongoing assessment is needed, because in the marketplace, even the mighty can fall. Recall that Yahoo in its prime sported better financial metrics than Google, but it proved to be a melting ice cube—not an overnight failure, but a trickle over time. If you had evaluated Yahoo by the poor quality of its decisions— such as a failure to invest and improve its search engine, as well as

---

3. Toyota sold its Tesla stake in June 2017.

the shortsighted move to maximize ad revenues by bombarding customers with annoying banner ads—you would have concluded that the stock was a trap. And you would have avoided it. Toyota could end up in similar trouble if it does not make the right decisions on next-generation technologies. It has so far bet that hybrids like the Prius, instead of a fully electric vehicle, are the way to go. Time will tell if this decision was sage or shortsighted.

In evaluating management teams, you must assess whether they are pursuing short-term KPIs (Key Performance Indicators) to meet incentive compensation targets, often at the expense of endangering long-term KPIs. It is crucial to know whether management is managing *earnings* (tends to line their own pockets) or *capital* (tends to line shareholders' pockets). Sadly, management incentives are often skewed toward near-term growth of earnings per share, which creates a bias to flatter earnings results today, often at the expense of long-term considerations. Beware of this predilection to shortchange the future for present gain.

In my opinion, this is exactly what played out at Coach (rechristened Tapestry), a premium handbag company. When management found that the profitability of their outlet stores was far greater than that of their high-street ones, they continued to expand their sales through the outlet channel to boost profits. This short-term expediency came back to haunt them, as it came at the expense of the brand's heritage and premium positioning. Fortunately, the company was wise enough to recognize it had overplayed its hand and corrected its strategy under a new management team. As we will see in chapter 8, Coach is now on its way to restoring its former glory. But this anecdote shows how measuring and managing aimed solely at near-term numbers can be damaging for the long-term health of a business.

Beware of management teams who make low-quality decisions in the name of high quality. One example: Using the proclaimed benefit of "optimal capital structure," there is a great deal of activism to encourage companies to borrow money to buy back shares, to boost earnings per share. The trouble is that people often confuse cost and risk, so on the surface poor decision-making can temporarily manifest as success. Such practices seem harmless in the good times but can prove very damaging in tough times. Having a cash cushion for a rainy day is good insurance. Borrowing money simply because it is cheap and readily available is not a smart move, as many homeowners discovered during the housing crisis a few years ago. The *cost* of the decision is not the same as the *risk* of the decision. Leverage in any form—operating or financial—is a source of risk to equity shareholders, and therefore highly leveraged companies fall squarely in the low-quality camp.

> **"The *cost* of the decision is not the same as the *risk* of the decision."**

Bottom line: *Quantitative* comparisons of outcomes (such as profitability or growth rates) should not trump *qualitative* assessments of the *drivers* of those outcomes. Do not judge companies on their numerical results alone; evaluating quality requires a balanced scorecard. In particular, instead of looking only at results, evaluate management teams on the quality of their decisions and the trade-offs they made that led to those results.

Is It a *Buzz* Model or a *Business* Model?

Many disruptive dotcom companies are known for their mouth-watering growth rates as they siphon customers and market shares from lumbering incumbents. You might think such challenger companies are high-quality businesses, but they are not. They appear to be successful in growing market share and revenues, but they are failures when it comes to making money. In fact, they often lose it.

Now, some people will dispute my claim, arguing that they *report* profits. The catch is that they appear to make money when they use non-GAAP accounting (not generally accepted accounting principles). With non-GAAP accounting, companies can blithely exclude certain legitimate business expenses to flatter results, often converting losses into profits. If you were to recast their earnings using generally accepted accounting principles, they are more likely than not to rack up large losses. Claiming one is profitable on a non-GAAP accounting basis but lossmaking if GAAP accounting is used is akin to a student telling her teacher: "If you exclude all my wrong answers, I would have aced my exam."

The lesson here is that many people confuse the narrative with the numbers. Simply because a company increases market share and revenues does not mean it makes money. In my opinion, a business that does not make money for shareholders is a *buzz* model, not a *business* model. It is best to think of it as a phenomenon to watch rather than a company to invest in. Many dotcom companies that emerged during the Nasdaq bubble period were buzz models that fizzled out, at great cost to their shareholders.

There are many examples; here are just two. Webvan, an online grocery company, went out of business in just three years and filed for bankruptcy in 2001. Pets.com did not last for even two years, despite advertising in the 2000 Super Bowl. It had the zany idea of selling products well below cost and trying to upsell and cross sell its customers to offset such losses. The strategy failed: losses grew faster than sales, and the company went under.

Many people assume a rising stock price is proof of success. This is a classic case of confusing cause and effect. Merely because a company appears successful, does not mean it is. A successful company is one that makes money, not loses it. Watch out for companies that have a big difference between GAAP and non-GAAP earnings (many tech companies in the United States tend to have the biggest divergence due to their widespread reliance on stock-based compensation expenses); it is a huge red-flag indicator of low quality and should give you pause. (The only exception is the owner-operated earnings construct used by Warren Buffett.) Likewise, be alert for huge disparities between reported earnings and free cash flows. This can indicate possible accounting chicanery; at the very least, it calls for the "five whys" interrogation.

Is Growth Driven by Acquisitive or Organic Means?

Companies that spend a significant amount of their own free cash flows in acquiring other companies are often ultimately revealed to be low-quality businesses as the acquisition strategy unravels. I call them serially acquisitive companies. Multiple studies show that most mergers and acquisitions fail to deliver on their targeted synergies or promised benefits; in fact, they invariably prove value destructive.

It is not difficult to understand why. Acquisitions usually suffer from a winner's curse: you win the auction, but only by paying an inflated price, resulting in a pyrrhic victory. Remember that all acquisitions are made with shareholders' monies, which means investors pay the high price while the CEO gets to walk away with the prize.

Acquisitions are such an easy way to drive fast growth that they tend to become addictive. Soon companies start leveraging themselves up to fund that addiction. Before long, the company becomes a house of cards. When that happens (and to be clear, it does not always happen), the company dismantles itself, often selling off its crown jewels to pay off debt. The best outcome one can hope for is that the company resets itself on a more organic path, something that they should have done all along. Serial acquirer Pearson Publishing is a textbook case of a debt-funded acquisition spree gone awry. For many years the company acquired companies with borrowed money to drive growth. When the strategy failed, the company found itself in distress and was forced to sell many prized possessions, including the iconic *Financial Times* and the *Economist*, to repay parent-company debt.

Serially acquisitive companies also have considerable latitude in creating cookie-jar provisions that enable management teams to manipulate reported earnings or even engage in corporate fraud. Typically, the larger the size of the acquisition, the greater the scope for a copious cookie jar to dip into.

Like a moth fatally attracted to artificial light that can kill it, myopic management teams can be so enamored with acquisitions and exhilarated by the adrenaline rush that comes from frenzied deal-making that they put their entire companies and careers at risk. Tyco under former CEO Dennis Koslowski and Valeant under former CEO Michael Pearson are emblematic of the disastrous consequences of such errant behavior. Both companies generated large losses for investors, and their chief protagonists were put behind bars on charges of corporate fraud.

Some people may argue that not all takeovers are value destructive, and I would certainly agree. Many CEOs are excellent stewards of capital, including when they make acquisitions. But they are so few and far between that I believe it is safe to generalize: serially acquisitive companies are generally poor-quality businesses that prove to be poor-quality investments. One famous exception is Warren Buffett's Berkshire Hathaway. It makes a lot of acquisitions but does not fit the mold of a serial acquirer. Rather than growth for growth's sake, Buffett is disciplined and acquires only if the deal represents judicious allocation of capital and adds value. Acquisitions can create value, but that tends to be the exception, not the rule. Think of Warren Buffett as exceptional in this regard—as he is in so many others.

Luck or Skill?

An example of a false positive is the performance of many high-cost basic-resource companies between 2003 and 2007. During this time, prices of copper, iron ore, oil, and similar commodities were so high that even uncompetitive, poorly managed, low-quality companies made a lot of money simply by being exposed to the bull market. If you mistook their luck for skill, you lost a lot of money when the tables turned.

The Brazilian oil and gas company OGX is just such a riches-to-rags saga. The company was formed in 2007 by billionaire Eike Batista, who bombastically claimed he would be worth $100 billion in ten years, which would make him the richest man in the world. Indeed, the initial public offering on June 12, 2008, raised an incredible $4.1 billion, with the promise that the company's oil ventures would yield a bonanza, despite not yet having produced a drop of oil. Five short years later, Batista filed for bankruptcy and OGX went under, taking shareholders' money with them.

The lesson here is that winning by *default* (being in the right place at the right time) is not the same as winning by *design* (strategically positioning yourself to win against the odds). Luck, in the form of tailwinds and externalities, may confer a fleeting victory to a company or industry but it will not stand the test of time. As commodity prices fell, many companies were forced to retrench, restructure, or even file for bankruptcy. Always ask the question: is this a high-quality business experiencing a tough time or a low-quality business experiencing a good time? The former is an opportunity; the latter is a red flag.

Tangible Patents Versus Intangible Know-How

Investors are typically impressed with companies that own patents but often fail to evaluate a more powerful form of intellectual property—know-how. Patents are tangible but perishable; they eventually expire. They can also be copied (with some tweaks) or challenged in court. Did you know that some of the worst-performing stocks over the past several years, such as Xerox, IBM, and Canon, are some of the largest patent owners? In my experience, patents are overrated, know-how is underrated.

Know-how is accumulated knowledge about a process or technique that is hard to decipher or reverse engineer. That means it can yield a competitive advantage for a long period of time. Consider ceramic resistors and capacitors made by Murata Manufacturing. These components are used in smartphones to minimize interference in the complex electrical circuitry embedded in most modern electronics. We use them every day but do not realize their value because they are not visible. Making a ceramic product is like making pottery. It is a complex mix of engineering design, carefully calibrated composition of materials, as well as the precise duration and temperature at which it is heated in the furnace. This is extremely hard if not impossible to reverse engineer. Such know-how is more precious and less perishable than a patent. Know-how can create high barriers to entry and yield not just superior but supernormal profits in a company.

High Tech Versus Proprietary Tech

In a similar vein as patents, investors often equate high tech with superiority and a marker of a high-quality business, when it may turn out to be the opposite. This is a mistake I made early in my career in the 1990s when investing in petrochemical-refining plants in Asia. I equated their technical complexity with high barriers to entry and competitive advantage. I was right about the *facts* but wrong about the *conclusion*. A petrochemical-manufacturing plant is indeed very sophisticated and complex. However, the technology and expertise to build and install the process-automation equipment in the manufacturing plant is owned by their suppliers, such as ABB, Siemens, and Emerson Electric, and they sell it to anyone who wants to buy it. There is nothing exclusive or proprietary about it. This explains why, despite being high-tech, petrochemical plants do not generate good returns on capital invested, which makes them low-quality businesses with poor value-creation prospects.

I almost repeated this research mistake a few years ago in 2013, when I researched State Street's new IT platform, which they touted as best-in-class and transformational for their business. The IT platform was supposed to be an inflection point for State Street because it enabled straight-through processing of data, provided real-time information on the cloud, reduced data-migration challenges, and expedited onboarding of new clients. This all sounded highly appealing. But having learned from my early mistake in the high-tech petrochemical sector, I asked whether the technology was proprietary or available to anybody. I learned that the technology was indeed state-of-the-art, but it was procured from a third-party vendor (IBM), which meant it was not unique, and anyone could buy or implement something similar if they chose to.

I therefore passed on owning the stock because I concluded that the new IT platform would indeed help with all the things State Street had described, but it would merely serve to *reduce a competitive disadvantage, not secure a competitive edge.*

Why? Because competitors like Northern Trust had their own proprietary IT platforms that already offered all the benefits that State Street was trying to secure with its new one. State Street had grown through acquisitions, and each acquired company had come with its own distinct IT system, creating a highly disparate infrastructure that needed an extensive revamp. This is why they needed to overhaul their IT platform at great expense while Northern Trust did not.

My initial misdiagnosis could have proven costly, but thankfully I course-corrected by asking the right questions, to ensure my final assessment was more on target. Several years have passed since the new IT platform was implemented at State Street. It has not resulted in any material market-share gains or conquest wins from competitors. Like its business, the stock has not had much traction either.

On the other hand, Northern Trust's proprietary IT platform was and remains both robust and versatile. Because it is more flexible, it can offer greater customization and bespoke services in its core asset servicing business, which lead to higher customer satisfaction. This in turn enables Northern Trust to charge a premium price and enjoy better margins.

This is yet another instance of where the facts were true, but the initial, conventional inference drawn from them was false. Not all investments or improvements, however transformational, create business opportunity. The new IT platform was a definite improvement over the old one, but it did not help State Street move the needle in winning new clients or growing revenues; it primarily helped to retain existing ones and lower the cost of servicing them. This underscores the importance of distinguishing high tech from proprietary tech. They are not the same.

Buyer Beware: Knowing Quality for What It Is

A final word on understanding quality: It is bad enough to fall for low-quality companies that are masquerading as high quality, but it is practically a crime to fall for low quality that is obviously low quality. I'm talking about companies with no competitive advantages or compelling customer-value propositions, who engage in poor corporate governance; have weak balance sheets, internal controls, or oversight; don't make enough money to cover the cost or risk of being in business; or have management teams who focus on short-term results at the expense of long-term value creation for customers and shareholders.

We are all familiar with the fraud perpetrated by Enron and WorldCom and the large losses inflicted on unsuspecting investors. Management teams such as those at Lehman Brothers, who focused on managing earnings instead of capital, blew up in the bonfire of their own vanities by taking on more risk than was prudent and exposed their employees and shareholders to both losses and humiliation.

What is noteworthy about these examples is not that their game was finally up, but that they could hide it for so long despite being audited by marquee accounting firms and being subject to stiff penalties under various regulations. As Warren Buffett points out, it is only when the tide goes out that you find out who has been swimming naked.

But the non-consensus investor understands that the key is to know who is swimming naked *before* the tide goes out, not after, because it is you who will end up losing money, not the swimmers.

Worse yet, some companies engage in fraud or accounting shenanigans that elude even regulators or auditors, let alone investors. This is truly a call for "buyer beware." Low-quality companies are more likely to resort to accounting chicanery to inflate their reported earnings. But no matter how clever the companies pretend to be, they can obfuscate reality for only so long. And deploying the research skills described in this chapter can help you avoid them. Here is one more real-world anecdote of how to question quality—or the lack of it.

In 2006, while researching QBE Insurance in Australia, I wondered how they had managed to report terrific earnings growth for several years when the underlying industry backdrop did not call for such performance. I could not understand the "why," so I walked away from a "what" that appeared too good to be true. It turned out to be a prescient move that spared me major losses. The stock plunged 65 percent, from a peak of A$35 in September 2007 to about A$10 through December 2018 (figure 7.4). It turns out there was no good reason for the company to have "made" those kinds of earnings. For several years thereafter, the company issued a series of profit warnings revealing that they had under-reserved for their liabilities (by implication, overstating past

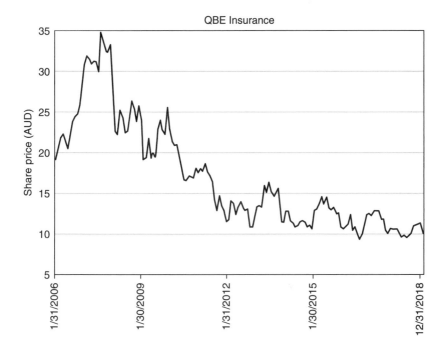

FIGURE 7.4 Share price performance: QBE Insurance, 1/31/2006–12/31/2018

earnings and book values). A once-revered management team fell from grace and was booted out by the board, while investors voiced their disdain by dumping the shares. This is the power of understanding *why* as opposed to merely *what*.

Quality Does Not Come with a Label, but It Does Have a Definition

To sum up, then, when it comes to investing, quality is not black or white but has many shades of gray. Neither businesses nor their stocks come marked with quality labels (unlike bonds, which at least have credit ratings). To understand quality holistically and correctly, you need variant perceptions and unconventional frameworks that go beyond the typical clichés and checklists.

In assessing quality, you must be vigilant about circular logic, in which you confuse cause and effect or conflate numbers with the narrative. As we have seen, often a business can appear successful because of a favorable trend, with a rising tide lifting all boats, or a competitive advantage that proves fleeting or fickle. The *symptoms* of success do not explain the *source* of success— or its sustainability. It is crucial to understand that sustainability, because earnings power without staying power can be a recipe for losing money. In markets, low quality often masquerades as high quality, and that is among the worst possible investment traps you can fall into.

Although quality does not come with a label, I will take a stab at providing a working definition. A genuinely high-quality business is one that offers exclusive and enduring value propositions to consumers and generates a fair return to justify both the costs and risks of lawfully engaging and reinvesting in that business.

In this chapter, we learned how to avoid the entrapment of mistaking low quality for high quality. In the next chapter, we will learn about the opposite—how to identify a high-quality company, ideally one that is mistaken for low quality. With those mispriced winners, you improve your chances of scoring upset victories and generating higher returns with lower risk.

Top Takeaways

1. What causes people to lose money unexpectedly and unwittingly? The answer is quality—or, more specifically, a misconception of quality.
2. Conventional thinking not only fails to diagnose quality, but often leads you to misdiagnose it, giving you the market equivalent of a false positive or a false negative test result.

3. Reset your reflexive inferences and examine the counter-factual. Brands, pricing power, leading market share, etc. are *symptoms* of quality, not *sources*.

4. Quality is a mosaic, not a metric; a capability, not a criterion; a latticework, not a label. It is not black or white but has many shades of gray. To find it, you need variant perceptions and holistic frameworks that go beyond the typical clichés and checklists.

5. A genuinely high-quality business is one that offers exclusive and enduring value propositions to consumers and generates a fair return to justify both the costs and risks of lawfully engaging and reinvesting in that business.

8

Ditch the Database, Embrace the Search Engine

Everyone wants to own a quality business, but if everyone is after the same quality, chances are it has already been bid up, which means it represents an overpriced booby trap, not a lucrative buy. Investment success accrues to those who identify and own what is missed, misunderstood, misjudged, and mispriced, while avoiding the crowded craze to own what is well understood, well loved, and well priced. Insist on quality, but look for it in a way, in a place, or at a time that few others are.

For investors, the puck has moved from the database to the search engine. A research edge is not secured from collecting information but connecting it. In a world where any public information can be Googled or Binged, looking for answers is a fool's errand because information (answers) that everyone has is not worth having. However, few have access to the right questions, which is why that effort has a better payoff.

This chapter provides the litmus-test questions investors should ask to identify non-consensus winners (and losers). Various examples, ranging from Toyota to Tapestry, illustrate how to figure out what, if anything, is misunderstood and mispriced.

Connect the Dots That Others Have Not

In investing, everyone wants to own high-quality companies—and that's precisely the problem. When everyone is after the same high-quality company, chances are the stock has been bid up and is overvalued. That makes it a booby trap (high risk, low returns), not a lucrative buy (high returns, low risk). Why waste time and energy chasing what everyone else is, when there is no money to be made even if you get your hands on it? Better to redirect your attention and efforts elsewhere. Insist on high quality, but look for it with a different lens.

> **"Big payoffs accrue to those who correctly identify high quality that *nobody* else has, not what *everybody* else has."**

Get off the obvious high-quality bandwagon and abandon the race to own businesses that are already well understood, well loved, and well priced. Big payoffs are more likely to accrue to those who correctly identify high quality that *nobody* else has, not what *everybody* else has. In this chapter, you will learn how to look around the bend to uncover the quality that is hidden in plain sight and, therefore, has been bid *down* instead of up. This allows you to own companies when they are undervalued instead of overvalued, improving your odds of generating higher returns with lower risk.

Quality: The Mother of All Mistakes and Mother Lode of All Opportunities

In the previous chapter, we figured out how to smoke out low quality that masquerades as high quality. In this chapter, I will show you how to find high quality that is mistaken as low quality and make money by arbitraging the difference. But before I show you how to do this, let me teach you how *not* to do it. In fundamental investing, research is about asking the right questions, not data mining the right answers.

Collecting information (getting the answers) is of little value, but *connecting* information (knowing what questions to ask) is incredibly valuable. When it comes to investing, assimilating a lot of information is just another form of intellectual chicanery. Simply because you know the historical financial performance of a company does not mean you understand the how or the why behind those numbers. Research is not merely about *knowing* a lot; it is about *understanding* a lot and, more importantly, *applying* what you know. Unfortunately, from kindergarten through college, most people are spoon-fed questions that lead them to "right" answers. We need to rewire these bad forms of learning, because they give us a knack for *accumulating* knowledge, not *applying* it.

The research puck has moved from the database to the search engine. In a world where any public information can be Googled or Binged, looking for answers is a fool's errand. Information that everyone has is not worth having. However, few have access to the right questions, which is why putting effort into knowing what questions to ask tends to have a bigger payoff. Once you know the right questions, the answers are at your fingertips. This counterintuitive approach to research puts you in a powerful position to connect the dots that others have not and convert ordinary information into extraordinary insights.

> **"The research puck has moved from the database to the search engine."**

Here is a list of key litmus-test questions that can be applied to any part of the market, whether a stock or a sector, a domestic company or an international one, a small cap or a mega cap. Obviously, while this list covers a lot of ground, it is by no means exhaustive.

Nine Questions to Nirvana

1. Where has apathy or pessimism degenerated into neglect?

If I told you that a country which instituted the shortest work week and levied among the highest corporate tax rates, offered you some of the finest investment opportunities in the developed world, you would not believe me. Suppose you did some additional research and uncovered two more troubling facts: Despite the highest public expenditure (57 percent) relative to GDP, this country had among the highest unemployment rates (10 percent). And despite repeated fiscal stimulus and budget deficits since 1981, it experienced among the lowest economic growth rates in the OECD.[1]

Knowing all that, you would think of this country as a loser and stay away. After all, how could such an economy, steeped in socialism and profligacy, offer capitalistic or profit potential? But that would be a mistake. Pessimism offers fertile investment opportunity because bad news is priced in, while good news is not. The country I am referring to is France, and yes, it is home to many world-class companies. If you care to look, you will find many French companies whose products we love and willingly pay up for.

From luxury goods (Louis Vuitton, Hermes, Gucci) to luxury beverages (French Champagne, Chivas Regal whiskey) to high-end Varilux lenses (Essilor) to state-of-the-art electrical wiring solutions (Legrand) to exotic perfumes (Christian Dior) to prestige cosmetics (L'Oréal) to premium tires (Michelin) to high-tech aircraft

---

1. The Organization for Economic Co-operation and Development, an intergovernmental economic organization with thirty-six member countries, was founded in 1961 to stimulate economic progress and world trade.

(Airbus, Dassault Aviation, Safran, Thales) to cutting-edge software and encryption technology (Dassault Systemes, Gemplus), France has produced many outstanding products and enterprises.

Many of these companies may not be household names, but they sell household products you recognize. If you use a cell phone or a credit card, chances are you have used a Gemplus product, because they make the SIM card or the CHIP card that authenticates you as the rightful owner. If you drive a car or ride in a plane, you are experiencing the 3-D engineering design software made by Dassault. If you wear prescription or high-end eyewear, chances are your lenses and the protective coatings that make them smudge free or scratch resistant were made by Essilor.

You are already familiar with the other companies mentioned above, so I won't describe them. But did you know that as of December 31, 2018, the stocks of Airbus and Kering (parent of luxury brand Gucci) have gone up eightfold since the market bottom in March 2009, a feat matched by only a handful of stocks in the rest of the world? Did you know that L'Oréal has quadrupled over that period, while its U.S. counterpart Procter & Gamble has barely doubled? Ditto for Essilor, which is up fourfold, and Dassault Systèmes, up sevenfold. You would be hard pressed to find so many successes anywhere, let alone in the large-market-capitalization range.

The point is, with approximately forty thousand listed stocks to choose from in the world, your best strategy is to look for countries or companies that suffer from disinterest or disregard. The wider you cast your net, the more fish you are likely to catch. This is why it makes sense to not restrict your investment choices to your home country but consider going abroad where many best-in-class companies exist. Sure, investing internationally can come with more risk but it can also reduce risk via diversification as well as offer opportunity. (Recall from chapter 6: there is a difference between being risk-aware and risk-averse.)

2. Where is failure priced in, but success is not?

Most investors devote enormous time and attention on success stories and want a piece of that success, often at any price. This is usually a recipe not to make money but to lose it. Here is my non-consensus advice: you are better off researching *failure*. Two benefits: it will sharpen your antennae for what can go wrong; but also, if it has already gone wrong and your research tells you a reversal is at hand, you can score an upset victory.

This was the setup when I researched Microsoft in 2012. It was a *well-known* but, in my opinion, not *well-understood* company. The consensus view at the time was that Apple would be the winner and Microsoft the loser. The bears pointed out that unlike Apple, Microsoft had neither a compelling mobile operating system nor a compelling device, and since the smartphone was becoming the handheld computer of choice, Apple's success would come at Microsoft's expense. Moreover, as desktop PC's became obsolete and declined, Microsoft would suffer as they derived a large portion of their revenues from that end market. This bleak view was reflected in a falling share price and lowly multiple.

My independent research led me to a very different, non-consensus conclusion.

For starters, I learned that the company had been developing a new Windows operating system that would not only work on PCs but also on laptops, tablets, and phones. This unified operating system would enable a seamless computing experience for users across various devices and reduce development costs for third-party software developers, making it a win-win proposition. In addition, the company was leapfrogging from the desktop to the data center by offering a cloud computing platform called Azure. Since the latter was expected to grow at a high double-digit clip, it would more than offset the decline in the traditional desktop market. More importantly, the company was pivoting from a product-centric offering to a service-centric offering which would provide more recurring and resilient revenues and command a higher multiple. Moreover, this transition to a software as a service (SAAS) business model would not only enhance its offerings but also expand its addressable market, allowing it to grow instead of being cannibalistic.

> **"When failure is priced in but success is not,**
> **the risk-reward balance becomes**
> **extremely attractive."**

The market anchored on the unsuccessful launch of Windows 8 phones and tablets as evidence of permanent failure. I was less concerned because I knew from long experience that Microsoft has a history of initially waning but eventually winning. For instance, the company had missed launching a browser in a timely fashion, giving Netscape an early lead. But they made a strong comeback with Internet Explorer. In the early days, Xbox was viewed as the poor cousin of the more popular PlayStation 2, but over time, it narrowed the gap.[2]

The consensus view was that Microsoft would stagnate or decline, whereas my research showed many opportunities for profitable and lasting growth. When failure is priced in but success is not, the risk/reward balance becomes quite attractive. As the company's strategy played out, earnings growth far exceeded initial consensus expectations, which forced the street to alter its negative view to a more positive one. Unsurprisingly, the stock has almost quadrupled from its 2012 lows of $28.50 to more than $110 in 2018, as what was once priced for failure and disappointing growth is now getting priced for success and steady growth.

---

2. And it now set to achieve a lead with the impending launch of XCloud—a video gaming as a streaming service à la Netflix.

3. Where are the babies being thrown out with the bathwater?

Every industry is subject to flux and declines. The key is to look beyond current events and prevailing sentiment to find money-making opportunities in the aftermath.

Over the past decade, the pharmaceutical industry experienced a seismic drop in profits as many lucrative blockbuster drugs went off patent and cheap generics appeared to take their place. Rising health-care costs and shrinking medical budgets further conspired to put a lid on the industry's profitability. As if that were not enough, scandalous revelations of unscrupulous behavior by some bad actors such as Valeant cast a pall over the entire industry. The result: even though the markets were scaling new highs, many health-care stocks were testing new lows (in terms of valuations, if not stock price).

I find that when both politicians and the media fall over each other to bash an industry, it is usually a sign of populist pandering as opposed to balanced analysis. The higher the decibel points, the greater the likelihood of a bottom forming in the sector being targeted as a punching bag, as the barrage of bad news blinds or scares investors away.

Non-consensus thinkers like me know from experience that there are two sides to every story and that industry fortunes tend to wax and wane. It is likely to happen in the health-care industry as well.

Ironically, I feel investors are giving up on the sector just as the green shoots are emerging. The health-care industry is on the cusp of major breakthroughs in treating life-threatening diseases such as cancer. Cutting-edge research and unconventional approaches to interrupting disease pathways are spurring a whole new paradigm of treating many debilitating or degenerative diseases. There is remarkable progress in areas ranging from gene-splicing to immunotherapy. In fact, contrary to perceived wisdom, many health-care companies are delivering more innovation than revered Silicon Valley upstarts.

The health-care companies that know how to conduct innovative research and produce drugs that score well on safety (side effects), efficacy (slower disease progression or cures), and novelty (differentiated mechanisms or pathways of treatment) are likely to decouple from the industry's challenges. My unconventional view is that for the companies rooted in science and skilled in doing R&D, *the industry's challenges are also their opportunities.*

On the other hand, the lucky health-care companies that were cruising along during the industry's heyday—not on the strength of their superior R&D, but on the back of their superior marketing mousetraps (seducing practitioners with promotional freebies or jaunts to exotic locations under the garb of hosting industry conventions)—will suffer their deserved demise.

The market is not wrong in derating and dumping some of the health-care stocks. It is simply wrong in not differentiating among them and devaluing all of them. If you can sort the valuable from the worthless, you can pick up the babies being thrown out with the bathwater and enjoy good gains. Companies with superior, diversified, and proven R&D platforms are likely examples of high quality. Single-product biotech companies with hit-or-miss prospects are more likely to be risky, low-quality investments, even if they have moonshot potential.

Of course, there are examples of such polarized opportunities in every sector and geography; the health-care sector is simply a more recent illustration of this principle. But I have come across similar opportunities in other industries throughout my career. For instance, in the late 1990s, when nobody wanted to own "old economy" stocks in the basic resources sector, best-in-class companies such as Rio Tinto were available for a song, even as the rest of the market was rip-roaring. In the decade that followed, an unexpected commodity boom catapulted the stock into stardom, yielding many contrarian investors a handsome profit.

On Wall Street, any company, sector, or geography can go from zero to hero to zero again in short bursts of time, with investors showing complete amnesia or denial to such round-trip excursions. A long-term approach to investing not only guards against such amnesia but takes advantage of it. In the next chapter, we will look at such behavioral biases and the compelling investment opportunities they present.

For now, note how non-consensus investing performs double duty once again. Not only does researching the full range of long-term outcomes help you go into an investment with eyes wide open (not narrowly squinted on just a few quarters ahead), but the same research effort serves to distinguish the professionals from the amateurs. By figuring out not only who survived the shifting tides but who prospered from them, you get a business that offers both defense and offense. And that is worth having in your portfolio. Grab such high-quality businesses when they are temporarily out of favor and go on sale; they invariably provide compelling investment opportunities.

4. Where is the future better than the past?

A potent example of where the future looks different from the past is the auto-components sector. The backward-looking consensus view was that manufacturers of auto components were mere widget-makers, vulnerable to boom/bust cycles and doomed to low commoditized returns because of their weak bargaining power with their key customers.

That was then; this is now. Over the past decade, the car has become more like a computer—think of all the electronic components in your car, from GPS navigation to electronic braking systems—the auto-component companies that switched gears from merely manufacturing pieces of hardware (standalone widgets) to adding software (integrated systems) came out winners. One such company was Harman. It is renowned for making high-quality audio speakers, making it the product of choice for major events ranging from rock concerts to political conventions.

For many years leading up to 2010, the company had seen declining sales and earnings, even as its peers in the auto-parts sector were experiencing robust recoveries. This is because the company had mispriced contracts, and as costs exceeded the contracted prices, they made losses instead of profits. In addition, they lost some key customers, which aggravated their poor cost position, as high fixed costs were amortized over less revenues.

The Board correctly grasped the gravity of the problems and appointed an outsider, Dinesh Paliwal, as a CEO. This change of management piqued my interest, so I did more research. I gleaned from various research reports and the company's website that the new CEO's transformation strategy was designed to do double duty—to fix the cost structure as well as grow the revenues by launching new products such as infotainment systems. His Chief Technology Officer, Sachin Lawande, was a key asset and ally in this transformational strategy so I met with both of them several times to thoroughly understand the scope and scale of the transformation. I came away impressed. My interactions told me that the company was moving from a product-based to a platform-based approach to manufacturing. I had seen this production strategy achieve great success at other companies, so I knew it had a good chance of working. The new modular production system would enable customization at low cost and allow the company to profitably make both high-end and mid-range products, significantly expanding their addressable market opportunity as they could serve both premium and mass market car companies.

From public press releases I kept learning that the company's new products were getting many design wins in new car models, providing further confirmation that the strategy was working. It was only a matter of time when this business success would show up in the financial statements as revenue and profit growth.

However, before that rosy future materialized, the prevailing earnings picture looked dismal as it reflected past mistakes which were still working their way through their financial results. This was a classic set-up where their past did not reflect the future, and my view was vastly different than the consensus. This presented an opportunity. If I was correct and proved everyone else wrong, an upset victory with its attendant rewards would emerge. Fortunately my research proved correct in this instance (as I have cautioned, not all research turns out to be correct), and I profited from it as the shares of Harman rallied from about $45 in 2013 to $111 a few years later, as investors (and its new owner, Samsung who bought it in 2017) began to appreciate the transformation underway.

5. Where is secular growth hiding behind cyclical volatility?

Growth companies can often hit an air pocket in earnings, not because their value proposition or competitiveness is eroding but because the end market is facing temporary weakness. Some businesses depend on large orders from a few customers. Or their product is a durable good that customers can postpone for a while (but not forever). Or sales may be seasonal. For such businesses, significant lumpiness in orders can occur from quarter to quarter or year to year, causing earnings volatility. Investors like visibility and detest volatility and often dump the stock out of impatience. When such stocks trade well below their intrinsic worth, they offer a lucrative investment opportunity.

One example was Tumi, the premium luggage and briefcase company. Tumi luggage is popular among road warriors, as it is built to take a bullet, not just a beating—literally. Tumi uses the same ballistic nylon material that the military uses in its bullet-proof vests. However, while it makes great suitcases and was likely to enjoy a significant growth runway under a new CEO who was expanding the product lineup to attract the more elusive women shoppers, the company experienced a slowdown in sales in 2012, when Europe underwent an economic and financial crisis. When travel plans are canceled or budgets are cut, it is typical for Tumi sales to suffer. This slowdown, combined with an increase in store rent expense, hurt earnings. The stock fell to $16 giving me a chance to add to my position. A few years later, in 2016, Samsonite saw the same potential and value in Tumi stock that I had seen and bought out the company at a price of more than $26.

6. Where is the exception that defies the rules?

Science, art, literature, music—these fields are known for breaking the rules and freely incorporating the skill and creativity of multiple disciplines. The same is true of high-quality businesses. Just because a business model does not subscribe to Porter's Five Forces or other business-school standards does not mean that business cannot succeed. In fact, outside-the-box thinkers deserve special attention.

Low-cost upstart Ryanair is a terrific example. In an industry dominated by complacent incumbents like British Airways and Lufthansa, which held all the key routes and charged high prices, Ryanair reintroduced the discount airline model at the right time and with a new flair. Rather than playing up "cheap and quirky," which served People Express Airlines well back in the 1980s, Ryanair launched a "cheap and reliable" service throughout Europe, giving the big players a run for their money.

Likewise, oil and gas company EOG took a page from Silicon Valley start-ups in its shale-fracking business. By decentralizing decision-making in the company and embracing iterative innovation with a Silicon Valley-esque "fail fast and fail cheap" mantra, EOG's horizontal drilling operations have disrupted the status quo of the oil industry. It is now among the lowest-cost producers of oil outside of OPEC, and its stock is up twenty-five-fold, from $4 in 2000 to $100 in 2018. Disruptive business models or technologies can be fertile sources of upset victories, provided one knows how to conduct such research. It often takes deep domain expertise about the industry and years of training and practice to parse the reality from the hype, so be sure to stay within your circle of competence.

7. Where are the setbacks that are due for a comeback?

Coach, the premium handbag maker now called Tapestry, had been a successful company for decades before stumbling in the marketplace. In chapter 7, I explained what happened when the company became overly reliant on its high-margin but low-end outlet stores at the expense of its high-end but lower-margin urban stores. But that wasn't all. To focus on selling through its own directly owned and operated retail stores, it had neglected the indirect wholesale department-store channel. That oversight proved costly, as it provided an easy distribution entrée to its competitor, Michael Kors, who stole a lot of mind share and market share.[3] During those dismal years of deteriorating earnings performance, the stock plummeted from the $70s in 2012 to the $30s in 2014.

Reeling from a declining brand, deteriorating same-store sales, and a plunging share price, Coach made the bold decision to reboot its strategy under the leadership of a new management team. It brought in a new CEO, CFO, and chief designer to turn

---

3. Michael Kors is an American fashion designer and the chief creative officer of his brand, Michael Kors, which sells men's and women's ready-to-wear, accessories, watches, jewelry, footwear, and fragrance. His gowns are favored by many celebrities, including Kate Middleton, Hillary Clinton, Angelina Jolie, Jennifer Lopez, Michelle Obama, Ivanka Trump, Heidi Klum, and Viola Davis.

the business around. The change in strategy and C-suite set the stage for a comeback. The ingredients were there, and the proof points kept coming, from excellent product reviews by fashionistas and critics to the brand resuming its former glory in the eyes of the consumer. Soon the company was able to raise the average price points of its handbags, instead of discounting them.

However, this turnaround needed upfront investments and expenditures, and that depressed short-term earnings. That, in turn, presented a marvelous contrarian opportunity. As the company found its stride, the stock recovered as well.

Despite the good ending in the Coach turnaround, I would caution against blindly owning turnarounds. Like a fixer-upper in a bad neighborhood, a turnaround can be tempting, but owning the best house on a bad block is not a good idea. Similarly, if a turnaround company belongs to a bad industry, its problems are likely to be more chronic than transient. Best to expend your efforts elsewhere.

However, when a good house in a good neighborhood has a temporary problem that is easily fixed, it behooves you to look past the short term and weigh the long-term past and future. Coach has been an iconic American brand for more than fifty years. Its quality and craftsmanship are legendary, and it occupies the premium sweet spot between mass market and luxury. There were many things to like and only a few things to dislike (which the management team was addressing anyway). When a franchise is underappreciated, underearning, and undervalued, it provides a good backdrop to make money. Coach was a good example of high quality mistaken for low quality.

You may remember from chapter 7 that I described Coach as an example of a low-quality company as judged by its poor quality of decisions. In fact, Coach, like many others, has gone from high quality to low quality and now back again to high quality (and may go back again to low quality). Fundamental research is about assessing such change. Owning stocks during such transformations can prove lucrative. As a non-consensus investor, one should *see the opportunity, not just the threat, in change.*

Another opportunity arose in the aftermath of the September 11 terrorist attacks in New York. But the story started six years earlier, with an important lesson I learned from my travels to the Middle East.

It was 1995. I had just made the switch from the sell side to the buy side and was excited by my very first business trip to Israel and Turkey. I was flying in from New York, so I would have traversed three continents in the span of a few days (if one considers Israel as Europe and Turkey as part of Central Asia). That would qualify as jet-setting. I was also secretly thrilled that I was going to get the red-carpet treatment when I landed in Israel. My boss at Soros knew some big shots, and they were going to send a stretch limo onto the tarmac to fetch me when my flight landed. It felt like a scene from a Hollywood movie.

It started out exactly as I imagined, but ended nothing like it!

I was in the car heading to Na'an kibbutz, where I had planned to stay over the weekend. Little did I know that, instead of a pretty little Amish village, I was going into a battlefield. Suicide bombings were happening all over the country (eventually leading to the assassination of Prime Minister Rabin later that year). I was totally unprepared and absolutely petrified. But what I found even more astonishing was that my Israeli hosts, living amidst a hostile neighborhood surrounded by enemies, took it in total stride. For them it was just another day. I realized then how blessed and safe America was, protected by oceans and friendly neighbors. It is one thing to study history and politics, quite another to experience it in raw, real time.

But shocking as this episode was, it helped me overcome a greater tragedy six years later: the 9/11 terrorist bombings that changed America forever. Investors panicked; stock markets swooned. I did not. In Israel, I had witnessed humankind's capacity to adapt and resume normal life in the face of grave dangers. I believed New Yorkers and Americans would show the same resilience. That gave me the courage to buy stocks when others were fearful and wondering whether life would ever be the same. I remember the stock of Porsche AG collapsing to pennies on the dollar as investors noticed that not a single Porsche had sold that month in New York (which accounted for more than a third of U.S. sales at the time). I did not know when sales would resume, but I knew that eventually the human capacity for resilience would stabilize business, so I doubled up on Porsche stock.

Paradoxically, not only did sales resume their upward trend, they went through the roof, as people who had been on the fence about buying their dream car became painfully aware of life's uncertainties. Suddenly, doctors, lawyers, real estate agents, and engineers, not just Wall Street stereotypes, decided to buy Boxsters and Carreras, iconic Porsche models.

Keeping the faith when everybody around you is losing it is a good habit to cultivate. I hope tragic events never occur again, but we all know that is simply not possible. Investing requires a horizon of many decades, and a lot of bad things can happen in the intervening period. Instead of succumbing to negativity, remind yourself that *setbacks sow the seeds of comebacks*. Whether tax or tariff wars, currency or cost headwinds, competition or regulation, companies (like humans) adapt to new realities and figure out ways to not only survive but thrive.

8. Where are the second-order impacts being ignored?

Let us say you conclude that defense spending (and therefore defense stocks) will go up if the Republicans win power. If they do, chances are you will pocket some money in the immediate election aftermath. This instant payoff may feel gratifying, but it is chump change compared to the big payoffs that come from figuring out second-order impacts, where one change results in another change, like a domino effect. Focusing on second-order effects is like watching a stone thrown into a still pond; take your eyes off the stone and instead note where the ripples go. Let's look at an example.

Consider the impact of building highways across America after World War II—it led to a boom in car sales. At that point, most first-order investors flocked to own stocks of automakers. Perhaps some ingenious investors extrapolated from the obvious and bought the steel companies and auto-parts companies that would benefit indirectly. But the truly farsighted investor bought suburban real estate because cars would bypass the need for public transport (which was typically only available near expensive city centers) to get to work. Not only was it the biggest beneficiary of consumers' newfound mobility, it was also inexpensive compared to costly urban land where the jobs were. Suburban land was neither perceived nor valued as a great investment opportunity, yet it was about to become a gold mine.

Connecting the dots that others have not and identifying second-order effects before everyone else may be harder to figure out and take longer to play out. However, they pack a powerful punch by securing lucrative upset victories.

9. Where are the "and" propositions?

I saved the best question for last. As we learned in chapter 2, people, products, and companies that deliver the "and" propositions are game changers and become the benchmark to beat. Those who settle for delivering the suboptimal "or" are soon left in the dust.

To visualize the difference between "and" and "or," think of a car tire. It needs to grip the road well to provide better handling and braking. But if it grips too much, gas mileage suffers. In the perfect design, the grip is less and more at the same time—which seems impossible! Manufacturers can solve for one or the other, but not both simultaneously. And that's not all. To ensure a comfortable ride in vastly different road and weather conditions, a tire needs to be both sturdy and flexible—again, seemingly mutually exclusive goals. Yet the Michelin tire company has done exactly that. Through its superior R&D and manufacturing prowess, Michelin has solved for multiple "and" propositions. Since 1946, when the company first developed and patented a key innovation, the radial tire, it has successfully exploited this and other technological innovations to disrupt incumbents and take global market share.

Today, all tire companies make radial tires, but Michelin tires still stand out for their better engineering and value proposition. As of 2017, Michelin's lifetime total of eighty-four awards in the J. D. Power Original Equipment Tire Customer Satisfaction Study, (starting in 1989 when the study was first launched), was nearly four times more than all other tire manufacturers combined.[4]

Companies that deliver products with "and" propositions tend to succeed for a long time because what they do is exceedingly difficult to replicate. You have probably seen copycats of Louis Vuitton bags, but you would be hard pressed to find a fake Michelin tire. This is because the rubber composite in the tire is not possible to reverse engineer. Michelin excels because of its superior manufacturing know-how and understanding of natural rubber and synthetic elastomers. Its tires not only offer superior handling and comfort, but they also provide better braking, fuel efficiency, and reduced wear and tear (notice the multiple "and" propositions). Michelin tires skew the curve up on so many fronts that competitors and bootleggers find it hard to match, let alone beat, them. But here is the kicker: Because their direct and indirect benefits deliver large savings to customers, Michelin tires also prove less costly despite their higher sticker price. These twin

---

4. See Michelin North America, "Michelin Sweeps Most Respected Survey of Consumer Satisfaction, Winning Four J. D. Power Original Equipment Tire Awards," *Cision PR Newswire*, March 29, 2017, https://www.prnewswire.com /news-releases/michelin-sweeps-most-respected-survey-of-consumer-satisfaction -winning-four-jd-power-original-equipment-tire-awards-300431214.html.

attributes—high quality *and* low cost—have made Michelin the world's leading tire company. And the market is beginning to recognize it: Michelin stock doubled between 2012 and 2018, outperforming the French stock market by a factor of two.

Shifting gears to another example of "and" versus "or" we need look no further than non-consensus investing. Non-consensus investors are always on the lookout for companies that make or deliver a product, service, or solution in such a compelling way that customers don't even think of trying an alternative because none exists. Such companies epitomize high quality and exude the "and" proposition on a multitude of vectors:

- They possess exclusive *and* enduring darwinian advantages.
- They offer higher quality *and* lower cost, delivering unbeatable value propositions.
- They generate surplus cash to reinvest in the business *and* distribute regular dividends to shareholders.
- They succeed in the present *and* build momentum for the future.
- They play good offense *and* defense.
- They perform well in good times *and* hold up better in tough times.
- They offer upside potential *and* provide downside protection.

In short, high-quality companies give us many ways to win and few ways to lose; low-quality companies are riddled with either/or propositions. But be very careful. A high-quality *company* is not a high-quality *investment* unless the stock is trading at a discount to its intrinsic worth and offers some headroom for error. This usually happens when the business faces temporary challenges or setbacks and the stock goes out of favor. By insisting on owning high quality with a margin of safety, non-consensus investors improve the odds of securing higher returns *and* lower risk.

Top Takeaways

1. Investment success accrues to those who avoid what is well understood, well loved, and well priced and instead seek and find what is missed, misunderstood, misjudged, and mispriced.
2. The research puck has moved from the database to the search engine. A research edge is secured not from collecting information but connecting it.
3. The mother of all mistakes—misunderstanding quality—can be the mother lode of all investment opportunities for those who know how to distinguish genuine quality from deceptive quality.
4. To find high-quality investments, one must connect the dots that others have not. This does not mean deciding the answer in advance and looking for evidence to support it; it means asking the right questions to arrive at the truth.
5. A high-quality company is not a high-quality investment unless the stock is trading at a discount to its intrinsic worth. This usually happens when the business faces temporary challenges or setbacks and the stock goes out of favor.

9

From Victim to Victor

Behavioral biases introduce subjectivity and limit objectivity; be aware of them, and overcome them. Failure is not a failing, but an opportunity for learning.

Avoid bias in research; seek to invalidate, not validate. Question what does not add up, not what does.

We confuse correlations and causation because we are wired for pattern recognition and neat explanations, even if they are misguided. These human instincts are great for survival but not for investing. These default factory settings need to be reset.

Failure Is Not a Failing If You Make It an Opportunity for Learning

Throughout the centuries, our species has singularly and spectacularly overcome its weaknesses. We have not only survived but prospered. Our early ancestors knew that other members of the animal kingdom outclassed them because they were faster, stronger, and better armed with claws, teeth, or muscles. Yet it was only by recognizing this overwhelming disadvantage that we were able to conquer the enemy. Instead of being handicapped by our weaknesses, we rose to the challenge. We figured out that the smart move was to avoid hand-to-hand combat with the predatory animals, because that would play to the enemy's strengths and our weaknesses. We applied our brains to make sharp tools as projectiles (with bows and arrows) to kill the enemy from afar because it was critical to maintain a safe distance. The predators now became the prey. They did not even see what was coming; the unexpected speed and distance of the projectile became their blind spot. We vanquished them before they could even put up a fight.

We know what happened next. The hunters fed on the rich animal protein, which further reinforced their brain power, leading them from strength to strength. Thousands of years later, our brains have been responsible for astonishing inventions, discoveries, and incredible progress. Our species is a triumph of brain over brawn.

> **"Failure is not a failing if you
> make it an opportunity
> for learning."**

But our brains can also play mind games with us, sabotaging our own best interests. This chapter will hold up a mirror to reveal the enemy within. It exposes flaws that we often believe to be our fortes. While you may not relish knowing your flaws, failure is not a failing if you make it an opportunity for learning. And that is exactly how you should think about your behavioral shortcomings—not something you succumb to, but something to surmount.

Behavioral Biases = Mental Shortcuts and Faulty Wiring

Our brains are wired all wrong when it comes to making sound investment decisions. We have been programmed for survival, not soul-searching. The brain consumes the most energy of any organ in our body, so evolution has designed it to be efficient. For example, we are endowed with quick pattern recognition to make life-or-death decisions instinctively, as in our fight-or-flight response. But what helps in life hurts in investing when our hard-wired decision tools play mind games and turn into behavioral biases. Academics give fancy labels to them, from the planning fallacy (poor planning by assuming best-case scenarios) to the endowment effect (overvaluing what one owns versus what one does not). In plain language, behavioral biases are nothing other than mental shortcuts that our subconscious mind uses to make fast decisions.

There is no escaping human biases when it comes to investing. We are genetically predisposed. However, we can train our reflexes to serve us instead of hindering us. This chapter shows how you can transform these behavioral vices into virtues. At that point, you take advantage of innate biases rather than suffering from them.

Flaw #1. Jumping to False Conclusions: The Availability Bias

This bias is easy to understand but difficult to defend against. Our brain relies on pattern recognition to form quick assessments of circumstances. It often extrapolates the recent past to forecast the near future. It is especially partial to what academics call the availability bias—using readily available information even if it is irrelevant.

The widespread use of price/earnings (P/E) multiples to determine valuations is a good example. Even though earnings multiples are in many ways flawed, inaccurate measures of value, investors routinely use them because they are readily available. On the other hand, even though free cash flows are the more relevant determinant of intrinsic value, they are not widely used because they are harder to calculate and therefore not readily available.

The human brain defaults to shortcuts. The necessity of making split-second survival decisions has programmed the brain to prioritize speed and ready availability over everything else. Fast-moving ticker tapes and TV shows with titles like *Fast Money* are designed to appeal to our baser instincts. Resist the urge. Investing is a marathon, not a sprint. Before you form any investment conclusion, take the time to collect all the facts, contextualize them, identify any disconnects, and resolve them.

Early in my career, I made this mistake while researching companies. I would devour copious amounts of research that was readily available—sell-side research, annual reports, investor presentations, news articles, and on and on. I felt I was being diligent and rigorous. But when all this effort did not result in investment ideas with a compelling value spread, I soon realized that all I had done was to review information that led me to the consensus view rather than formulate a non-consensus one.

The Fix: Go Outside the Sandbox

I went outside the usual sandbox. I searched out ideas from a wider range: academic papers, interviews with key division heads in specialty trade publications, books written by former employees of companies I was researching, memoirs of former CEOs, case studies of analogous challenges faced in other industries, and so on. I began to understand businesses from the inside out rather than the outside in. This helped me ask the right questions, which led me to the correct and often non-consensus answers.

For example, I considered investing in companies that had won power-project contracts in Asia in the late 1990s. The readily available information was this:

1. There was an acute shortage of electricity, but governments lacked money to invest in multi-billion-dollar power generation infrastructure projects.
2. The lack of infrastructure was proving to be a big bottleneck to GDP growth and affecting quality of life.
3. To incentivize foreign investment, many governments such as those in China, Malaysia, Indonesia, and the Philippines

set up private-public partnerships (PPPs) with high guaranteed rates of returns.

4. The logic was so compelling and the guaranteed returns so mouthwatering that there was a gold rush for these investment opportunities.

5. Many institutional investors, such as U.S. university endowments, invested in these PPPs. Retail investors who could not invest directly in them latched onto this gravy train vicariously by owning stocks in companies that were winning the contracts, such as Hopewell Holdings, which was listed on the Hong Kong Stock Exchange.

Clearly, the readily available information suggested this was a win-win, with both governments and investors acting in rational self-interest. As an early student of behavioral finance (which studies the role and impact of human biases in investing), I knew I should look beyond the readily available information. I looked for PPPs in other industries and found that they were commonplace in building highways and bridges—often referred to as toll road projects. My findings startled me. There were far more failures than successes. Often, when consumers found out about the high tolls they had to pay for using the roads, they protested, forcing governments to capitulate and default on the contracts. Or the builders faced massive cost overruns, which the contracts did not cover, causing losses for shareholders and defaults on bondholders.

I feared a similar predicament awaited the PPPs in the power generation sector and avoided them. My concerns proved well founded. The gold rush turned into a minefield. Many governments went on to renegotiate or renege on those PPPs when costs proved too prohibitive. The endowments, as well as infrastructure stocks such as Hopewell Holdings, took big write-offs on their investments. On the other hand, my dollar saved became my dollar earned.

Flaw #2. Falling Victim to Vividness: The Recency Effect

A close cousin of the availability bias is the vividness/recency effect. It is the tendency to measure frequency by our ability to think of examples, which in turn produces a tendency to over-weight recent developments. For example, we believe flying is less safe after we see news of an airplane crash on TV. Even though the belief is baseless, it rings true because of the vividness of the imagery.

The recency effect is very similar. The human mind extrapolates recency into certainty. If you recently made money in the market, making money suddenly seems more likely or even a sure thing, even though reversals are just as likely. There is a 50–50 chance that the market could go down just as much as it could go up, but our brain believes otherwise because today's headlines over-shadow more distant memories.

This effect often manifests itself in pro-cyclical asset alloca-tion decisions. When emerging markets do well, investors flock to them. When the markets correct, the investors rush for the exits. When international equities do poorly versus U.S. equities, many investors lament the underperformance and switch over to what's working only to lose out or get whipsawed when the situation reverses.

The Fix: Think Long Term

Extend your time horizon and think long term. Ask what can go right when everyone around you is worrying about what can go wrong. It will help you make a balanced decision and stay the course. Long-term patient investors (and I am one) recognize the recency effect for what it is and tend to resist its pull. But it can be very seductive. Early in my career I made the mistake of having business news shows running in the background on my computer. The streaming headlines led me to subliminally focus on topical newsflow that explained recent developments or price action rather than inputs that affected the intrinsic worth of the business.

The fix was simple. I no longer watch live TV. I stay abreast of day-to-day news by reading newspapers instead of watching on the big screen as the vividness effect is a close proxy of the recency bias. (Moving images and sound are more vivid and tend to draw the viewer in emotionally while words tend not to have the same impact and allow one to consume information more dispassionately.)

Flaw #3. Monday-Morning Quarterbacking: Hindsight Bias

It is easy to believe we are smart when we make the correct call after the fact. I call it the "but of course" bias; academics call it the hindsight bias. You may recognize it as the Monday-morning quarterbacking syndrome.

Observed outcomes appear inevitable and predictable. If you already know which team won, you can look back and think the victory was inevitable and therefore predictable. Likewise, many who invested in Apple purely by fluke believe they just *knew* (with or without research) that the company was going to be a spectacular success story. They now view themselves as savvy investors, which may prove dangerous when they try their hand at picking the *next* Apple. Luck and skill are not the same thing.

I made this mistake myself when I invested in some stocks in the mid-1990s. I thought I had made the right call because they went up a lot. Fact of the matter is I did not have a good grasp of their business models or intrinsic values, but I thought I did because I made money. Several years later, when the air came out of these stocks, I got whipsawed by their volatility, not knowing whether I should double up or quit, as I had no basis to anchor my investment decisions. (This also goes back to the concept we learned in the previous chapter of markets rewarding correctness, not confidence.)

The Fix: Parse Luck from Skill

To give yourself a much-needed reality check down the road, take time to investigate before you invest, write down your investment theses and quantify your qualitative expectations in a spreadsheet. Then track how things are going in the business versus how you modeled it. This will enable you to separate out the luck from the skill. Most professional investors do this.

Flaw #4. Banking on Best-Case Scenarios: The Planning Fallacy

We all know that when the stakes are high, we should not count on the best-case scenarios, but instead plan for the worst. Yet most of us hope for the best and tune out the rest. In investing, such wishful thinking can prove problematic. I don't know anybody who can afford to play Russian roulette with their life savings. This is why we must insist on a margin of safety in our investments: it's like having insurance against large losses.

I made this mistake with a family-owned food products company. The company was enjoying great success in its dairy products' division as yogurt consumption was witnessing a resurgence among Western consumers. However, growth stalled when regulatory authorities stopped the company from advertising unsubstantiated health claims of probiotic benefits in its yogurt. I had assumed that they would launch other products or

158

market them differently, to offset this headwind. Instead, they chose to be acquisitive and bought growth instead of achieving it organically. They acquired a high-growth infant-nutrition business, at what I judged to be an extremely high valuation. To make matters worse, they funded this expensive acquisition by taking on loads of debt.

I had fallen for the planning fallacy. I had not considered the possibility that they would satisfy their growth envy through acquisitions, no matter how expensive or risky. I had assumed that because the management was also the largest shareholder, they would be excellent stewards of capital. But simply being aligned with shareholders is not enough for the best outcomes. Even well-intentioned, well-incentivized management teams can make mistakes in allocating capital. It was clear that I should have considered worst-case scenarios, not just planned on the best case. The company remains highly indebted, and the stock has had no traction for about a decade ending December 2018, a period when most equity markets around the world have appreciated considerably.

The Fix: Play Devil's Advocate

I believe in debating my investment theses with someone else who plays the role of a devil's advocate to weigh the strengths and weaknesses of an investment case. By the way, this is not an original idea—I borrowed it from the world's greatest investor, Warren Buffett. In my opinion, Charlie Munger is Buffett's de facto sounding board and devil's advocate, whether he sports the title or not. Frankly, it is what we all do in our daily lives—naming a designated driver when we go out drinking. Similarly, the job of the devil's advocate is to stay sober and balanced, even if the person advocating the investment case has had one beer too many.

Flaw #5. Overvaluing What You Possess, or Denial on Steroids: The Endowment Effect

The endowment effect is the tendency to overvalue what you own over what you do not. It means rationalizing a decision once it has been made, whether or not it was made on valid grounds.

The endowment effect can dull the brain. We get lulled into a comfort zone and stop scrutinizing our holdings. Growth managers often fall in love with their high-flying stocks, justifying their rich valuations by endowing them with qualities that are easy to pitch, even if they do not truly exist. This flaw comes back to haunt when growth disappoints and the stock craters. Complacency is not a good reason to continue owning overrated stocks well past their prime.

The Fix: Practice Zero-Base Thinking

This flaw can be fixed using the same idea management consultant Peter Drucker used with GE's CEO Jack Welch. Drucker challenged Welch: "If you weren't already in this business, would you enter it today? And if the answer is no, what are you going to do about it?" That single question reset the trajectory of the company. It transformed the way Welch thought about running a conglomerate. Likewise, you should ask yourself a similar question: "If I didn't own the stock already, would I buy it today?"[1] This is known as zero-base thinking.

---

1. Note that many corporations are adopting a variant of this question: If you did not incur this expense before, would you incur it today? It's called zero-based budgeting.

Many hedge-fund managers guard against the endowment effect by forcing preset stop-loss limits on trades. They automatically sell the stock when the limit hits. The manager can then reassess whether to reinstate that position by buying it back. Some would regard this as suboptimal from the standpoint of transaction cost: it costs money to liquidate and reinstate a position. But the smart money considers it a small price to pay to guard against the larger cost of suffering from the endowment effect. In fact, because the benefits can outweigh the costs, in many hedge funds this is a standard risk-management policy.

In hindsight, I suffered from this syndrome when I owned Ericsson in the mid-2000s. Ericsson makes telecom equipment that carries about 40 percent of the world's mobile-phone traffic. Its base stations allow mobile phones to access cellular signals so we can make phone calls or surf the internet while on the move. A key element of my thesis was that the company would benefit from consolidation in the industry, and both revenues and margins would improve. This seemed a reasonable assumption, given the demise of Motorola and Nortel and the mergers of Lucent-Alcatel and Nokia-Siemens. Unfortunately, it did not play out as I hoped. Stiff competition came from Chinese vendors ZTE and Huawei, who were willing to offer ultra-low pricing to gain entry into the global market, even at the expense of profitability.

As it happens, I was aware of this threat. However, I did not take the competition seriously because Ericsson's management led me to believe that their technology was a differentiator and their costs were competitive. I also liked management's strategic pivot toward offering professional services—persuading their telecom customers to outsource the running of their wireless networks to Ericsson. The computing world had found success with outsourcing back-end infrastructure, so it seemed logical to assume the same benefits would apply in the communications' networking world.

Sadly, that did not prove to be the case. Unlike IT customers, who are numerous and can derive scale benefits from outsourcing, telecom companies are a small handful, no more than three to four in any given country. So unless everyone in that country outsourced, there would be low to no synergies. Last but not least, the largest telecommunications companies typically had a large and long-serving employee base, so their severance and pension costs were prohibitively expensive. This meant they had a *disincentive* to outsource.

I wanted to believe that the company was well positioned, but there were growing signs that my thesis was not holding up. Despite management's assertion of technological superiority and cost competitiveness, I had noticed that the Chinese company Huawei was winning contracts with big customers such as British Telecom. When I questioned the management of Ericsson about this potential threat, they dismissed the win as small potatoes; the contract, they pointed out, was for a tiny territory like the Isle of Man, a mere outpost for British Telecom. What they (and I) did not realize is that those small wins were test beds to secure learning curves; they turned out to be precursors of larger contracts down the road.

Even though I suffered from the endowment effect and believed in the company's capabilities and strategy, I did not suffer from confirmation bias (see Flaw #10). I kept looking for evidence that undermined my thesis. Once I had gathered enough evidence to the contrary, I sold the stock in 2006 and 2007, even though it meant taking a loss. That decision proved to be the right one. A decade later, the company and its stock have continued to struggle (figure 9.1).[2]

---

2. For more details, see Matthias Verbergt, "Ericsson Shares Dive on Profit Warning," *Wall Street Journal*, April 6, 2016, updated October 12, 2016, https://www.wsj.com/articles/ericsson-warns-on-profit-as-demand-dries-up-1476254597.

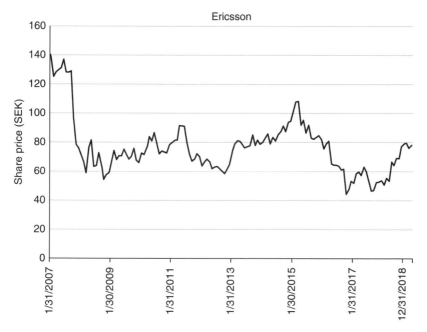

FIGURE 9.1 Share price performance: Ericsson, 1/31/2007–12/31/2018

Flaw #6. Ignoring a Wrong Instead of Righting It: Loss Aversion

This is a close cousin of the endowment effect, and the antidote is the same. People resist taking losses on failed investments because they do not want to acknowledge failure or defeat. To make matters worse, instead of quitting, they often double down. Cutting your losses ensures two salutary outcomes: you learn from your mistakes, and you spare your portfolio further damage from an investment that is headed south.

The best way to figure out if one is wrong, rather than simply ahead of others in an investment call, is to compare how the underlying *business* is performing (as opposed to how the *stock* is performing) versus one's expectations in the original investment thesis. If the business (not the stock) is tracking my expectations, I hold onto or even average down on my investment. However, if it is performing worse than my expectations, I force myself to rethink my thesis and apply the fix discussed below. As we have seen throughout this chapter, the worst part of a mistake is not the mistake itself but how soon you identify it, acknowledge it, and address it. Loss aversion only compounds one's mistakes.

The Fix: Acknowledge Reality and Cut Bait Quickly

Over the past few years, many value investors have continued to cling to their investment in the hitherto successful but now troubled British food retailer Tesco, hoping that a new management with a different strategy will restore the company's profitability. This behavior stems from both anchoring (past success is etched in people's heads, described next) and loss aversion (denial).

Initially, in 2012, I shared this view. By 2014, I changed my mind as new facts emerged. I realized that the competitive dynamics of the UK market had permanently shifted and management's profit targets would miss by a mile. Tesco's hypermarket formats would struggle to compete with the biggest hypermarket in the world (Amazon) in general merchandise as well as with discounters (Aldi and Lidl) in groceries. Consumer preferences for choice and low cost were met by these two distribution channels, which sat at opposite ends of the spectrum. Tesco sat in the middle and got squeezed by both. In response, it embarked on a major cost-cutting program to restore competitiveness and win back customers. However, contrary to what management had guided, even if it worked, profit margins and profits would reset to a materially lower level and stay there. What made matters worse is that the company tried to disguise or delay acknowledging these profit shortfalls by extracting unfair and unsustainable rebates from suppliers and reporting earnings that had not really been earned. The poor quality of management decisions raised corporate governance concerns in my mind. The returns were falling while the risks were growing—the opposite of the attributes I seek. I saw the writing on the wall and cut my losses by selling out of my position. Better to acknowledge that my thesis had been busted and cut bait to redeploy the proceeds elsewhere.

I mentioned before that failure is not a failing but an opportunity for learning. I zeroed in on the root causes (there were many). A key lesson was that the hypermarket/supercenter format was structurally vulnerable to the threat from e-tailing, and therefore best avoided. To apply this learning, I identified many other retailers in the world with similar formats and competitive dynamics and made a note not to own them.

Flaw #7. Clinging to the Past and Being Slow to React to Change: Anchoring Bias

You are stuck in the past, refusing to admit that things have changed. In the case of investing, it means fixating on a certain point of view.

Many companies generate high profits when times are good, not necessarily because the company itself is good. When the tailwinds turn to headwinds, the company flounders. The mind takes time to process this changed reality. Academics call this anchoring—the tendency to adjust prior estimates insufficiently when presented with new information. In simpler terms, it means human beings are slow to react to change and prefer to cling to a point of view even though it is no longer valid.

Many investors prefer to invest in industries that do not change, such as consumer staples. Actually, I think it may be time for these investors to change. Change is inevitable, but the anchoring bias is preventing investors from sizing up and pricing in the emerging risks in the sector. Instead of glossing over these risks, one should take a hard and honest look. The price transparency on e-tailing platforms such as Amazon is giving a headache to manufacturers of branded goods. For instance, it is commonplace for the same product to be priced higher in the convenience store channel than the supermarket channel, which in turn would be higher than the price charged at a warehouse club. However, the days of easy markups and price discrimination among different distribution channels may be behind us. In the online world, the consumer is king. Consumers can readily search for the product with the lowest price and highest value, marginalizing retailers and manufacturers who do not adjust to this new paradigm. Eventually, investors will be forced to question whether the pricing power that anchored their favorable investment view of the "fast-moving-branded-consumer-goods" sector still holds.

Historically, established branded-goods companies had the upper hand in securing distribution, as shelf space is scarce in a retail storefront. But in the digital arena, shelf space is unlimited; anyone with a compelling product can reach consumers. The distribution access and advantage that only big brands once enjoyed is fading.

Big advertising budgets used to be another barrier to entry for upstart brands. But in the digital world, a one-to-one marketing campaign is eminently feasible. In this paradigm, not only is advertising expense far lower, but it is a variable expense and success-based. The large upfront costs incurred by the behemoths on prime-time TV, with their hit-or-miss results, are becoming hard to defend.

Branding used to be a huge competitive advantage for consumer-staple companies. However, millennials are proving more resistant to advertising and tend to be influenced by user reviews and transparent side-by-side product comparisons, which are readily available online. The opportunity to charge large premiums on branded consumable products with generic quality are shrinking, as trusted retailers and e-tailers offer their own private-label alternatives.

Anchoring bias may be preventing investors from seeing this changed reality. Consumer staples still trade at large premiums despite the emerging threats. This is no different from many brick-and-mortar retailers who ignored, then resisted, the emerging omnichannel world. By the time reality caught up, many business models and stocks had been decimated.

Investors in many former blue chips suffer from this syndrome. Consumer-staple stocks such as Kraft Foods (which merged with Heinz Ketchup) come to mind. In February 2019, Kraft's owner, 3G Capital, announced a massive write-down as cost cuts failed to offset declining revenues. Investors finally saw the writing on the wall, and the stock collapsed by more than 25 percent in a single day.

Anchoring represents an innate human desire to ignore change in the hope that it won't happen, using denial as a coping mechanism.

The Fix: Adopt Clean-Slate Thinking

To overcome this bias, it is best to appoint someone else to do clean-slate research so that original or contradictory points of view emerge. That person needs to be ruthless and relentless in looking for information that invalidates, refutes, upends, or discredits any or all beliefs about company X. For individuals who don't have someone they can count on to play this role, perhaps an investment club might be a good forum for such a debate (although investment clubs are not a panacea as they can be a case of the blind leading the blind—be sure to enlist someone who has the expertise to understand industry trends and also apply that knowledge to specific companies and what is priced into their stocks). Or you can role-play, using the techniques described later in this chapter, and make a concerted effort to look for information that negates your views.

The Opportunity: Turn This Behavioral Vice Into an Investment Virtue

Because many investors can be slow to react to changes in a business, even one that is improving, you can take advantage by being early in such investment opportunities. Not only does this offer high returns, but it can also come with low risk. That's because bad news is expected and priced in, while good news is not. Here is an example.

For several decades leading up to the mid- to late 2000s, the auto-components sector had rightly been regarded as a dog of a sector. A fragmented supplier base had a poor bargaining position against a concentrated original equipment manufacturer (OEM) customer base. Reflecting this weak position, the sector had traditionally traded at a large discount to the market. However, as more electronics began to be embedded in a car, many auto components were no longer discrete parts but part of a larger system solution glued together by software rather than nuts and bolts. Suppliers who were part of such tightly integrated system solutions could not easily be swapped out, which gave them greater pricing power. This improved bargaining position would eventually result in better profit margins for those companies, but the markets were anchored in their old point of view and slow to price in this change. Astute investors could exploit this bias just as we saw in the case of Harman, the misunderstood and mispriced auto-components company described in chapter 8.

Flaw #8. This Emperor Has No Clothes: Relying on Intuition Over Data

Billy Beane confronted this syndrome in baseball, where team owners lost both games and money by basing their decisions on instincts instead of information. Listening to your gut instead of checking the facts is what academics describe as intuition bias: relying on intuition over data.

Sometimes headlines seduce you into believing there is substance when there is only sizzle. Many people buy companies that advertise during the Super Bowl, confusing familiarity for fact-checking. In the same vein, many investors think if they like a company's product, it must be a great investment as well. GoPro is a great action-adventure camera, but that does not necessarily make it a great investment. Like many consumer-discretionary products, it can face severe ups and downs. In fact, GoPro stock has crashed, even though their cameras work just fine. The growth rates and profit margins proved unsustainable, and when the business did not perform to the lofty expectations priced into the stock, it fell hard from a peak of $87 in late 2014 to a low of $4 in late 2018.

The Fix: Collect and Connect Information

Take the time and make the effort to collect the relevant data to make a well-informed decision. But be careful not to go overboard. As we will see in the next section, too much data collection can itself be a behavioral flaw.

Flaw #9. Knowing Less Than You Think You Know: Overconfidence Bias

Of all the personality traits we tend to value and envy, confidence leads the pack. We are told to raise confident children, be confident in our careers, approach new situations with confidence, wear our clothes with confidence, and so on. Yet confidence contains the seeds of big problems, which begin to sprout when healthy self-esteem turns into overconfidence and arrogance.

In fact, you might call overconfidence the original sin of investing. Thinking we know more than we do, certain that we are right, works against having the humility—or the common sense—to know when our judgment is off. Several landmark studies have shown that most people think they are above average—obviously impossible. Sometimes called the superiority illusion, this tendency manifests itself as overconfidence.

Human beings are prone to overestimating what they know and underestimating what they do not know. Confucius put it best when he described knowledge as knowing the extent of one's ignorance. The worst part of this behavioral flaw is we do not know what we do not know. So we underestimate the uncertainties of the future and invest as if we knew all there is to know. Such blind faith leads us to bet the farm on investments that appear to have great promise because we ignore what can go wrong.

In the mid-2000s, many investors were so convinced of the super-cycle in commodities that they poured money into this sector, only to lose vast sums of money when the seemingly surefire bet unraveled. Many portfolio managers fell prey to overconfidence and converted their hitherto diversified portfolios into a concentrated thematic bet, overweighting anything directly or indirectly linked to commodities, such as copper stock Freeport-McMoRan, or a country linked to the commodity such as Chile. Just a decade prior, investors had made the same wrong bet in overweighting tech stocks, especially internet stocks. Of late, in my opinion, that insanity has found a home in loss-making unicorns which are going public at egregious valuations as investors buy into hyper growth rates lasting far out into the future.

Sadly, just as trees don't grow to the sky, most hyper growth companies flame out instead of meeting or beating expectations (as we saw earlier with the GoPro stock example). Excessive optimism is usually a marker of overconfidence, not a plausible real-life scenario. High multiples are often a manifestation of high *confidence*, not high *earnings prospects*. This often proves to be the undoing of growth investors, who tend to suffer from this bias more than any other kind of investor. In fact, high growth is the exception, not the rule, yet investors routinely overestimate growth. The commonly used valuation method, discounted cash flow (DCF) analysis, turbocharges the value of a company that is forecasted to have high profit and high growth. Note how the DCF formula works: the wrong input (high growth) will give you the wrong output—accurate, but wrong. It is not the fault of the formula; it is the fault of the forecaster in believing and estimating the wrong growth assumptions.

Overconfidence in the sustainability of growth often leads growth investors to inflate their earnings forecasts as well as the multiples they are willing to pay for such rosy forecasts. If reality sets in worse than expected, the stock sinks, hit by the double whammy of both earnings and multiples resetting downward. The opposite is true for value investors; they tend not to pay, let alone overpay, for a rosy future and insist on owning companies where expectations are low.

Another form of overconfidence that overtakes investors is home-country bias. Familiarity breeds comfort and confidence. Because these investors feel most knowledgeable and secure about their home turf, they overweight investments in their own country even if better opportunities are available abroad. But familiarity is no substitute for research. In fact, it is more likely to breed ignorance than awareness. In investing, as I have said before, ignorance is loss not bliss.

Many Canadian investors learned this lesson the hard way when their portfolios reflected a home-country bias toward stocks listed on the local Toronto Stock Exchange (TSX), whose benchmark index had a large 33 percent weight in Nortel during the mid-2000s. In January 2009, when Nortel filed for bankruptcy, it triggered a 99 percent drop in its stock price, from about C$15 a year prior to under C$0.15 by the time of the announcement. At the time, the bankruptcy case was the largest in Canadian history, and it left pensioners, shareholders, and former employees with enormous losses. Fortunately, since that fateful episode, Canadian investors have made significant headway in diversifying their equity investments to have more global exposure and less home-country bias.

The Fix: Accept What You Do Not and Cannot Know

Think in terms of odds rather than outcomes or certainties. Evaluate scenarios ranging from best case to worst case. Accept that you are dealing with known unknowns and unknown unknowns. Acknowledge that where there is data, there is uncertainty. All data are subject to error, so statisticians always assign confidence intervals denoting the margin of error and prefer to supply ranges instead of precise numbers. But long footnotes do not make for a pithy headline, so they are invariably omitted by the media outlets. This gives the illusion of precision when in reality there is significant room for error. Give up the ghost of precision. Accept what you do not and cannot know.

"Think in terms of odds rather than outcomes or certainties."

I made the mistake of owning a large position in British Petroleum (BP), the British oil company. I lost 40 percent in a matter of days when news of the Deepwater Horizon oil spill emerged in April 2010. Before the accident, I had viewed BP as a well-positioned and well-managed company. Like many others, I had failed to understand the safety risks associated with poor maintenance of their equipment.

When the fire occurred, my initial assessment was that the damage was limited to the cleanup costs for the oil spill in the immediate vicinity of the ship. Over the next few days, even though the fire was contained, new information emerged that the company and its vendors could be sued for negligence. This meant a jury could hit the company with *triple* damages. In the following weeks, I learned that the oil spill was spreading because the currents in the Gulf of Mexico were carrying it toward the Florida coastline instead of keeping it closer to the Louisiana shore. This shift in wind patterns mattered because damages for lost business in an area with higher commercial property values are far greater than in poorer regions.

The cost of cleaning up the oil spill and damages awarded literally depended *on which way the winds blew*! If they shifted course, then the oil spill would not reach the coast of Florida. It became clear that no amount of data-gathering would help me to handicap the outcome; there was simply no way for anyone to know. After stress testing the numbers for various potential outcomes, I was unable to rule out bankruptcy in the worst-case scenario. The stock had become too risky, so I exited the position.

The lesson learned is that investing comes with uncertainty. No matter how much you to try to handicap all outcomes, unexpected things happen. No amount of research would have uncovered this accident. Sometimes all you can do is reassess the risk/reward of an investment as new facts emerge, and then take appropriate action.

Ten years after that ill-fated accident, the stock traded around $43, well below its pre-spill level of $60. Even though BP avoided bankruptcy, I believe my decision to sell was the right one. The risk of being wiped out was real and large. The only way to manage the tail risk was to avoid the stock completely.

Flaw #10. Believing What You Believe Instead of Questioning It: Confirmation Bias

I saved the worst for last. As biases go, this one tops the list because it engenders a false sense of security instead of exposing your blind spots. As Claude Bernard, a French physiologist, quipped, *"It is what we think we already know that often prevents us from learning."*

Imagine yourself on a beach on a warm July afternoon. All around you are lots of people enjoying the day. You quickly conclude this is a safe zone and you have nothing to worry about. You see, the mind believes in visual cues. To avoid expending undue energy, it trusts what it has already concluded. So in this case, you would ignore the many posted signs warning of dangerous undercurrents close to the shore. Because you don't see them, they do not exist. Your mind gets its confirmation from seeing all the other people on the beach laughing and playing. This leads you to lower your guard, to the point of risking your life if you swim into one of the invisible riptides.

That's confirmation bias. It can cause risk to disappear, making you more exposed to danger than you bargained for. This is what happens in markets. When a stock is going up and lots of people own it, you get complacent and stop looking for the warning signs, until it is too late.

> **"Figure out what does not add up,
> instead of what does. Actively look to invalidate
> rather than validate."**

In investing, you cannot let your guard down. Beliefs are not facts. Assumptions are not proof. In day-to-day life, such distinctions may not matter if they work, but in investing, ignorance is not bliss but loss. Our instinct to believe what appears to be true in our minds is so hardwired that we tend to look for confirming evidence and tune out anything that contradicts it.

However, in investing, we need to do the opposite. Figure out what does *not* add up, instead of what does. Actively look to invalidate rather than validate. This is not normal behavior for most people. As a species, we have benefited from getting along and going along. And it is distinctly uncomfortable to question long-held beliefs. Yet that is exactly what sound investment research requires of you.

The Fix: Look to Disprove, Not Prove

Research is a quest for truth, not a confirmation of predetermined beliefs that we have concluded to be true. It must be conducted without an agenda. You should not care what truth will be revealed, as long as your process reveals the truth. Investors who go about their research to validate a preset conclusion are doomed to fall into the confirmation trap. For example, it is commonplace for investors to screen or shortlist companies that meet certain financial criteria, such as a high return on equity or a net cash balance sheet. Such screening criteria make an implicit assumption that they are markers of high-quality businesses, and therefore that the people using them are fishing in a high-quality lake.

But facts can mislead. For example, many investors believe that if a company or a security is rated AAA, that indicates high quality. On the face of it, this hardly seems like a mistake. But the error is assuming that a high rating is some kind of foolproof guarantee. I believe this was a significant factor at the root of the 2008 financial crisis. Many investors and analysts zeroed in on securities in the financial sector with AAA ratings and took comfort when they were able to verify that the securities indeed had AAA ratings. But verification is a form of confirmation bias. It seeks to validate rather than invalidate. Triangulation, not verification, is the right research approach. If you asked whether that particular security or company deserved the AAA rating, if you looked for evidence to figure out if the rating was warranted, you would have ferreted out the deeper truth and perhaps avoided the extraordinary losses that ensued. I did my own investigation at the time and concluded that the rating was undeserved which led me to sell my position in the mortgage insurer Dexia, even though it was AAA rated. My clients were spared the pain that ensued when the company faced bankruptcy and had to be rescued by the authorities. As an aside, this explains why naïve risk-management or audit teams often fail to unearth risk: they accept superficial labels such as AAA ratings without questioning its validity, a form of confirmation bias.

Too many investors inadvertently set themselves up for confirmation bias by favoring companies that score well on a checklist of desired attributes. The non-consensus investor should do exactly the opposite—look for what does not fit one's desired investment criteria, or things to dislike. I actively seek to eliminate bad ideas instead of selecting good ones. When I cannot find much to dislike, I know I am onto something. Only then do I dig deeper to find things to like.

I do my own independent assessments of companies that are highly financially leveraged, instead of subordinating my judgment to third parties such as credit-rating agencies. My research shows that many bonds currently rated as investment grade (BBB) should actually be rated as below investment grade (commonly referred to as junk bonds or flatteringly referred to as high yield). Their financial ratios and metrics simply do not stack up to warranting a higher credit rating. This substantial and perilous grade inflation has caused me to avoid the stocks of many BBB-rated companies. In the next crisis (which I believe will be a balance-sheet-led crisis in which financially leveraged companies may go bust or be severely handicapped), this latent risk exposure is likely to prove costly to those who blindly rely on ratings, without doing their own independent homework.

Wrong Fix: Chasing Quantity Over Quality

Can you do too much research? Absolutely. Do not assume that doing more research will solve the overconfidence bias; in fact, it might reinforce it. The more data you collect on a subject, the more confident you feel about its validity. Now you are in danger of confirmation bias. When you seek out information that does nothing more than confirm what you already "know" to be true, you have swapped confidence bias for confirmation bias.

Remember that confidence is irrelevant in investing. Correctness is everything. Being confident about incorrect answers only multiplies your losses and flushes both your ego and your money down the drain. The art of smart research is to know when you have reached the point of diminishing returns, when additional information is noise as opposed to signal. Working alongside experienced practitioners will help you navigate this continuum. If you are an individual investor, try role-playing, described next.

Another Fix: Role-play

Fast-forward to the future, and imagine the company misses a product cycle, or earnings. Will you double down or quit? Why? What signposts will you look for to conclude that the challenge is temporary and not structural? After the changed reality, what does your endgame look like? Role-playing forces you to empathize. It gives you a preview of how you will behave when the future unfolds differently from what you believed.

Yet Another Fix: Remind Yourself of Unexpected Developments

A few years ago, did you imagine that GE would lose its AAA rating? Or that Alan Greenspan would go from being revered as a perfect central banker to being reviled as the worst offender? Or that the UK would exit the EU? Or that oil prices would collapse? Or that interest rates would be low or negative in many parts of the world?

Acknowledging such surprises trains your brain to guard against overconfidence in what you believe today, so you are better able to handle tomorrow's unexpected realities.

Conclusion

It has become an article of faith in the world of investing that humans are doomed to failure and our (biased) minds represent our undoing. As a corollary, many believe that quantitative or algorithmic investing that is devoid of such human bias is programmed to succeed. But to accept this premise is to short sell the human race. Those who promote such defeatist views of human behavior would be wise to remember that as a species, our predicted destiny could have been death and extinction, yet we lived and multiplied. For all our human frailties, humankind has one overwhelming advantage that we can always count on: we do not believe in giving up. It is that spirit that has kept us marching upward and onward. A few behavioral biases are no match for our innate ability to not just overcome the odds but defy them.

Yes, our minds can play simple tricks, but they can also solve complex conundrums. How we use them is up to us. This chapter shows you how to improve your mental agility, by not just focusing on facts and figures but by fostering a state of mind in relation to them. Here is a summary of the top five mental states a non-consensus investor would do well to cultivate:

1. Skepticism (poke holes, insist on triangulated validation)
2. Optimism (consider what can go right)
3. Pessimism (stress-test what can go wrong)
4. Pragmatism (don't bet the farm on on some hunch or belief)
5. Stoicism (be equanimous amid adversity or euphoria)

Although this chapter requires you to surrender your fantasies, illusions, and habits of denial, it also shows you where other investors are likely to stumble. Knowing that you have certain blind spots and hidden biases is humbling. Knowing that other investors suffer from the same is a potential opportunity, because the very brain that is burdened by biases is also loaded with antidotes. For every flaw, there is a fix.

Flaws	Fixes
1. Availability bias	Go outside the sandbox
2. Recency effect	Think long term.
3. Hindsight bias	Parse luck from skill.
4. Planning fallacy	Play devil's advocate.
5. Endowment effect	Practice zero-base thinking.
6. Loss aversion	Acknowledge reality and cut bait
7. Anchoring bias	Adopt clean-slate thinking.
8. Intuition bias	Collect and connect information.
9. Overconfidence bias	Accept what you do not or cannot know.
10. Confirmation bias	Look to invalidate, not validate.

It is true that our conscious mind is wired for efficiency and expediency, not elaborate and exhaustive analysis. This division of labor between the conscious and subconscious serves us well in life, but not in investing. We need to (and can) overcome our instinctive impulses and tap into the subconscious mind to separate the deeper truth from the superficial reality. This takes effort and willpower, which not everyone wants to engage in. But those who do can reap rewards at the expense of those who do not.

Top Takeaways

1. We may be flawed, but we are also gifted. The very mind that suffers from biases also holds the antidotes to overcome them. Flaws need not be failings if we make them

opportunities for learning, allowing us to profit from them instead of suffering from them.

2. For every flaw there is a fix. The power to change is within us. We can be prey or predators; it is up to us.

3. We can play to our strengths instead of being handicapped by our weaknesses, by cultivating the five "isms"—skepticism, optimism, pessimism, pragmatism, and stoicism.

4. Those who give in to their predispositions lose out to those who transcend them. Rainbows emerge for those who don't run away when it rains.

5. We can choose to surmount not succumb to our biases and be a victor instead of a victim. We can define our own (investment) destiny with our strengths or let it be defined for us by our weaknesses. The choice is ours to make.

10

Value Investing = Margin of Safety

This chapter exposes the biggest sin in value investing: confusing price (or valuation) with value. This is the crime for which value investors are rightly penalized with doing time. Headline cheap stocks may prove Faustian bargains—seductive initially but a bad trade eventually. Prices and valuation multiples are red herrings, not metrics that denote value. Value is not relative—not to sector, market, or history—but absolute and intrinsic.

You must know what you are getting, not just what you are paying, because value is the spread between the two. This explains why valuation multiples should not be used as a screen (before you know what you are getting) but as a sanity check (after you know what you are getting). The same applies to growth rates. There is nothing wrong with growth, but what matters is not the growth rate itself but what that growth rate is worth. Since markets readily tell you what you must pay, in the form of the stock price, you should focus your research efforts on figuring out what you are getting for that price—such as the quality, risk and growth profile of the business.

Price Is Not Value: Price Is What You Pay, Value Is What You Get

It is one of those cool summer mornings on a lazy weekend. You decide to go shopping at your local bazaar, an open market overflowing with colorful trunks and a dizzying assortment of merchandise. As you saunter toward the market, you hear a fast, musical tempo wafting through the air, beckoning you to pick up your pace. When you arrive, the place is teeming with bargain hunters and merchants, each side surreptitiously plotting to get the better of the other. You are excited by all the action around you and cannot wait to be a part of it.

You see a merchant wildly gesticulating to get your attention. He compliments you on your good judgment in visiting the open bazaar where great bargains can be had. He proudly points to his array of woven jute bags that appear to be full of trinkets and casually inquires how much money you want to spend.

You think to yourself, does this guy take me for a fool? Why would I volunteer that kind of information? But you like all the attention he is showering on you, so you coyly but cleverly tell him a lower number than what you have in mind.

"I have $100 to spend."

The merchant beams. "Well, I have something for you that I sold for $125 just last month. But because you are my first customer today, you can have it for just $100."

You are mightily pleased that his opening salvo has begun with a discount, and you decide to engage. Feigning indifference, you coolly ask, "What will I get for $100?"

Instead of answering you, he tells you that someone offered him $100 just a few minutes ago, but he did not strike a deal and is regretting it and does not want to repeat his mistake, so he will let you have it for $100.

You repeat your question. "What will I get for my $100?"

He still does not answer you but offers an extra 20 percent discount if you buy in cash right now.

Now your heart is racing. You smell the desperation on the other side. The merchant is dangling lower and lower prices. You pretend to be uninterested and start to walk away.

The merchant comes running after you. "Final offer," he says. "You can have the bigger bag for the same price as the smaller one if you seal the deal right now."

Smugly satisfied that you have secured a large bargain, you hand over $80 and grab the big bag he is holding in his fist. You eagerly open the bag and your heart sinks. Inside are a dozen apples that have almost rotted. You suddenly realize you have been had. You complain to the merchant and ask for your money back.

"Why?"

"Because $80 for a dozen rotting apples in a vintage jute bag is not a bargain at all!"

"Tough luck," he responds. "You should have checked the merchandise before buying it."

Lesson learned. The merchant kept directing your attention to *the price* while you should have focused on *the merchandise on offer*. Knowing one without the other is of no use. Until you know what you are getting, you have no idea whether the price you are paying represents value or a value trap. Price is not value.

By now you are thinking, no smart person would fall for that trap—certainly not you. Surely you would know what you are buying before bidding for it. And yet many investors, even and especially value investors, fall for this trap. Replace the words "merchant" with "Mr. Market," "merchandise" with "stock," and think of "you" as the "equity investor."

The first negotiation ploy (someone offered $125 in the past) appeals to "reversion-to-mean" investors who believe that if the stock traded at a higher price or multiple in the past, it will do so in the future. However, markets do not reward nostalgia. "Reversion-to-mean" investing relies on the hope that history will repeat itself. Remember what Henry Kissinger said: *"Hope is not a strategy."*

The second negotiation ploy (someone else was willing to pay $100) is designed to deceive you with the "greater fool theory," or what I call "optical value." Just because someone else was willing to pay a higher price does not mean you should. The other person may simply be a greater fool, not a smarter investor. It is foolish to invest based on wishful thinking that some sucker will come along to bail you out of your mistake and pay you top dollar for junk. *Value investing is about buying at the right price, not hoping to sell at an inflated price.*

The third negotiation ploy (compared to $100, you can have it for $80) appeals to "relative value" investors. In relation to something else, it can be made to look cheap, so it appears to be a bargain even if it is not. You have seen plenty of "relative" value traps even if you didn't know the name. When a retailer offers huge discounts from merchandise that was marked up in the first place, that's a relative value trap. Savvy shoppers know that not everything on sale is a bargain.

The fourth negotiation ploy (if you want this, you must buy it right now) is to trick you into making a hasty decision without having all the necessary information. Investing before investigating is risky; you are playing the game blind and relying on luck rather than skill. Do not fall for this ruse. Take your time to do your research.

The fifth negotiation ploy (offering you more for less) appeals to "distressed value" investors. It appears as if significant value is being offered because a large bag is twice the size of a small one, so you are conned into thinking you are getting the better end of the bargain, whereas it was the merchant who got the better of you. In my opinion, distressed-value investing tends to compound your problems (you now must deal with a larger bag of rotten apples instead of a smaller one), not your returns.

As you have guessed by now, merely adding the word "value" after these labels (reversion-to-mean value, optical value, relative value, distressed value) does not magically make them a value proposition. They all suffer from the same syndrome of confusing price or price action with value. Quantitative or factor-based investment approaches are also guilty of this type of "value" investing. Their "value" factors are either statistical, optical, or relative, but they are not intrinsic, because computers cannot be programmed to calculate intrinsic value.

Even Warren Buffett and Charlie Munger learned a costly lesson on the difference between price and value due to a misstep. In 1993, Buffett bought the shoe company Dexter for about $400 million, paying for it with 22,500 shares in Berkshire Hathaway. Dexter would eventually fail and become worthless. Buffett and Munger have candidly admitted that instead of making sure Dexter was a high-quality business intrinsically worth $400 million, they focused unduly on what they considered at the time an attractive purchase price. Worse still, because they paid for Dexter in stock instead of cash, it actually cost several billion dollars, as Berkshire Hathaway stock appreciated dramatically over the next several decades. This multi-billion-dollar mistake serves as a stark reminder of the importance of understanding the quality of the business you are getting. Value is driven by what you are *getting*, not just by what you are *paying*.

Valuation Metrics May Be Used as a Sanity Check, Not as a Screening Tool

Most value investors start their investment process by screening for low multiples or share-price drops. (Note that my non-consensus investing approach is an exception.) Once they have culled such a shortlist of stocks from a larger universe, they then proceed to investigate whether each investment is genuinely (or deceptively) attractive. This does not seem like a bad idea in theory, but it tends to be in practice. A low valuation multiple is tangible and tempting, whereas figuring out the quality of the business is intangible and daunting. Chances are the brain will default to its mental shortcuts and fall into the availability bias and confirmation bias (see chapter 9, "From Victim to Victor"). You start to think, "If the stock is cheap, it must represent value." Before long, you end up owning value traps instead of value.

Of late, this is how many value investors rationalize their overweight exposure to banks despite ample evidence that the quality and economics of the business have materially and structurally deteriorated. Returns on equity for most banks around the world have halved from about 20 percent to 10 percent as capital requirements have doubled and interest rates have collapsed, but the allure of cheap headline multiples continues to seduce. In my opinion, many bank stocks are more likely to be a value trap than a value proposition.

Looking at valuation metrics first is to put the horse before the cart. Valuations should not be used as a screen (*before* you know what you are getting) but as a sanity check (*after* you know what you are getting).

> **"Valuations should not be used as a screen (before you know what you are getting) but as a sanity check (after you know what you are getting)."**

Since markets readily tell everyone what they must pay (the stock price), your research efforts are better expended on figuring out what you are getting—the quality of the business. This explains why I dwelt extensively on understanding and not misunderstanding quality in previous chapters. It is a prerequisite to practicing intrinsic-value investing as opposed to all the misguided forms of "value" investing described earlier. Intrinsic-value investing focuses on arbitraging the difference between business worth and stock price. Without knowing what the business is worth, you cannot determine whether value exists.

You may have guessed by now that I am an intrinsic value investor. My non-consensus approach to research and contrarian approach to investing is the means by which I find value (or more specifically *intrinsic* value). This is how non-consensus investing is joined at the hip to intrinsic value investing—it is a highly symbiotic relationship where one leads to the other and feeds off each other. Indeed, while Warren Buffett is known as the world's greatest (intrinsic) value investor, he should equally be described as the world's most non-consensus or contrarian investor. Not only does he want to own high-quality businesses, he insists on a large value spread or discount to intrinsic value, which he is able to secure by investing against the grain. He is greedy when others are fearful and fearful when others are greedy. Borrowing from Mark Twain, I would aver that to describe my approach as non-consensus investing and intrinsic value investing is to repeat oneself.[1]

Stock Prices and Valuation Multiples Are Red Herrings

Like a magician who tries to distract you from what really matters, markets try to redirect your attention to "52-week" highs or lows, "P/E" or "P/Book multiples," and a litany of other misleading metrics. Do not let yourself be conned. Stock prices and valuation multiples are red herrings; neither are measures of value. You need to stop looking at things that do not matter and focus on things that do—the quality of the business. In fact, *value investing is not about low multiples, but about low risk that arises from a margin of safety.* Low valuations are a necessary but not sufficient condition to secure a margin of safety. Values are absolute and intrinsic, whereas valuations are relative and conditional (they only matter in relation to what you are getting). This is so important, it bears repeating: *Price is what you pay; business worth is what you get. The difference between the two represents value.*

Historical or falling stock prices are yet another form of distraction. Anybody who has gone shopping knows that buying something that is marked down after being marked up is not the definition of a bargain. Too many investors focus their efforts on studying stock prices and headline valuations instead of the

---

1. Hence the book's title is non-consensus investing, not non-consensus intrinsic value investing, which would be redundant.

underlying business. This does not make you an investor, let alone a non-consensus, intrinsic-value investor. If you base your investment decisions on information that everyone (the consensus) has (stock prices, headline valuation multiples), it confers neither an advantage nor profit.

This is why information that is readily available is not worth having. What is unknown is the future trajectory of the free cash flows. Spending time, effort, and money to figure out the business's power to generate free cash flows is a more profitable pursuit. Once you know the answers to these questions and can quantify them in a financial model, you can estimate the intrinsic worth of the business by using a discounted cash flow (DCF) valuation method, among others.

The DCF method is just a formulaic equation. Many finance websites and online tutorials provide and explain the formula, so it does not warrant repeating here. The challenge is not in knowing the formula, but in knowing how to determine the inputs. If the inputs are wrong, so is the output. This is commonly referred to as GIGO: garbage in, garbage out. At its core, fundamental research is about figuring out the correct inputs, such as understanding why a company makes money, how much money it will make, for how long, and what risks it is exposed to in doing so. If your inputs are correct and non-consensus, you typically are able to identify investment opportunities with a reasonable value spread. The more non-consensus (and correct) your point of view, the larger the value spread. A larger value spread not only means a large reward, it usually comes with more downside protection and a greater margin of safety. Conducting superior, differentiated, non-consensus fundamental research on a business is the cornerstone of successful active investing—without it one cannot uncover misunderstandings or mispricings on a systematic basis. This explains why this book predominantly focuses on how to do such research. It is what helps one become a better researcher and therefore investor. I am disheartened by the fact that many analysts assiduously analyze stock performance and financial statements when they would be better off researching the business. Stats and stock-price charts are backward looking; business models, capabilities, and strategies are forward looking. No amount of stock-price navel-gazing is going to tell you what is going on in the business. Good (or terrible) things happen in the business first, then they manifest themselves in the financial statements, and finally in the stock price. By doing research at the front end (the business), you give yourself a lead.

Once you figure out what can go right and wrong in the business, estimate the worth of that business under various scenarios ranging from best to worst. Now you have established the boundary conditions within which you are prepared to engage. Only after you have decided what you are willing to pay should you look at the share price to ascertain where the market is willing to sell the business to you. If it is closer to the optimistic or best-case scenario price, move on; the upside has already been priced in. Even if you are right about the business prospects, others got there ahead of you and already imputed it in the price. You are too late to this party. However, if the share price corresponds to your pessimistic or worst case, you should open your checkbook. When the market wants to sell you for a song what you wanted to buy, go for it. When the market wants to charge you an arm and a leg, walk away.

Luck Favors the Prepared: Patiently Wait to Get "Lucky"

Value investing is about sitting tight and letting the investment opportunity come to you, instead of chasing it. The one thing you can count on in markets is mood swings—from greed to fear, euphoria to panic, and optimism to pessimism. All these throw up investment bargains, but you must be patient.

"Value investing is about sitting tight and letting the investment opportunity come to you, instead of chasing it."

Luck favors the prepared, so use this waiting time wisely. Do your research. Develop a pre-vetted inventory of investment ideas that you are ready to act upon should the market present them to you during one of its mood swings. With this proactive and measured investment approach, you call the shots, not the markets.

Seek and Ye Shall Find: Bargains Exist Where You Least Expect to Find Them

Even in bull markets (which typically offer slim pickings for value investors), there are pockets of pessimism and neglect that provide fertile ground for the contrarian investor. For instance, the pharmaceutical sector has disappointed and derated over the past decade. This is in stark contrast to the lofty expectations priced into the sector in the 1990s, when it was bid up as a surefire play on aging baby boomers. Ironically, even though this premise remains valid, the sector got pummeled.

What happened? Many things. Hitherto blue-chip companies became victims of their own success, as drugs that went off patent had been such blockbusters that it became impossible to fill the large void created, let alone replace them with something even larger. Even when new drugs were launched, the relative lack of innovation led to many similar drugs being launched at the same time. This created rampant price discounting in an effort to move undifferentiated product. After the arthritis drug Vioxx was found to trigger cardiovascular disease and caused an estimated sixty thousand deaths, regulatory changes necessitated larger expenditures on clinical trials, hurting profit margins and delaying new drug approvals. Reimbursement price pressures and bargaining power exerted by wholesale purchasing organizations such as Express Scripts added another nail to the coffin. Last but not the least, an echo chamber of negativity reverberated through the news cycle about a decade later, when the media, public opinion, and politicians alike found a convenient villain in Valeant to cast aspersions on the ethics of the entire sector, even though Valeant's egregious price increases were the exception, not the rule.

All these adverse developments were a far cry from the giddy growth expectations anticipated and priced in by investors during the golden years. As hopes deflated, so did investor interest.

All Bad Things Come to an End

It has taken about two decades for the pharmaceutical sector to go from being revered to reviled, and investors have dumped the sector in droves. But just like all good things, all bad things come to an end too! Even hot stoves cool down, and you can touch them then and not get burnt. Over the past few years, I have found many high-quality companies with a proven track record in research and development and promising product pipelines trading at attractive discounts to their conservatively estimated intrinsic values. Yet few investors are interested in these bargains because of the behavioral bias of anchoring and recency discussed in chapter 9.

In good times, people focus unduly on what can go right and ignore what can go wrong. In troubled times, people dwell unduly on what has gone wrong and overlook what can go right. Non-consensus investors can take advantage of such predictable patterns of behavior. For example, in the pharmaceutical sector, the market has priced in the bad news of patent cliffs and price pressures but is ignoring the many remarkable R&D breakthroughs underway. Analyzing financial statements of pharmaceutical companies will not help at this stage because current reported earnings lag the leading indicators of better times ahead. This is because the improved drug profiles and pipelines (based on clinical-data read-outs) have yet to hit their full stride in the marketplace, either because they have not yet launched or have just recently launched, necessitating large upfront investments in R&D and marketing. When these new and improved drugs prove their merit, they will confer pricing power and reimbursement rates commensurate with such value added. Earnings and cash flows will grow, and upward surprises will eventually attract broader investor interest.

Note that contrary to conventional wisdom, higher drug prices can be a win-win for society at large. In the United States, drug costs account for only about 10 percent of the total cost of treating a patient, while hospital and other acute-care costs account for a whopping 90 percent. If a $100 drug is improved such that it prevents the need for surgeries or hospital stays, even if it costs a 20 percent premium ($120), it is still a stupendous bargain if it saves $900 worth of hospital costs.

Notice how, once again, price is not value. A 20 percent increase in the price of a drug can deliver tremendous value, whereas a 20 percent discount on a drug may not be worth it if it does not work as effectively. Long-range decisions such as managing health and wealth require strategic, second-order deliberation, not tactical, superficial thinking.[2]

In long-cycle industries such as health care and basic resources, it is not uncommon to go from feast to famine and back again. You should pay careful attention to where you are on this continuum, as the transition from peak to trough is large and long. This saga of great expectations turning to great disappointment

---

2. I cannot help pointing out that the same logic applies when comparing price versus value of passive versus active investing. Instead of judging alternatives by their price propositions (headline fees or prices), you should measure them on their value propositions (outperformance after fees).

is routine in markets if you examine cycles over decades, not years. This is the primary reason that growth investing fails in the long run: it overpays for a very rosy future that often fails to materialize, and investors are left holding the large bag of rotten apples with deflating prospects and derating multiples. Ironically, despite their poor long-term track record, growth stocks mesmerize people to the point of blinding them. In my investing experience, intensity is overrated while longevity is underrated. I prefer steady growth that lasts longer to heady growth that peters out.

> **"Intensity is overrated while longevity is underrated.**
> **I prefer steady growth that lasts longer to heady growth**
> **that peters out."**

Although value investors do not consciously pay up for growth, they unconsciously do so by failing to distinguish between value and value traps. To illustrate this phenomenon, I will draw parallels between two stocks, one from twenty years ago and one from today.

Value Traps or Value?

Consumer-electronics companies are hits until they are misses. When they are hits, it is hard to fathom they could miss. When they have a string of successes over several years, it is harder still to imagine they could fail. And if you layer on a series of product-family successes, they appear almost invincible. No, I am not talking about Apple and its decade-long success with the iMac, iPhone, and iPad. I am taking about Sony and its success with the Walkman, Discman, and PlayStation.

The semiconductor revolution, which allowed engineers to pack ever more circuitry into ever smaller componentry, proved to be a bonanza for consumer-electronics companies such as Sony. As miniaturization enabled portability, gadgets suddenly went from being communal to individual, spurring an explosion of demand. Sony rode this wave and enjoyed enormous popularity and profitability. The stock followed suit, doubling and quadrupling during the 1980s and 1990s, to a peak of ¥16,300 in early 2000. But as with most growth stocks, the good times rolled over and tough times set in. In the process, investors lost their shirts, because whether you bought the stock at ¥4000 in 1998 or at ¥16300 in 2000, you lost 75 percent or 94 percent a decade or so later as the stock plummeted to below ¥1000 in 2012.

Investors who were betting on Sony's continued dominance paid the price. Over a decade, Sony went from being a growth stock to a "reversion to mean" value trap to succumbing to the "greater fool theory" to being perceived as "relative value" to finally being regarded as "distressed value." Frankly, it never represented value but a value trap, as all these value frameworks are false ways to assess value.

From an intrinsic-value standpoint, it was clear to me as early as in 2001 that the business was deteriorating and Sony had lost its competitive advantage. My research had led me to conclude that the transition from analog (bulky picture-tube TVs) to digital (slim flat-screen TVs) would advantage semiconductor companies such as Samsung at the expense of analog-component companies such as Sony. I therefore ignored the prevailing hype and refrained from owning the stock. Such abstinence helped me avoid the painful losses and reset in the business, and eventually in the stock. Recall that in chapter 6, we learned the preeminence of avoiding losses. Knowing what not to own, and why not to own it, is crucial to investment success.

Sony is a good example of a value trap that was mistaken as value. It is hard for investors to imagine that soaring blue chips can turn into lumbering dinosaurs. In fact, in free-market economies, it is often the norm, not the exception. This explains why you must learn to parse between value and value traps; not doing so is among the biggest and costliest mistakes made by value investors.

Is Apple the Next Sony?

Fast-forward to 2018. I fear this mistake may be being repeated in a different but similar stock: Apple. Like Sony, Apple is renowned for its quality and cool gadgets. Like Sony, Apple appears invincible, with an almost cult-like following among consumers and investors, not to mention a stock price that has doubled and quadrupled since 2007, when the iPhone was first launched.

Popular wisdom in 2018 is that Apple is the cheap man's tech play on 15x earnings. This looks like a bargain when compared to other tech stocks such as Nvidia or Netflix, which trade on heady earnings multiples of more than 50x. But remember that I cautioned you against falling for such "relative value" traps. To figure out whether Apple is a value proposition or a value trap, you need to know what you are getting, not what you are paying. To understand what you are getting, you need to wear the hat of a business analyst and understand the company's capabilities and opportunities, its challenges and threats. Here are some highlights from my business analysis of Apple in 2017–2018:

1. You are getting a consumer-electronics company, not a technology company. Gross profit margins of Apple are around 40 percent, whereas those at tech companies with proprietary moats such as Microsoft or SAP are at twice that level.
2. You are getting a company with single-product risk. Despite the popularity of products such as the iPad and iMac, the iPhone contributes the bulk of the profits.
3. The replacement cycle of the iPhone had come down to as low as eighteen months. If it were to expand by just a

few months, say to twenty-four months, the annual run rate of sales could easily fall by double digits. Sales for a consumer-electronics company are a hamster wheel; they must sell new devices at a faster rate to keep growing.

4. The pushback provided by the company and market bulls is that every new iPhone is sold at a higher price than its prior generation, so even if volumes slip, upselling will make up the difference. This thesis has been undermined as consumers cringed at the $1,000 sticker price of the new iPhone 10X, which was a failure even by the low bar set for its sales.

5. The bulls will try to redirect your attention away from the mature and saturated U.S. market (where both volumes and pricing have been disappointing) toward the burgeoning emerging market, where billions of consumers are waiting to get their hands on an iPhone. The problem with this argument is that most emerging-market consumers cannot save several hundred dollars to make a down payment on a house, let alone splurge such precious money on an ultra-expensive iPhone. Cheaper Samsung and Xaomi phones are far more popular in emerging markets, and the iPhone has found it hard to address its lack of price competitiveness.

6. The bulls (and CEO Tim Cook during the November 2018 earnings call) will try to redirect your attention from challenging product sales to growing services revenues. Sadly, even this argument does not hold water. Services contribute less than 20 percent of profits. Were the installed base of iPhones to shrink, so would the services opportunity, as it is the caboose that pulls the wagons. Apple could then become a melting ice cube. Think about Yahoo, which has experienced the same fate, even though it retains its incumbent position as a personal email domain and garners some advertising and subscription revenues from it. There is also a risk that the high double-digit distribution commission (levied by Apple on its app providers such as Spotify)

could be viewed as an anti-competitive business practice, threatening this lucrative service-revenue contribution.

7. If all these points and counterpoints do not give you pause, let me call out one that should. It is the biggest risk in any business model: when a competitive advantage turns into a competitive disadvantage. This is where the iPhone finds itself: caught between a rock and a hard place. It must charge higher prices to sustain its luxury image and protect its back book and financial metrics. But without added value, the high price point is turning off consumers. Apple's phones used to have features that competitors lacked, such as Gorilla Glass or aluminum casings, which allowed it to charge a premium. Today, Apple still charges a premium, but the features are no longer unique, making the iPhone uncompetitive in the marketplace. In fact, iPhone was behind the curve in introducing beveled edges, wireless charging, and fast charging, among other things.

8. To add insult to injury, many of its new products have failed to reach the same heights. Products like iHome, iTV, and iWatch have all disappointed, relatively speaking. Siri and iTunes are hardly monopolies. In fact, most apps on the iPhone are found on other phones too. There is nothing exclusive or proprietary about them.

This can morph into a very risky setup. If the flagship product stops offering compelling value, so could the stock. A 15x PE multiple may not offer a margin of safety if earnings fall by 30 percent. Could that happen? All it would take is 10 percent lower sales and a 5 percent reduction in gross margin. At that point, the stock would be trading on 20x multiples—theoretically. Actually, it is unlikely the stock would trade on 20x. Much more likely it would derate to, say, 10x as lower growth expectations typically cause investors to lower the multiple they are willing to pay. This means you could lose 50 percent on your investment.

It is tempting to believe this time is different. Surely this cannot happen to Apple? Remind yourself that this is exactly what investors in Nokia and BlackBerry thought when their products were selling like hotcakes. This is the fate that often awaits most consumer-electronics companies sooner or later. Don't pay for it, prepare for it. When a company's future rests on the shoulders of a single product like the iPhone, the risk exposure is large and binary. When the product is a success, the stock can be a moonshot; but when it flops, the stock can become a blowup. Note that I am not arguing that consumers will stop using the iPhone. They will simply not replace it as often or pay higher prices for uncompetitive or unnecessary bells and whistles.

And if you are impressed with the fact that Apple has sold more than a billion phones, you have fallen prey to the trap of investing before investigating. If you did your homework, you would have learned that Nokia sold more than 1.5 billion of its successful Series 40 phones back in the day. Despite that, we all know that Nokia's handset division took a nosedive when its products lost favor with consumers. In its heyday, BlackBerry was nicknamed "CrackBerry" because people were addicted to it. Executives and employees alike loved having email at their fingertips, and BlackBerry delivered the fastest service. But as with all consumer electronics, consumer preferences change, and yesterday's winners became tomorrow's losers.

Recall from chapter 8 that fundamental research is about asking the right questions, not knowing all the answers. The litmus-test questions for any intrinsic-value investor are:

1. Is Apple's business model bankable or binary?
2. Will the company miss, meet or beat consensus growth expectations priced into the stock in the years ahead??
3. What is the impact on its earnings if sales flatten or decline instead of growing?

4. Can growth in its service revenues offset shortfalls in product revenues?
5. What is the downside risk compared to the upside potential if the intrinsic worth is significantly lower than what current consensus expectations have priced in?

To imagine the fate that may await Apple if the iPhone loses its luster, take a look at figure 10.1. It's a snapshot of what happened

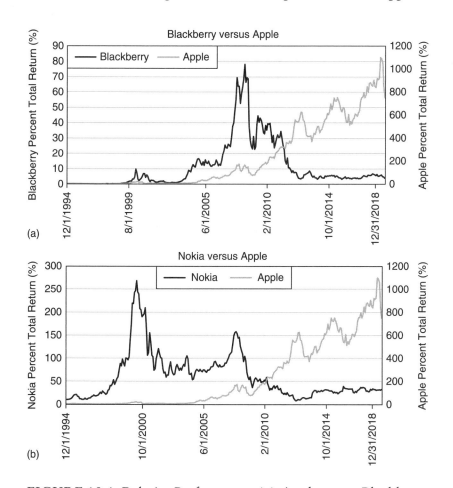

FIGURE 10.1 Relative Performance: (a): Apple versus Blackberry; (b) Apple versus Nokia 1995–2018

to two other iconic phone manufacturers, Nokia and BlackBerry. Note that I am not predicting Apple's demise (even Nokia and BlackBerry still exist today) but questioning the sustainability of its growth and profitability, the risk inherent in its business model, and the large losses that could ensue if the current lack of product competitiveness persists. Keep in mind that to cause massive losses for its investors, a company does not have to *disappear or die*, it just needs to *disappoint*.

Top Takeaways

1. Price is not the same as value. Price is what you pay; business worth is what you get. Value is the difference between the two. The larger the value spread, the greater the reward and lower the risk.
2. Since markets readily tell everyone what they must pay (the stock price and headline valuation multiple), research efforts are best expended on figuring out what one is getting: the quality of the business.
3. Do not fall for hype or headlines. Focus on analyzing business quality to find the blue chips of tomorrow instead of clinging to icons of yesterday.
4. Distinguishing between value traps and value propositions is key to successful investing.
5. Intensity is overrated; longevity is underrated. Steady growth that lasts longer is better than heady growth that proves short-lived. Growth companies don't have to disappear or die, they just need to disappoint, to cause big losses to their investors.

11

Sizzle Fizzles, Patience Prospers

Investing is about making correct and prudent decisions. The process and principles by which those decisions are made matter more than the decisions themselves. Similarly, understanding what drives outperformance matters more than the performance itself.

Confusing luck with skill is endemic in investing because the short term and the long term often diverge and investors tend to confuse frequency and severity. Short-term performance provides instant gratification and (false) validation, while underperformance, even for good reason (such as a manager being prudent), puts one on the defensive. Investors want to avoid pain at all cost, but successful investing often entails taking short-term pain for long-term gain.

The patient, contrarian investor prefers to lose the battle and win the war, while the short-term investor focuses on winning the battle even if it means losing the war.

Performance Evaluation Through a Different Lens

The stock market is my life. You've probably figured that out by now. People tell me that when I'm describing a stock I like or a company that has intrigued me, my eyes light up and I start talking faster. They mean it as a compliment—I think.

But I do realize that not everyone feels the same way. Not everyone thinks that digging up new market information that no one else has yet noticed is the greatest thrill in the world. They are quite happy putting their energy elsewhere and letting a professional make investment decisions for them. And that's OK too.

Perhaps that describes you. If so, how do you know whether your fund manager is doing a good job? Or if you are at the stage of thinking about hiring one, how should you evaluate them and choose?

That is the heart of this chapter. Its mission is to give you perspective, through several lenses, on evaluating the performance of your money manager.

Statistics: What They Reveal Is Suggestive, But What They Conceal Is Vital[1]

In most areas of life, we tend to measure success statistically, whether it is a grade point average or gross revenues at the box office. So it seems logical to look at the past performance numbers of a money manager to assess how your investments are doing. In fact, historical performance remains the most important determinant of asset-allocation or manager-selection decisions. However, that would be no different than driving by looking in the rearview mirror instead of at the road ahead.

If you heard about an athlete who had won every major competition in a certain sport for several years in a row, you would conclude that he (or she) was a high performer with great skill. But several years later, if you learned that he had been taking steroids to boost his performance, you would have a vastly different view of his prowess. The same is true in money management: it is critical to understand not just the performance outcomes, but the performance

---

1. Source: The Late Prof. Aaron Levenstein, associate professor emeritus of business at Baruch College. This heading is a subset of his original quote: "Statistics are like bikinis. What they reveal is suggestive but what they conceal is vital".

drivers. *Why* is once again more important than *what*. In the fullness of time, more facts will emerge that put earlier facts in wider context, and you may end up forming a different conclusion.

> **"In money management: it is critical to understand**
> **not just the performance outcomes,**
> **but the performance drivers."**

Sometimes an athlete might perform well simply because of rookie luck or a home-court advantage. He may not be able to repeat that performance at different times or in different environments. The same is true of money managers. Were they smart, or just lucky? To answer that, you have to analyze multiple data points over many years in varying conditions. You also have to consider the planning and preparation that drove the outcome. In investing, skill is best assessed not just by looking at a performance track record, but by understanding the philosophy and process that underpin that performance. You also need to take into account the headwinds and tailwinds that might help or hurt over various time periods. Differently put, performance must be judged in context and over an extended period, not in isolation or in short intervals.

Luck or Skill: A Bad Manager Having a Good Time, or a Good Manager Having a Bad Time?

In the early to mid-2000s, buying real estate in America was widely considered a surefire way to make money. Cocktail party conversation inevitably turned to home renovations. HGTV became one of the most popular TV channels. Sprucing up your house, or buying a vacation home, became the national pastime. The fast money went a step further: not only owning real estate but flipping it.

Before long, the average person on the street thought they could moonlight as real estate investors and strike it rich. In fact, you felt like a sap if you did not get on the bandwagon.

Between 2001 and 2007, anyone who owned real estate looked smart, and those who did not (such as me) looked dumb. We know how that turned out. People who sat out the bubble were ultimately proven smart as they picked up bargains when home prices fell precipitously.

My decision not to own real estate stocks from 2001 to 2007 would eventually prove smart, but at the time I looked very foolish. To make matters worse, I got unlucky. I happened to own reinsurance stocks when a "1 in 150 years" event unexpectedly occurred in 2005—a record-breaking hurricane season, including notable storms such as Dennis, Elma, Wilma, Katrina, and Rita. In addition to the tragic loss of life, the hurricanes caused catastrophic and costly damage (the highest on record at the time), resulting in many billions of dollars' worth of insurance claims on Swiss Re and Munich Re, whose stocks I owned.

These two unrelated investment decisions—being underweight in real estate and overweight in reinsurers—conspired to make my short-term performance look unbelievably bad. Eventually my performance did turn around, but it took several years. In the intervening period, I was pegged as unskilled, even though I was just unlucky.

On the other hand, many of my competitors owned both real estate and refinery stocks in their portfolios and did very well, not because they had the foresight to know that the hurricanes would cause many refineries along the Gulf of Mexico to shut down and create temporary shortages, but because they happened to be in the right place at the right time. As those stocks went up, they looked skilled, even though they were just lucky. An untimely confluence of unpredictable disasters and uncorrelated developments meant that my performance record took a big hit.

In investing, unexpected stuff happens—the proverbial unknown unknowns. No amount of fundamental research could have uncovered those outcomes. But what happened next was in my opinion a function of skill, not luck.

My research told me that after every catastrophic natural disaster, the reinsurers would initially suffer but eventually benefit, because they would be able to raise prices substantially in the next renewal season. I doubled up on my reinsurance stocks as they fell and enjoyed the gains that followed a few years later when their stocks rose. My other decision—to not own real estate—also paid off several years later when the housing boom turned into a bust. Both these non-consensus calls eventually contributed to my better performance numbers, when measured against the benchmark and my peers, but in the meantime my record suffered.

In the short run, luck can hurt or help a manager's performance. In the long run, skill tends to drives performance. This can be true for markets as well—in the short run they can be lucky or unlucky due to noise, newsflow or need, but in the long run, fundamentals are likely to prevail. For example, during 2013, Mexican stocks suffered collateral damage from a financial and political crisis in Brazil and declined by almost 20 percent, which is bear-market territory. Emerging-market managers sold Mexican stocks simply because of their *need* to raise cash to meet redemptions; it was Mexico's bad luck to be in the wrong place at the wrong time. This correction represented volatility, not risk, because the price action was driven by flows not fundamentals. Recall from chapter 3 that volatility can be an opportunity instead of a threat. Mexican stocks were providing potential investment bargains to contrarians who could stomach the temporary sell-off.

However, buying when everyone else is selling is painful because a falling stock hurts a manager's performance in the short run. You look dumb even though you are being smart. On the other hand, buying into a rising market makes you look smart for a while, even though you are being dumb. *Looking* smart or dumb versus *being* smart or dumb makes a world of a difference in investing.

And the same goes for looking at *annual* versus *annualized* performance, which is the topic of the next section.

Lose the Battle to Win the War: Consistent Returns Come at the Expense of High Returns

We saw in chapter 6 that severity (order of magnitude) matters more than frequency (which is just another word for consistency). A money manager can underperform more than half the time and still deliver superior performance over time. Yet, investors continue to mistakenly focus on batting averages, which are a measure of frequency, not severity. In investing, you can lose many battles and still win the war. In fact, you often need to.

> **"In investing, you can lose many battles and still win the war. In fact, you often need to."**

Let's revisit the the performance table of the hypothetical risk aware active manager in chapter 6. Even though the hypothetical portfolio underperformed in six out of ten calendar years, its cumulative performance over the decade still beat the benchmark by a wide margin, with annualized returns of 8 percent versus 4 percent. A few things to note here: First, the risk-aware actively managed portfolio does not deliver outperformance every year (*annually*), just over time (*annualized*). Second, it is important to look at performance data in terms of "growth of a $100" investment, which reflects absolute returns over time in addition to relative returns annually; Third, by itself, underperformance in any given period is meaningless. The money manager may be avoiding popular but expensive stocks and owning unpopular stocks with more compelling values. Understanding *why* your manager is underperforming is more important than the frequency or degree of underperformance.

In investing, you can lose many battles and yet win the war. The key is to understand the difference between *annualized* and *annual* returns: Expecting high returns or outperformance every single year is wishful thinking and dooms you to disappointment. This is because persistent alpha (risk-adjusted returns relative to a benchmark) is rarely consistent (year in and year out), and consistent alpha is rarely persistent. In fact, as far as I know, only one money manager even pretended to deliver this fairy tale, a fellow named Bernie Madoff. And you know what happened to him—he went to prison for defrauding investors. This anecdote should make clear how impossible it is to constantly deliver both superior *annual* and *annualized* performance—one often comes at the expense of the other.

Consider another example. In the long run, small-cap stocks have delivered higher returns than large caps, but they rarely do that consistently (aka annually). In fact, in many years, large caps will outperform small caps. That does not mean small caps cannot deliver higher *annualized* returns over time; they simply may not do so *annually*.

This is true of most performance numbers; short-term and long-term outcomes may diverge a lot. In fact, it is fairly typical for the vast majority of top-performing managers over a ten-year period to have three straight years of underperformance. My own experience corresponds to this. Even Warren Buffett, the best money manager of all time, has underperformed from time to time. As he puts it, "We are happy to sacrifice a smooth 12 percent for a lumpy 15 percent." Compounding of capital is a long-term game. Lumpy but higher is better than linear but lower.

Astute money managers know that consistent returns can come at the expense of high returns. You should realize it too. In fact, I would go as far as to say that *if your portfolio manager is not underperforming with some frequency, you might want to question whether such performance is sustainable.*

Marathon, Not Sprint

Think of investing as a marathon, not a sprint. If you try to win every lap, you are likely to lose. Unfortunately, most investors think investing is a sprint, a test of *speed* instead of *stamina*. So they measure the wrong thing: how their manager is performing every quarter or calendar year, rather than in the fullness of time. This creates pressure on their money manager to not lose out in the short run. The cheapest trick in the book to achieve good short-term performance is by chasing momentum, owning whatever is in vogue at the moment, a subterfuge that enables a money manager to show *consistency* even if it is at the expense of *persistency*.

But chasing momentum is nothing other than following the herd. By the time you discover that your money manager's investment process was no more than a case of the blind leading the blind—which is what herd investing is—you have lost both your money and your mojo. Better not to put yourself in such an awkward position in the first place. Stop measuring and incentivizing short-term performance results. It results in unintended and perverse consequences, where consistency is prioritized over longevity and returns are prioritized over risk.

Investing is an Endurance Test, Not an Endearment Test

It was December 1995. I had just joined the multi-billion-dollar money manager Oppenheimer Capital in New York as an Asian-equities analyst and portfolio manager. Back then, Asian stocks were all the rage. Global investors were enamored with the region and clamored to have more exposure in their portfolios. It was the classic crowded trade filled with confirmation bias: nobody looked for what could go wrong; everyone focused on what could go right. And their unbridled optimism had plenty of company.

Experts from the International Monetary Fund, the central banks, and the credit rating agencies were falling over each other to compliment the local governments and regulatory bodies for their success while simultaneously and self-servingly taking credit for it, as if their economic and monetary policies had led to the spectacular growth rates and market performance. The media fed this frenzy of good news, and everyone was palpably cheerful and confident. Nobody dared to question let alone look for evidence that contradicted those expert assertions, which were passing off as truth. The worst part was, even though investors were clueless and unprepared for the brewing storm, they felt as if they were "in the know" because they were engulfed by glowing headlines in newspapers and ebullient predictions on TV by experts who were telling them all was well.

Amid all this, I stood out like a sore thumb because I saw things very differently. My due diligence suggested that the heady growth rates were the result not of sound economic policies but of unsound lending practices. I foresaw that a debt-fueled binge would unravel badly and cause a lot of losses in its wake. Where others saw an Asian *miracle*, I saw an Asian *mirage*. My research led me to be prudent and own utilities while my peers chose to be profligate and owned banks. I paid the price for this non-consensus positioning by underperforming.

While I was looking out for my clients' long-term best interests, they thought I was hurting their pocketbook. Even in internal investment-committee meetings, my colleagues and fellow portfolio managers were getting frustrated with me. Not only was I not giving them ideas to buy in Asia, I kept hammering home reasons to sell. Out there in the real world, they were hearing an entirely different story, and it was hard for them to support me, let alone sympathize.

As days turned into weeks and months into quarters and then years, I felt tormented. Even though I knew I was doing the right thing, if I was not proven right soon, I could lose my job. And that would mean losing my ability to stay in the United States because I was on a work visa. I sometimes wondered which would crash first: my dream to prove myself on Wall Street or Asian stocks. It would have been convenient to fold, especially when I had a lot on the line—not just unemployment, but deportation.

I knew Asian stocks (and banks in particular) were risky and overvalued, so I did not invest in them. But while those stocks were going up, my colleagues and clients felt I was letting them down. I found myself in a quandary of "failing" them or "cheating" them. I chose to "fail". My performance stank because I prioritized risk management over return management. I had no doubt it was the right thing, but I paid a steep price.

Recall from chapter 6 that the cost of risk management is incurred in the *present*, but the benefits are secured in the *future*. The result is that many money managers sacrifice risk management at the altar of return management. This risk-taking behavior is often unknowingly and unwittingly blessed and incentivized by the very clients whom it ultimately hurts. This is what played out during the Asian bull market. The money managers who chased momentum and stock-market favorites looked like geniuses, even though they were taking remarkably high risk, while managers who were prudently sitting out the fads underperformed and underwhelmed.

Naturally, I was ostracized while my peers were feted. They received accolades and assets while I struggled to secure credibility, let alone clients.

Finally, on July 2, 1997, the tables turned. The Thai baht halved against the dollar, crashing from ฿26 to ฿54 in a matter of months, setting off a firestorm of currency devaluations around the region. Surprise turned to shock and then full-blown panic. Investors who had vied to get in now rushed to get out. Asian markets and currencies fell like dominoes. Governments were toppled. Crony capitalism and corrupt practices were exposed. Widespread defaults and layoffs occurred. Suddenly and sadly, *the region that could do no wrong became the region that could do no right.*

The rest is history. I went from being zero to hero inside my firm. Not only was I not fired, I was promoted. Clients and money soon followed.

"What Matters May Not Be Measured and What Is Measured May Not Matter." (Albert Einstein)

If you measured a five-star chef on speed of service instead of quality of food, he would probably flunk. Likewise, if you tasted gourmet food before it was ready, it would taste awful, even if the finest-quality ingredients were used. Measuring the wrong thing or over the wrong time frame risks yielding an erroneous conclusion. Despite this, human beings feel obliged to measure progress and performance along preset timelines.

In investing, the danger here is twofold. Managers know their clients require performance reports at preset periods, such as quarterly or yearly, so they oblige by delivering what is undeniably short-term information. What is worse, they make decisions specifically designed to give good results in that time frame. In other words, they manage to those preset periods, knowing they will be measured on them. This reinforces the bad habit of measuring what does not matter (short-term data) and not measuring what does (process and prowess). If you meticulously monitor your portfolio's performance at short intervals, you run the risk of losing sight of the endgame, which is to compound capital in the long run.

Worse still, frequent measurement of performance is not only futile, it actually proves counterproductive. This is because investors tend to feel losses more intensely than gains of the same magnitude. The more often they look at performance numbers, the greater the emotional cost over time, and the more likely they are to act on those emotions rather than resist them. The result is that investors experience worse returns than the market averages because they make buy/sell or hire/fire decisions based on recent—and misleading—performance.

Manage Expectations: No Pain, No Gain

The ideal scenario is a money manager who has built an investor base with a common investment philosophy, time horizon, resolve, and tolerance for underperformance. Only then can a manager maintain the stable capital base required to see his contrarian philosophy through to a successful conclusion. Unfortunately, many investors want instant (and constant) gratification, so their financial adviser may feel compelled to serve up the fast-food equivalent instead of offering the choice of fine dining. We know that fast food is comfort food; it feels very satisfying when you are hungry. But indulging in short-term quick fixes to ease your hunger comes at a very steep cost: it jeopardizes your long-term health. Also, you miss out on a wonderful experience and the satisfaction that comes from enjoying a gourmet meal. In life, you have learned the importance of good eating choices. The same principle applies to investing choices. Superior short-term numbers may be easy to serve up and comforting to digest but will likely prove injurious to your long-term wealth.

This is about managing *expectations* rather than managing *money*. Most people know it takes far more time to prepare a gourmet meal than fast food, so they are willing to wait patiently for their meal with positive anticipation. However, if the fine dining restaurant-did not tell them at the outset that the meal would take time, they would soon complain, and perhaps rush to a fast-food restaurant that would quell their hunger (but not satisfy their appetite).

No one would insist that a chef prepare a sixty-minute dish in thirty minutes. It's equally foolish to insist that a money manager deliver good results in a short time frame. In my view, managing expectations about performance is better than managing performance on a short leash.

Balanced Scorecard: Assess Prudence and Prowess
Instead of Performance

Often, the challenge for individual investors or their fiduciaries is the inability to assess whether a good money manager is experiencing a bad time, or a bad money manager is experiencing a good time. If you are not supposed to judge prematurely, how do you conduct evaluations in the intervening periods? After all, the long term is a series of short terms.

The correct approach to evaluating performance is in a multifaceted way, using a balanced scorecard. Here is a framework to consider:

1. Look at performance over a long time frame, such as a full market cycle that comprises both bull and bear markets. Short-term performance numbers contain a lot of noise and therefore have limited power to predict a manager's skill. In his book *Active Portfolio Management*, published in 1995, Ronald Kahn demonstrated through a series of equations that it takes sixteen years' worth of performance data to prove skill over luck with a high degree (95 percent) of statistical confidence. To evaluate a strategy or manager, it is important to look at long-term performance data spanning not just years but several cycles of bull and bear markets.[2]
2. Look at performance in absolute dollar terms as growth of a $100 investment (as shown in table 6.1), not just relative returns every calendar year.
3. Understand the *context* of the performance data, not just the *content*. Were there tailwinds or headwinds that helped or hurt performance? Did elements of good or bad

---

2. Richard C. Grinold and Ronald N. Kahn, *Active Portfolio Management: Quantitative Theory and Applications* (Nashville, TN: Probus, 1995).

luck play a role? Luck equals things that could not have been foreseen; skill equals predictable performance outcomes under certain conditions.

4. *Why* a strategy is performing is more important than knowing *what* its performance is. Look at performance attribution data (this is an analytical report that deconstructs the drivers of performance), not just raw performance numbers. Your goal is to analyze what contributed to or detracted from the performance. Was it driven by factors within the manager's control, such as his/her stock theses playing out, or did some unexpected externality influence results?

5. Evaluate whether the performance attribution is broad based, with many small things contributing, or whether it came from one big call. My preference is for performance to be driven by multiple, independent theses working out over time, not a single stock or theme driving the numbers, as that tends to be less repeatable.

6. Do not simply analyze the returns; analyze the risks taken to achieve them. In particular, check if leverage has been deployed to juice up returns. Sometimes higher returns may be a function of higher risks assumed. This reflects aggression, not skill. You may recall from chapter 6 that a significant portion of the returns of private equity came from loading portfolio holdings with debt, which is a risky way to generate them. Look at risk-adjusted returns, not returns alone.

7. Look at performance metrics such as Jensen's alpha, appraisal ratio, and upside and downside capture ratio.[3]

---

3. *Jensen's alpha* is a measure of the excess returns earned by the portfolio compared to returns suggested by the CAPM model. The *appraisal ratio* is a ratio used to measure the quality of a fund manager's investment-picking ability; it compares the fund's alpha to the portfolio's unsystematic risk or residual

Many independent, third party databases provide such data. Looking at a multitude of metrics and ratios helps provide a more holistic understanding of the drivers of performance.

To assess process, make a concerted effort to understand why the manager's investment approach should work in long run. Ask the following questions:

- What market inefficiency is the strategy trying to exploit (understand the investment philosophy and approach)?
- What skill is being brought to bear to uncover and arbitrage this inefficiency (consider the training and experience of the practitioners)?
- How long will it work? This is about repeatability: will it stand the test of time, or is it a fluke?
- How much will it work? This is about scalability: will it deliver the same results at higher levels of investment, or is it capped by size?
- Where will it work? Is it limited by factors of geography, certain sectors, etc.?

Finally, I would not ignore the soft skills. Investing is as much about stomach as it is about smarts. I prefer money managers who have a track record of staring temptation, fear, and contempt in the eye and not capitulating for short-term gain. I would also seek managers who have been baptized in the school of hard knocks and not given in or given up. It takes character and fortitude, not just caliber and intellect, to succeed in this profession.

---

standard deviation. An *upside capture ratio* over 100 indicates that a fund has generally outperformed the benchmark during periods of positive returns for the benchmark; a *downside capture ratio* less than 100 indicates that a fund has lost less than its benchmark in periods when the benchmark has been in the red.

I think it is clear from the above discussion that there is no shortcut to assessing performance—it is a multidimensional exercise that requires looking at a lot of numbers but also the narrative behind those numbers. Look at the hard facts but don't ignore the soft factors.

Understand Potential for Future Returns; Do Not Invest Based on Past Performance

In chapter 4, we learned how to distinguish a genuine investment management strategy from a gimmicky asset-gathering strategy. Often, strategies appear compelling because they are easy to explain and understand, not because they are sound or effective in practice. When launching a new product, it has become easy to impress investors with back-testing statistics that predict high performance potential. That kind of statistical evidence can seem very convincing but be careful. It may be none other than fanciful data mining that fails in practice because implementation costs are too high, or the targeted inefficiency is so small that it is unlikely to produce any meaningful returns. Evaluating skills and capability has predictive power; looking at historical performance does not. Sadly, data, however misleading, wields more power because it is tangible to look at, while skill is hard to figure out. But easy does not equal right.

In the 1990s, hedge funds reported spectacular returns, and many people piled in, seduced by the compelling performance data. Few tried to understand *why* these funds were performing so well. It turns out that most were leveraged long-only funds: their investment portfolios were augmented with borrowed money to lever up their assets and returns. Leverage turbocharges performance in a bull market but decimates it in a bear market. Instead of figuring out whether those managers had good skills in shorting, which would enable them to perform in bear *and* bull markets, investors simply looked at performance data to make their decisions.

> **"Often, strategies appear compelling because they are easy to explain and understand, not because they are sound or effective in practice."**

A decade later, the hitherto terrific performance had turned terrible, and investors realized they were paying high fees for less than stellar skill. Since the issue of skill had never been evaluated (but assumed based on performance data), the only thing left to do was to bail at the first sign of trouble. This is neither smart nor responsible. It is easier to blame the hedge fund managers than to take responsibility for failure to ask the right questions. It is your responsibility to evaluate performance drivers using the framework provided earlier.

Sadly, instead of learning from their mistakes of the past, many investors are making new ones in the present. Their asset-allocation decisions are driven by their need for and assumption of a certain level of actuarial returns based on past performance, rather than the potential for achieving those returns, especially net of costs and fees.

In my view, the recent trend toward allocating to private equity, junk bonds, and passive are glaring examples of this. These three decisions are risky and also highly correlated, although few view them through that lens. Here are the common denominators from my vantage point:

1. They show classic signs of being crowded trades, but investors looking at their high historical performance find it easy to justify their allocation decisions (even though it is common knowledge that past performance is no guarantee of future results).

2. They have benefited from low interest rates and quantitative easing (QE: loose monetary policy by central banks, which boosts the appetite for and price of risky assets) and are likely to suffer when QE is unwound. Private equity has used low-cost loans to lever up their portfolio companies. Junk bonds have benefited from investor appetite for high yield which in turn has reduced the margin of safety with respect to future default risk. Passive has turned into an "all night long" momentum party where nobody questions whether what it owns is overvalued or undervalued, so long as it is delivering high absolute returns.

3. Their sales pitch tends to focus on a single metric to the exclusion of other equally important considerations. Private equity talks up its lack of correlation to other asset classes. Junk bonds flatteringly rechristen themselves as "high yield." Passive draws attention to its low costs.

4. They have large and growing risks (as described in earlier chapters), but since they have not materialized, they get a free pass (Recall from chapter 6 that investors overlook risk *exposure* and overly anchor on risk *experience*).

5. They are likely to have disappointing future returns compared to their past, given their high valuations. (This is my research opinion—I could be wrong).

Recall from chapter 9 that we humans are reductionists by nature. We want to simplify things to the point of zeroing on one thing at the expense of everything else. Such blind spots introduce risks. In forming any assessments, one should be balanced and weigh the positives and negatives, the upside as well as the downside. I am not arguing these asset classes may be wrong investment choices for you or forever, I am simply saying you should make well-informed decisions and consider their risks as much as their returns.

The one question that should be asked before making any asset-allocation decision is this: Based on available value spreads, what are future returns likely to be? Future returns are predominantly determined by whether the asset class is under or overvalued. Unfortunately, despite the SEC's familiar and very clear warning, "past performance is no guarantee of future returns," most investors still extrapolate past high returns and believe they can reliably generate them in the future. This is a risky assumption to make; there are no guarantees in investing. Assuming a high return *in theory* does not mean it will be generated *in practice*. In fact, the opposite is more likely. After a prolonged period of high returns, typically low returns set in. Bull markets tend to become both crowded (everyone wants to get in on the action) and overvalued. To restore efficiency, markets undergo corrections to wipe out such overvaluation. Unfortunately, markets can overshoot, and the sell-off can be larger and longer than warranted, to the point of correcting so much that stocks become undervalued instead of fairly valued. This pendulum swing from overvalued to undervalued and from crowded trade to lonely trade presents advantageous opportunities for the contrarian investor.

However, exactly when the opportunity to make money is highest, investor interest is lowest. An out-of-favor asset class, sector, geography, or stock offers rich pickings for those who are willing to be contrarian. But contrarians tend to be in short supply (read the next chapter to understand why). Instead of availing themselves of contrarian opportunities and stepping away from the herd, investors gravitate toward it, and the vicious cycle of prioritizing consistency over longevity, returns over risk, and short-term over long-term continues. Your investment portfolio should try to take advantage of such greed/fear pendulum swings by allocating countercyclically instead of procyclically. One leading indicator of excess is when a lot of new products or funds are being launched in a given category or sector. They are usually asset-gathering strategies pandering to investor appetite, instead of investment strategies with genuine return potential. I covered this in more detail in chapter 4.

Optimize, Do Not Maximize: Practice Prudence Over Profligacy

Some investors want to pounce and go all in at the lows and all out at the highs. This may sound like a great idea in theory, but it is impossible to execute consistently. After all, we only know the highs and lows of a stock in hindsight, making such market timing a fool's errand. The art of building a position and gaining exposure to your desired investment ideas and subsequently exiting them when your theses have worked out (referred to as portfolio construction) is about optimizing, not maximizing. The goal is not to bottom tick or top tick a stock. The idea is to capture the "meat of the trade" by generally buying closer to the lows than the highs. To ensure the juice is worth the squeeze, your investment idea must possess a large difference between where you accumulate and where you pare back, to have both a reasonable margin of safety and a decent margin of upside. In other words, there must be a large value spread to exploit between your view and what is priced in by the consensus.

The principle of optimizing instead of maximizing also applies to portfolio construction, where you must own neither too many stocks nor too few. Owning too many stocks results in an active manager turning passive, mimicking the benchmark instead of differentiating from it. Owning too few stocks makes a portfolio quite risky as it does not possess adequate diversification.

So how do you both concentrate *and* diversify your portfolio? This may sound like an oxymoron, but it is not. The key is knowing that what you leave out of your portfolio is as important as what you put in. Active investing is not about owning everything in the benchmark (that is passive's prerogative and obligation), but about knowing what *not* to own.

It is also about doing your homework and being very discerning. If you can only send twelve men to the moon, you will be incredibly careful about which twelve you choose. Likewise, in investing you can choose from thousands of stocks around the world, but you must choose only the very few that will do better than the rest. This scarcity/abundance paradox—you can choose from a lot, but you must only choose a few—is key to successful active management and portfolio construction. For this, we need to apply the lessons learned in chapter 6: rejecting low-quality businesses is as important as selecting high-quality ones, because it is the weakest links that break the chain. Also, to reduce concentration risk, individual investment ideas and theses should be uncorrelated as far as possible.

Do Not Judge a Book by Its Cover

When an athlete takes shortcuts by consuming steroids, this can pay off temporarily but proves costly and risky eventually, not just to the athlete but to the sport itself, as spectators and sponsors lose trust. In investing as in sports, winning at any cost or through any means is in my opinion a form of fraud, not a feat. In investing, it is better to choose a money manager who *looks* foolish but is *being* smart, who prefers to "fail" rather than to "cheat", and who may disappoint you in the short run but will impress you in the long run, rather than the other way around.

Finally, for investment success, it is not just your manager's discipline that matters. Your discipline matters too. Both parties need to:

a. Practice patience (endure short-term pain for long-term gain).
b. Possess perspective (recognize that a lumpy 15 percent is better than a smooth 12 percent).
c. Exercise prudence (not sacrifice risk management on the altar of return management).

Last but not least, humans are programmed for survival and gut reactions, not soul-searching or delayed gratification. Our mind and body prioritize the short term over the long term because if one is dead, the long term does not matter. However, most investment decisions are not about survival or life or death, and our instinctive fight-or-flight response proves counterproductive. With practice and persistence, these factory settings can be reset, and practitioners like me have spent a lifetime doing this. However, if this is not your forte or desire, you can still enjoy the fruits of patience and prudence. Simply outsource your investing needs to the right professionals who have mastered this discipline, and go about your business.

Top Takeaways

1. Do not confuse performance with prowess. It may simply be a function of being in the right place at the right time. In the short run, it is hard to distinguish skill from luck or aggression.
2. Premature judgment is likely to be erroneous judgment. Wrong behaviors are incentivized, and right behaviors are disincentivized.
3. What matters may not be measured and what is measured may not matter.
4. A money manager can have a poor batting average (*annual* outperformance) yet outperform on an *annualized* basis over a full market cycle. It is not uncommon for even top performing managers, to have three straight years of underperformance over a ten year period.
5. High returns and consistent returns are typically mutually exclusive. Lose the battle of chasing consistent returns in the short term and win the war of generating higher returns in the long term.

12

North Star

This chapter brings together all the principles presented previously, to explain how a non-consensus, intrinsic value approach to investing can help to square the circle of generating returns and reducing risk via differentiated research and countercyclical investment behavior. The epic battle between active and passive investing is none other than being a contrarian. The more contrarian you are, the more active your portfolio.

By being correct, contrarian, and courageous, as well as holistic, prudent, and patient in your investment decisions, you can buy what you wanted to all along, on sale instead of paying full price, thereby improving the odds of making money instead of losing it.

Despite such desirable outcomes, few people practice non-consensus investing because going against the grain is very uncomfortable. There is no easy road to investment success, but there are some classic if counterintuitive precepts that can serve as your north star—that is what this chapter is about.

Non-Consensus Investing: A Research and Behavioral Framework to Generate Superior Risk-Adjusted Returns

Wall Street pundits and ivory tower academics have very little in common. But one thing they seem to agree on is that high returns and low risk are mutually exclusive and therefore it is impossible to accomplish both. I refuse to settle for this suboptimal choice. My non-consensus investment approach tries to square this circle by turning conventional investment norms on their head. Instead of being a dense database, it seeks to be a smart search engine.

Instead of picking winners, it focuses on avoiding losers. Instead of letting our flaws become our failings, I believe we can use them as opportunities for learning and profit from them instead of suffering from them. This chapter brings all these precepts together so that a full picture emerges.

Non-consensus investing is about mastering certain intellectual and behavioral principles.

1. Being correct: understanding and not misunderstanding quality
2. Being contrarian: conducting differentiated research and investing countercyclically
3. Being prudent: avoiding losers and losses and prioritizing risk management over return management
4. Being holistic: understanding what can go right and wrong to figure out the upside potential as well as the downside risks
5. Being patient: waiting for opportunities to come your way rather than chasing them
6. Being courageous: standing resolute in the face of ridicule and backlash

Non-consensus investing is about buying what you always wanted to own but waiting for the right opportunity to present itself when others are ignoring it, misunderstanding it, or fearing it. Because you are buying on sale instead of paying full price, you improve the odds of making money instead of losing it. That is the essence of contrarian investing. It is about selling or patiently waiting on the sidelines when everyone is chasing the stock up on unrealistic expectations or unsustainable valuations; eschewing the crowded trade in favor of the lonely one and investing countercyclically instead of procyclically; waiting for clamor to give way to capitulation as sentiment waxes and wanes on different sectors, countries, or companies.

A non-consensus investor can find asymmetric risk/reward investment opportunities in many ways. Here are a few key ones:

1. Conducting differentiated research to identify what is misunderstood and therefore mispriced by the consensus.
2. Taking advantage of excessive pessimism that focuses unduly on negative developments in the near term while ignoring what can go right in the long term.
3. Investing countercyclically to other people's investment appetite when the sentiment swings from greed to fear or reverence to repulsion.
4. Looking at pockets of the market suffering from sheer neglect.
5. Arbitraging differing time horizons, taking advantage of people's inability or unwillingness to think long term.

Some of these attributes can exist simultaneously, as the following examples will demonstrate.

The Popularity of a Trade Is Often Inversely Correlated with Its Profitability

What is very popular rarely remains profitable, yet popular feels safe. Excessive popularity of a theme, geography, sector, or security is called a "crowded trade" in markets. This means that the crowd's hot pursuit brings inflated stock prices, invariably making them overvalued. Markets penalize such price distortions with losses. This is why crowded trades are often doomed to failure. When too many people latch onto a trend, they bid it up to the point where valuations inflate like a balloon and are just a pin prick away from bursting.

This also explains why growth stocks tend to underperform in the long term. Their very popularity proves to be their undoing.

When high expectations are built into the stock, it gets priced for perfection, and even minor setbacks cause major sell-offs. People expect that high growth to continue; if it slips—and it inevitably does—that can cause the stock to plunge. In the late 1990s, with the advent of the internet, networking-equipment stocks such as Cisco became crowded trades. They were attractive businesses with good prospects, but their high valuations provoked a meltdown. Between late 1997 and early 2001, Cisco stock went up tenfold, from $8 to $80, then crashed by 85 percent to $12 in under two years when growth disappointed. As of December 2018, Cisco stock has recovered to $43, but that still wiped out about half of net worth for those who had chased it at the start of the century.

On the other hand, an unpopular or lonely trade can be very profitable. When sellers abound but buyers don't, stocks get marked down, throwing up bargains. A good example is the Japanese equity market in 2012. After a large and laborious market correction of 75 percent from January 1990 through December 2012, Japanese equities became so out of favor that Japan was disparagingly christened the "submerging" market, a little market humor meant to draw contrast with the high-growth "emerging" markets that were still the rage at the time. Ironically, just a decade prior, investors had craved Japanese equities as they soared 450 percent between January 1980 and 1990. Over the next twenty years, Japanese equities swung wildly from adulation to derision as the economy suffered from debt, deflation and successive downturns.

However, during those difficult years of decelerating growth and debilitating deflation, many companies swallowed the bitter pill of restructuring and deleveraging to become more competitive, profitable, and resilient. These efforts paid off. Leading companies such as Canon and Kao went from sprawling conglomerates to more streamlined businesses and from net debt to net cash. In addition, many younger companies such as Murata and Keyence leveraged their technological expertise in electronic and industrial components to become market leaders in their respective industries. Companies such as Daito Trust Construction developed new manufacturing techniques to reduce the need for manual labor in the housing-construction industry. Nomura Research Institute developed and offered infrastructure and software as a service, well before it became a buzzword in Silicon Valley. Last but not the least, corporate governance improved, with companies raising their dividends and/or share buybacks to return surplus cash to shareholders.

Ironically, these structural improvements did not attract much investor attention. Investors had experienced so many false starts in the country that they had become weary and wary (an example of the anchoring bias we learned about in chapter 9).

An unprecedented natural disaster in 2011, the costliest in Japanese history, coupled with a weak economy and strong yen were hurting near-term earnings, further sapping investor appetite. So, despite the substantive progress by the corporate sector, sentiment remained sour, and many blue-chip stocks were available at depressed values. This combination of high-quality businesses trading at large discounts to their intrinsic business worth created an attractive setup. Many Japanese equities were both under-earning and undervalued, simultaneously offering low risk *and* high returns.

Around the same time, emerging markets had become a very crowded trade as investors were drawn to their high growth (while ignoring their high risks). While there were many attractive companies in emerging markets, my research revealed them to be overvalued relative to their business worth, so I avoided them. On the other hand, in true contrarian form, I scooped up many out-of-favor Japanese gems at bargain prices.

I was not surprised when the Japanese market, which was priced to submerge, stunned market participants by soaring 52 percent from 2012 to 2015, while the much-sought-after emerging markets

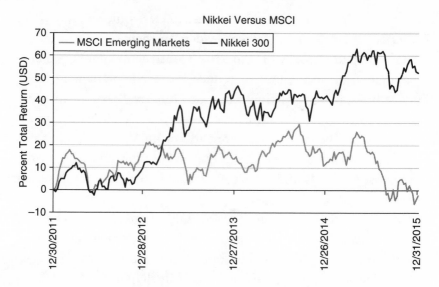

FIGURE 12.1 Relative Performance: Nikkei 300 versus MSCI Emerging Markets index, 12/30/2011–12/31/2015

declined 2 percent in dollar terms (figure 12.1). A $100 investment in the lonely trade (say an ETF mirroring the Nikkei 300) would have become $152, while going long the crowded trade (say an ETF mirroring the MSCI emerging market index) would have resulted in a decline to $98, a difference in performance of more than 50 percent.

Buy a Depressed Market, Not a Distressed Asset

There is a profound difference between a depressed market and a distressed asset. "Depressed" refers to a temporary dislocation driven by antipathy or indifference rather than permanent dysfunction. The short-term fundamentals diverge and disappoint, but the long-term prospects and capabilities remain intact. When neglect or pessimism becomes widespread, it is natural for multiple investment opportunities to emerge from a single thesis and for an entire sector or subset of the broader market, or even the market itself (Japan in our earlier example), to go out of favor. This is what I call a depressed market—earnings expectations and what investors want to pay for them are repressed.

"Distress," on the other hand, refers to a real danger that could prove fatal. A distressed asset is typically a low-quality business that I would not own at any price, including a distressed one. You can take advantage of a depressed market by investing in it countercyclically. But a distressed asset, even if it is optically cheap, is more likely to take advantage of you.

The weak performance of derivative exchanges such as Deutsche Börse is a good example of a *depressed* market opportunity that emerged several years ago in 2012 in Europe. Exchanges thrive on transaction activity in various financial markets, such as equities, index futures, interest rate swaps, and the like. In the wake of quantitative easing, volatility decreased dramatically, reducing the need for hedging as markets moved in a singular direction. This hurt transaction activity and near-term earnings, which in turn caused their stocks to lag.

However, I knew that such low activity levels were unlikely to last forever, and as they rose, so would their earnings and stock price. Six years later as of December 2018, the stock had doubled while the BE500 (European equivalent of the S&P 500) benchmark was almost flat. This is a good example of high returns without necessarily taking on high risk. It also demonstrates how active stock picking can generate returns, compared to investing passively in an index fund that mirrors a benchmark like the BE500 that has yielded practically no returns over the same timeframe.

Many international banks are examples of *distressed* assets, especially in Europe. While American banks have recapitalized in the aftermath of the 2008 financial crisis and now boast surplus capital, many of their European counterparts remain undercapitalized and should be viewed as distressed. I have avoided owning these international banks as their headline "cheap" valuations are a trap. Just because they are out of favor and nobody wants them does not mean you should chase them.

Another example of distressed assets is highly leveraged companies. Their bonds are typically rated below investment grade. Often, they sport a cheap multiple and appear to be a bargain, but do not fall for such optical illusions. Leveraged companies are highly risky, and equity investors should avoid them. Some would argue that the risk is accounted for in the cheapness of their valuations. I disagree. Risk is risk. Just because you are avoiding valuation risk does not give you a free pass to take on massive balance-sheet risk.

One word of caution with respect to owning depressed markets: It is not a license to go long on a wholesale basket of such stocks or sector or geography. Careful stock picking remains paramount, as the quality of business models and discounts to intrinsic worth vary even within the same sector or country. While taking advantage of a substantial portion of the market where value clusters, you must be careful not to cross the line from constructing a highly selective bottom-up portfolio to turning it into a thematic portfolio. Curation is critical to exploiting the power and payoff of non-consensus investing; what you leave out is as important as what you put in. A big loser in the basket can negate the gains from the winners.

Wait for the Sentiment to Swing—from Good to Bad, Greed to Fear, Clamor to Capitulation

For contrarians, bad news is good news because it gives you the opportunity to own something you always wanted to, except now you get to pick it up when you are being paid to take the risk of adverse developments. Crowds tend to buy stocks where good news is playing out and priced in, but no company or country or industry is immune from bad news. Wait patiently and let the investment opportunity come to you instead of chasing it.

For example, in Mexico in 2012, after the election of President Enrique Peña Nieto, which returned the Institutional Revolutionary Party to power after a twelve-year hiatus, the Mexican stock market became a favored investment destination, especially among investors focused on emerging markets. The regime change was expected to boost economic reforms and growth. This positive outlook contrasted dramatically with the economic and political disarray that investors expected in Brazil, where the unraveling of a corruption scandal led to the president's impeachment and caused the economy to spiral down into a full-blown recession. Unsurprisingly, by late 2015, the Bolsa Mexicana index was trading close to its highs (up 40 percent from the lows it had reached in August 2011) while Brazil's Bovespa index was on its knees (down 35 percent from the highs it had reached in March 2012). I avoided the popular and expensive Mexican stocks and instead bought inexpensive, out-of-favor Brazilian stocks such as Itaú bank.

A few years later, the tables had turned. Fresh elections in Brazil led to a more market-friendly president being voted in. On the other hand, an unexpected and protracted oil slump caused Mexican stocks to drop. In addition, over the prior few years, the Mexican peso had depreciated by more than 50 percent, reducing the probability of further falls (it is typical for a currency to stabilize after a large devaluation). This dramatically improved the risk/reward of the investment because both valuation risk and currency risk had diminished.

In the meantime, as prospects and sentiment recovered in Brazil, Itaú bank stock had gone up a lot. I took profits there, as investors had priced in the good news and were increasingly overvaluing the stock. Several months later, in early 2017, I used the proceeds to buy Walmart de Mexico, which had become a fallen angel as investors priced in bad news, making it undervalued. Over the next two years, Walmart de Mexico ADRs (American Depositary Receipts traded in the United States) went up 100 percent in dollar terms.

I tell you this story to illustrate how active management can win in the marketplace:

1. By actively redeploying capital from overvalued to under-valued stocks, it makes money for clients.
2. By contributing to fair-price discovery and reducing price distortion, it gives the market what it wants, which in turn rewards it for performing this double duty.

Long-Term Horizon: A Flower Is Far More Valuable Than a Seed

In investing, a difference in time horizons alone can yield pay-offs, not just a difference in your research. Very often, perfectly sound investment ideas are left by the wayside because there is no immediate catalyst in sight to warrant an upward rerating. If a stock lacks near-term momentum, the investment community often shuns it, as it tends to be obsessed with instant gratification. Those who can tolerate delayed gratification can benefit from such shortsightedness. Instead of buying and selling seeds, you wait for the seed to blossom into a flower. A little patience creates a lot of value because a flower is far more valuable than a seed. Do not leave this money on the table. In a world filled with short-termism, a long-term horizon can be a reliable source of excess returns.[1]

Markets need to reward people for postponing consumption. The longer you give up your use of money by setting it aside, say

---

1. A long-term horizon benefits from a statistical concept known as the square-root-of-time rule, sometimes used in conjunction with the term "time diversifica-tion." The latter suggests that, on a relative basis, more volatile assets become relatively less risky over time. The square-root-of-time rule dictates that while drift (expected return) grows linearly with time, standard deviation grows more slowly at the square root of time. In other words, volatility dominates the return-generating process over short periods of time, but in the long run drift eventually emerges as the more dominant factor as noise washes out.

in a time deposit instead of a checking account, the higher the interest rate you will earn for forgoing its immediate use. This is how patience puts more money in your pocket and why a long-term investment horizon is the only free lunch in investing.

Cultivating patience is especially important in non-consensus investing. Even if your thinking is correct, it takes time for non-consensus calls to become consensus. In the meantime, you must learn not to capitulate. Temporarily, it makes you look foolish, even though you are not. This takes character and courage, and it is one among the many reasons that investors do not practice non-consensus investing, even though in my view, the pros outweigh the cons.

No Good Deed Goes Unpunished

Besides patience being in short supply, there are several other reasons why investors fail to take advantage of contrarian investing despite their potential for delivering superior returns with lower risk.

Prime among them is that contrarians are guilty until proven innocent, and their proof statement comes much later. Investment theses take time to play out, and the more non-consensus your views are, the longer it takes. In the intervening period, you are often in solitary confinement. This is a tough pill to swallow. To add insult to injury, you are always the defendant, never the plaintiff. The burden of proof is on you, while the benefit of the doubt is given to the status quo.

Second, short-term pain precedes long-term gain, and few have the stamina for it. Even if contrarian managers are doing right by their clients by avoiding risky crowded trades, they are dropped like a hot potato when their performance fizzles while the benchmark sizzles.

Jean-Marie Eveillard of First Eagle Funds faced this in the late 1990s when he underperformed the benchmarks by refusing to invest in expensive and risky tech stocks. Legend has it that in less than two years, his investors redeemed in droves from the mutual fund he was managing, which went from over $6 billion in assets to just under $2 billion at the end of 2000. When a top executive at his parent company told him that if that continued, he would no longer have any money in his fund, he replied, "I'd rather lose half of my shareholders, which I did, than half of my shareholders' money, which I did not."

Those who stood by him reaped the benefits. His fund outperformed handsomely in the bear market that followed. In 2003, he went on to receive a Fund Manager Lifetime Achievement Award, created by Morningstar to recognize "mutual fund managers who throughout their careers have delivered outstanding long-term performance, aligned their interests with shareholders, demonstrated the courage to differ from consensus, and shown the ability to adapt to changes in the industry."

Third, human beings are social creatures who crave company. In fact, we are genetically predisposed to seek strength in numbers because it protects us from predators in the physical world. Nature programmed us to stay with the pack, not stray from it. In the intellectual world of investing, this urge proves very counterproductive, to the point of being self-destructive. Contrarians, on the other hand, are typically iconoclasts, which also makes them outcasts. They do not fit in; they stand out. Most people find it hard to be contrarian; it goes against their very being.

Fourth, we humans prefer to take the path of least resistance, whereas non-consensus investing demands the path of most resistance. It is tough to buy when everyone is selling and sell when everyone is buying. Even Stanley Druckenmiller, a proven veteran investor (and my former boss at Soros Fund Management) who has the distinction of delivering 30 percent annualized returns per annum over a thirty-year career, confessed to this in a Bloomberg interview on December 18, 2018: "I have never made a buy at a low that I didn't feel terrible about and was scared to death making. It is easy to sell at the bottom. You can go home that night and it relieves you of your nerves. But when you follow a process of investing based on reason and analysis rather than on emotion or by following the crowd, you will soon know and understand that you are on the right long-term path."

Finally, when you march to your own tune, nobody except you can hear the music. Everyone else is dancing to a different song, and you will look awkward and out of sync while everyone else will appear graceful. When your portfolio is positioned differently and your views are not yet playing out, your performance will struggle and make you look out of step. Few can tolerate this kind of discomfort; most find it easier to simply march to the same drumbeat by following the crowd.

Sometimes, this profession can be cruel and gut-wrenching. If you have selected non-consensus money managers to handle your investments, support them with patience and approval—and maybe some brownies from time to time! Being a contrarian can be hard and lonely. Support groups have proven their worth for people going through tough times, and investing is no different. It is important to connect with like-minded investors to help you stay the course. Feel free to visit my website, www.nonconsensusinvesting.com, to swap notes. I may also post some exclusive content, investment puzzles, inside scoops about the book or what I am up to—so check in from time to time.

Get Performance, Not Fashion Statements, with Your Portfolios

Herding, crowded trades, and momentum employ a common ruse: they offer the seduction of a chase that gets even more alluring when more join in. Mob psychology takes over in crowded trades. An auction-like frenzy develops, where the thrill and adrenaline of outbidding overtake the dispassionate evaluation of what something is worth. The non-consensus investor treats markets as a shopping mall where things periodically go on sale as opposed to an auction house where you must bid the highest price to get what you want. By waiting patiently for your desired items to be discounted, you can get what you want *and* not pay up for it.

> **"The non-consensus investor treats markets
> as a shopping mall where things periodically
> go on sale as opposed to an auction house
> where you must bid the highest price to
> get what you want."**

In investing, you should cast your net wide in any pocket of the market or part of the world that is suffering from neglect, pessimism, or misguided fears. These tend to be fertile grounds for generating high returns with low risk, provided they meet the tests of high quality. You can always count on something to go wrong somewhere and provide contrarian opportunities. Your job is to figure out whether what has gone awry is temporary or permanent.

Whenever investors pursue a fad or a fetish, there is usually money to be made by looking at the opposite end of the spectrum. Often when investors favor U.S. markets, opportunities surface in neglected international markets. When some sectors are in vogue, it pays to direct your attention to sectors that are being ignored. If small caps are in much demand, moneymaking opportunities may lurk in mega caps.

If these examples sound too obvious, try this: Look at companies you are researching with a different lens or barometer. The recent craze to own companies with *hyper* growth may have left the door wide open for contrarians to invest in companies with *sturdy* growth. For instance, over the last few years while investors were chasing heady growth and bidding up the FAANG (Facebook, Apple, Amazon, Netflix, and Google) stocks, they were in my estimation overlooking and mispricing the MAANG

(Michelin, American Express, Amdocs, Nippon Telephone, and Gilead)—companies with steady growth but not in as much vogue.

Another obsession afflicting the market is the fixation toward passive and away from active. Such a polarized crowded trade, in my view, sets the stage for a strong comeback of truly active money managers. I believe the pendulum is likely to swing away from passive strategies when investors realize they cannot rely on beta (broad equity market exposure) alone to generate compelling absolute returns. They will have no choice but to seek performance from alpha (idiosyncratic returns that can be derived from superior stock picking). In financial speak, beta is systematic risk that is reflected in the benchmark's returns; alpha is the extra (risk-adjusted) return generated compared to a passive benchmark. Only active managers have the potential to generate alpha because the benchmark cannot, by definition, exceed its own returns. As I point out later in this chapter, benchmark returns are likely to be low or negative in the coming years as rich valuations and weak balance sheets cap the upside. If you do not want to resign yourself to such unattractive returns, you owe it to yourself to explore active investing.

However, even the few who are brave enough to invest actively are falling for another herding trap: favoring quantitative (quant) approaches over qualitative ones. Quants have driven a wedge between passive and active by occupying the middle ground. Note that passive is itself a quant approach that replicates "dumb" beta, while quant or factor-based investing tries to offer "smart" beta to generate alpha. By being different from the benchmark, quant can call itself active.

Quants have curried favor with investors by highlighting the scientific and algorithmic modeling that underpins their investment decisions compared to the more eclectic and artistic approaches of stock pickers. This preference for precision has all the makings of yet another crowded trade. It offers the illusion of proof via back testing; stock picking, in contrast, cannot explain itself as a neat formula or set of rules. While I appreciate the difficulty of comprehending the art of stock picking, that does not mean it is an inferior approach, just a different one.

Think of stock pickers as jazz musicians and quants as musicians who play classical compositions. Classical musicians faithfully follow notations in sheet music, but jazz musicians follow their finely honed instincts. Jazz is not about reproducing someone else's musical score but composing one's own tune. It is constantly adapting and improvising, not scripted or formulaic. Yet despite that, it never descends into cacophony, always rendering a soulful melody. Non-consensus investing is akin to playing jazz. It is not a regurgitation of the consensus view or readily available information but a quest for originality to develop differentiated insights. It is opportunistic yet disciplined. It constantly adapts and iterates to find overlooked or misunderstood investment opportunities to generate superior risk-adjusted returns.

While quants use computers to decipher relative value, non-consensus investors use judgment to figure out intrinsic value. To think of one as superior or inferior is to miss the point. The two are simply different approaches, and if they stay true to themselves, each can render a good performance (although as I pointed out in chapter 10, I would caution against thinking of relative value as value investing).

I think it is no coincidence that jazz is an American invention. American ingenuity and entrepreneurship are the envy of the world because, like jazz musicians, we dare to improvise. Creativity has been the foundation of our economic success and is the key to our investment success as well. Of course, like entrepreneurship, stock picking is hard. It is neither error-proof nor stress-free. Failure is a by-product of greatness, and just as many entrepreneurs fail, so do many active managers. However, just as a society in which everyone wants to be an employee and nobody aspires to be an entrepreneur would become stagnant instead of vibrant, a market where everyone invests passively and avoids taking any active risk becomes static, not dynamic.

The prevailing negative view of active investing reminds me of the premature and incorrect verdict passed on American capitalism after the great financial crisis of 2008. Not only has the American economy recovered, it has prospered, thanks to the very capitalism it was criticized for. From shale fracking to gene-splicing, American enterprise continues to push the boundaries of innovation to develop an original symphony like no other. Stock picking (aka truly active investing) is no less an expression of individual creativity and ingenuity than jazz or entrepreneurship—and in my opinion, destined to be just as successful.

Active Investing Is Dead: Long Live *Truly* Active Managers

As of February 2019, the S&P 500 index traded at 2800, more than tripling in value from the market lows of March 2009. A disproportionate amount of this increase has come from valuations going up rather than earnings or free cash flows going up. As a result, equity markets are richly valued on a variety of methodologies, such as those used by Nobel Prize–winning economists Robert Shiller and James Tobin, investment gurus like Warren Buffett, or independent analysts such as Stephen Jones. All of them point in the same dismal direction: future expected annualized equity-market real returns in the United States are likely to range between +2.5 and –4 percent as shown in figure 12.2.[2]

With the U.S. ten-year government bond yielding close to 3 percent as of December 2018, equity indices will have a tough time competing against fixed income—not to mention, who wants negative returns? Investing passively in equities means you lock in such potentially low or negative returns. This is a potentially

2. See J. T. Crow, "Warren Buffett and Robert Shiller's Long-Term Models Show Where S&P Is Going," *Money and Markets*, January 24, 2019, https://moneyandmarkets.com/buffett-shiller-long-term-sp-500-prediction-method/.

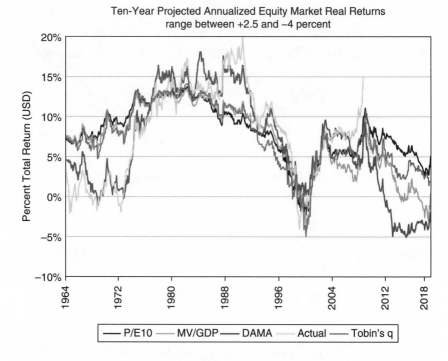

FIGURE 12.2 Ten-year projected S&P 500 real total return as of December 2018, using widely respected methodologies

dire outcome for many pension plans and retirees who have expected and assumed far higher returns (about 6 to 8 percent) on their equity portfolios. Before you despair, remember there is an alternative—active investing.

Not only has truly active investing delivered outperformance in the past,[3] it is likely to continue to do so in the future because the opportunity set is larger. The excessive popularity of passive and the diminishing proportion of active have made markets

3. Recall the study referenced in chapter 4 that showed that truly active managers beat passive by more than 2 percent per annum on a gross basis.

less efficient, creating more moneymaking opportunities for truly active managers.

> **"The excessive popularity of passive and the diminishing proportion of active, have made markets less efficient, creating more money-making opportunities for truly active managers."**

Your goal, therefore, should not be to give up on achieving higher returns than the benchmarks, but to pick those money managers who are truly active (recall the distinction in performance of *faux* active managers versus *truly* active managers from chapter 4). Yet investors continue to choose passive because of their singular focus on lower fees. This is a case of the tail wagging the dog. The goal of investing is to generate the highest returns with lowest risk, not to incur the lowest fees. Most pension funds and retirement nest eggs remain underfunded and will need higher returns than passive investing can potentially deliver in the decade ahead, if the expert forecasts of low to negative real returns in the S&P500 are right. Those managers and investors would be wise to follow the example of the man I consider the dean of active investing, David Swenson, who oversees Yale University's $29 billion endowment, which has generated outstanding results by astute asset allocation supplemented by use of talented active managers. According to their website, over the past thirty years ended June 30, 2018, Yale's investments have returned an unparalleled 13.0 percent per annum, adding $31.6 billion in value relative to the Cambridge mean. Relative to the median endowment, Yale's superior active manager selection contributed an additional 2.4 percent of outperformance per annum. Incidentally, this 2.4 percent outperformance corresponds very well to the findings of the studies done by Professors Cremers and Petajisto referenced in chapter 4.

Passive: Penny Wise, Pound Foolish?

As I have said before, I am not against passive per se. I think John Bogle, the pioneer of low-cost passive investing, rightly called the bluff of money managers who pretended to be active but were not (such as the closet indexers or low active share managers referenced in chapter 4). Markets need healthy competition, and consumers should have choices. My concern is that the pitch on passive has become so one-sided (everything else is inferior) and one-dimensional (low costs) that investors do not see the full picture. Investing your own savings or overseeing someone else's is too important to not hear all sides, especially the dark side of passive investing.

Investors see the active-versus-passive debate primarily through the lens of *cost*, but it should also be viewed through the lens of *risk*. To refresh your memory on the litany of risks I outlined in chapter 2, here is a recap:

1. Crowded-trade risk
2. Valuation risk
3. Redemption risk
4. Liquidity risk
5. Front-running risk
6. Permanent-impairment-of-capital risk
7. Behavioral risk
8. Momentum risk
9. Reflexivity risk
10. Market-inefficiency risk

Popular Wisdom Is Often a Contrary Indicator

It is worth recalling the pronouncement on the cover of *Business Week* magazine in October 1983: "The Death of Equities." This popular view not only proved ill-timed, it proved dead wrong. Equities went on to deliver their best returns in the decades ahead. I believe that the October 2016 *Wall Street Journal* headline "The Dying Art of Picking Stocks" will prove equally ill-timed and incorrect.

Passive is typically a bull-market phenomenon, when equity markets are delivering high absolute returns as they have done in the past decade. Active tends to do better in bear or choppy markets, which is where I believe we are headed. The contrarian in me would argue that you should consider seeking the other side of the trade when others are unwilling or unable to step up to the plate. In figure 12.3, notice how the pendulum swings over

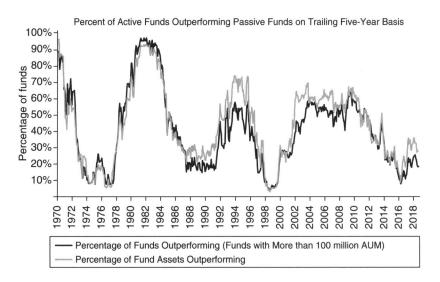

FIGURE 12.3 Percentage of funds (and fund assets) outperforming S&P 500 on a five-year basis *Note:* The figure shows the percentage of U.S. active equity mutual funds (black line) and fund assets (gray line) outperforming the total return of S&P 500 based on trailing five-year performance, after fees. Funds are those in existence for five years or more and include U.S. growth, growth and income, and income funds (based on CRSP fund-objective code). For percentage of fund outperformance, only funds with more than $100 million in total net assets are considered. Percentage of fund-assets outperformance is calculated as the ratio of total net assets of U.S. active equity funds outperforming the S&P 500 over total net assets of all U.S. active equity funds. Period of analysis is from January 1970 through December 2018.

the decades—historically when the majority of active funds under-perform passive over a five-year rolling period, it tends to mark a bottom, which then sets itself up for a dramatic reversal.

Keep in mind that investors need to put trillions of dollars to work in equity markets. The capacity of any active manager to manage assets is in the billions if not millions. Just as any popular sporting event or concert with limited seating capacity sells out quickly, active capacity is equally limited and could fill up quickly. Better to dig your well before you are thirsty and get those soon-to-be-coveted truly active money managers before they are full up and close their doors to new clients.

For Every Boglehead, There Needs to Be a Contrarianhead

In my view the epic battle between active and passive is none other than that of being a contrarian. The definition of passive is to toe the benchmark, while active is about being different from it. The higher the active share, the greater the disagreement with the benchmark of what is mispriced (undervalued or overvalued) and needs to be arbitraged to its fair price, thereby restoring efficiency to markets.

While this book seeks to pay homage to equities as an asset class and to truly active investing as an investment approach, it does not guarantee that they will always beat the competition for all time to come. From time to time, when the sentiment swings too far in one direction, it may be appropriate to take the other side of the trade. When I was putting the final touches on my manuscript in early 2019, fixed-income and passive approaches dominated investment preferences if not allocations; equities and active investment approaches were still viewed with skepticism. By the time you read this book, that trend may have abated or even reversed. My core message is on the power and payoff of non-consensus investing and how it can help to improve the risk and return profile of an investment decision. It is one among many ways to approach investing. The decision of what makes sense in your circumstance is ultimately yours. I am merely presenting a choice, hopefully a compelling one.

I did not write this book to champion one asset class or investment approach at the expense of the other, but to ensure that all sides are heard. It is true that not *all* active managers can outperform the market; after deducting fees and expenses, it is mathematically impossible. And by definition the sum of all active is passive, which is the market itself. However, this notion has been taken too far that *no* active manager can outperform markets. Everyone can't be above average, but that does not mean nobody is.

I hear so many investors talking up the virtues of passive and the vices of active but failing to consider the other side. Passive is increasingly perceived and pitched as the default choice, which is a short distance from becoming the only choice. When you take away choice, you take away freedom. Without the freedom to choose, democracies turn into dictatorships and markets become pawns of flows rather than fundamentals. This is not good for markets or society. We owe it to ourselves to consider all points of views—especially the non-consensus and counterintuitive ones—before passing verdicts of right or wrong, good or bad. Passive is a prisoner's dilemma; if everyone chooses it, everyone is likely to be worse off. Just as democracies need plurality to prosper, markets need diversity (of views) to flourish. In my view, for every "Boglehead", there is a role and room for a "Contrarianhead".

Top Takeaways

Investment opportunities abound if you know how to look for them. This book describes a road map that has proven useful to me in different types of market environments—bull or bear, developed or emerging, domestic or international, new or old economy led as well as in small to mega caps. I have shared my practitioner's perspectives and insights on how to spot opportunities and improve the odds of making money instead of losing it. No insight in and of itself is a silver bullet, but together they can pack a powerful punch. Here is a recap of the top ten precepts underpinning the practice and payoff of non-consensus investing which are explained throughout the book:

1. Counterintuitive thinking can help to crack the code of delivering the "and" proposition in investing,
2. Conduct differentiated research that is correct *and* proves the consensus wrong
3. Get the biggest bang for one's research buck by scoring upset victories
4. Avoiding losers and losses is more important than picking winners
5. Misunderstanding quality could be the mother of all mistakes as well as the mother lode of all opportunities
6. Connect the dots that others have not and buy quality on sale
7. Avoid behavioral biases and emerge a victor instead of a victim
8. Know what you are getting, not what you are paying

9. Lose the battle and win the war
10. Non-consensus investing can serve as your north star as you walk down "the road not taken."[4]

---

4. "The Road Not Taken" is a poem by Robert Frost, published in 1916. Although there are many interpretations, to me it champions the notion of following your own path, especially one that few would have dared to choose, and how game-changing that can prove to be. The poem begins like this: "Two roads diverged in a wood, and I took the one less traveled by, and that has made all the difference."

A Special Message from Me to You

AS A GLOBAL EQUITY MONEY MANAGER, I have traveled extensively around the world—from far-flung islands in Indonesia to manufacturing hubs across Europe, from poverty-stricken Pakistan to glitzy Dubai, and from capitalist America to communist China. Everywhere, I encountered people, practices, and cultures that seemed vastly different from one another. But on reflection, what my travels really revealed is not how *different* we are, but how *similar*: the same aspirations, if not the same ideals; the same values, even if not the same religion; the same basic human needs, wants, emotions, and vulnerabilities, even if expressed in different forms.

One thing I have learned from this exposure is that women are the same all over the world. We make the same mistakes, fall into familiar traps, and hold ourselves back—everywhere. We don't raise our hand, don't feel qualified to seek promotions or confident of assuming leadership roles. Many don't believe they deserve more or better and resign themselves to a lifelong second-class citizenship. Those who believe they could do better professionally choose not to do so for fear it will set them back personally, ruin their relationships, or make them unsuitable partners. Even those who have the ambition often lack the validation; they wonder whether the struggles and sacrifices will be worth it. Often, we don't see enough role models to believe that it is possible, let alone worth fighting for.

As a woman who has experienced and overcome many of these feelings, I am sharing certain aspects of my own journey in the hope it will help to dispel many of these concerns by offering some advice and encouragement.

Like me, my mom grew up in India and saw women being sub-jugated in many subtle and significant ways. It was commonplace for women to be financially dependent on their husbands. This dependence meant constant compromise: toeing the line or doing things against your will because you were dependent on someone else for your well-being. On the other hand, she saw the freedom and latitude men had. As heads of the household, they controlled the purse strings and could do as they pleased. Like her, many of her educated and talented classmates were shortchanged, as their parents married them off at a young age. They regret that they were forced to become housewives and were determined not to let that destiny fall on their daughters.

My mother was one such woman. She encouraged me to think for myself and pursue a career so I could stand on my own feet. She freed me up from household chores so I could focus on my studies. She encouraged me to apprentice at a young age so I could learn from the best.

Just as higher education became my passport to intellectual freedom, work paved the way for my financial and emotional sal-vation. No matter how meager my stipends were, they represented cash flow and independence. When you are not beholden to any-one or anything, it is the most liberating feeling in the world.

While I had my mom's moral support, I did not have a men-tor or role model. My own experience has been that, although

I longed for them, they were not a necessity to get ahead in the business world. The fact is you are your own best cheerleader. Your inner strength, motivation, and dedication are more crucial than any person, book, or TED talk. I am not saying you can't have a helping hand, only that you don't *need* one.

However, if you are going to have a life partner, make sure he or she is fully supportive of your priorities and aspirations. My husband knew from the time we started dating how important my career was to me; I neither hid it nor underplayed it. It helps to set the rules of engagement clearly from the start. If there's one thing married people know only too well, it's that people don't really change. It is best to reveal your true self to the person with whom you hope to spend the rest of your life. My own experience of being happily married for the past twenty-five years has taught me that professional success does not have to come at personal cost, provided both sides sign up for it.

Not only did I not have any mentor, I did not even have a master plan. I just kept walking in the direction of my destination until I got there. Here is how it all began.

I had just finished high school and wanted to get hands-on work experience in finance. I did not want to join my dad's stockbroking business because I wanted to make it on my own. At the time, Citibank was the best foreign bank in India, and it fit my dream of going to America. So I decided to get my foot in the door via an internship there. In the phone directory, I found that the highest title listed was country head. I wrote to him but did not hear back. I called, but his assistant managed to stonewall me. So I decided to plead my case in person. (The internet did not exist back then, so emailing was not an option.) I went to the Citibank headquarters in Mumbai and sat outside his office, waiting. I don't know why his assistant did not simply boot me out. I managed to get an audience with him by following him to the elevator bank. I rode with him and used those few minutes to express my keen desire to work there. He tried to dodge me by quoting the bank's policy of only recruiting MBA students and said I looked like an undergraduate. I told him that even though I did not have a formal degree, I was fascinated by the world of finance and wanted to work in it. As we talked, I think he could tell that even at my young age (nineteen), I knew more about markets than the average MBA student. He asked me to come back with a summer project idea, since he had none in mind for me. A week later, I went back with five. He rejected all of them but gave me an internship anyway, because he was impressed with my enthusiasm.

That summer, I worked on Citibank's foreign-exchange desk, where I learned how to trade the dollar against the sterling, or the "cable" as it was called back them. I must admit, I had no business being on that desk. I could hardly contribute. In hindsight, it was nothing but an act of charity, but it was one that I am eternally grateful for.[1] The lesson I learned from this experience is that life is about taking chances and giving chances; it sets off a flywheel that is unstoppable. One success set me up for another because I acquired self-confidence, among the most important ingredients in the world of business.

"Life is about taking chances and giving chances."

On graduation, my rookie success emboldened me to seek a full-time job at the premier financial institution in India at the time, Industrial Credit and Investment Corporation of India. They too did not recruit people without an MBA, and I had only a bachelor's degree at the time. Through a friend, I managed to meet with the head of the investment banking division. I told him that if he gave me a shot, he could lower his costs. I also promised him that I would simultaneously pursue a master's degree in banking and

---

1. As my silent thank-you, my family has been and remains a lifelong customer of Citibank for our checking accounts as well as primary credit cards.

finance, so that in two years' time I would have the minimum educational qualification he was looking for. Once again, I was able to persuade my future boss to take a chance on me. It was among the best training grounds I could hope for, from project finance to loan syndications to merchant banking and even venture capital.

Frankly, before this, I had no idea finance had so many facets. Partly that's because at the time few women explored a career in finance. Unfortunately, in many corners this is still the case. Most perceive it as mind-numbing number crunching or staring at spreadsheets all day long. Many are put off by the lack of work/life balance. Some think finance is crass and crude compared to the nobler pursuits of, say, medicine or teaching. The less charitable view is that finance is full of dirtbags or windbags who are driven by money and machoism instead of morals. To make matters worse, most women think of money as a taboo topic, and since finance is equated with money, it is easily overlooked as a career choice. This may explain why the proportion of women in finance is staggeringly low; it should be half, but it is less than a quarter. Even in challenging fields such as medicine and law, the ratio has edged up to 50 percent, but somehow women are turned off by a career in finance, especially Wall Street.

It is true that many aspects of the finance profession can be daunting or undesirable. Take investment banking. It requires grueling hours or camping in the client's office while working on an important deal. Other paths such as sales or marketing of financial service products may require you to be a road warrior or network outside of usual business hours. This can seem unpalatable to people who value a more predictable routine or those who are introverted by nature.

But it does not have to be this way. *Your job is what you make it.* And finance can be a terrific platform for women because it is a meritocracy. Wall Street cares about performance and results above everything else, so your work can speak for itself—you don't have to. And you have choices. If you don't want to travel, you can work in an area of finance that does not require it, such as accounting or commercial banking. If you prefer the people side, you can be in client servicing at a financial services firm. If you are more analytically inclined, you can consider equity or fixed-income research. The possibilities are endless, and there are lots of support groups that can help you navigate your options, address your concerns, give you advice, or offer a head start. In the United States, they range from 100 Women in Finance to Girls Who Invest to the Forte Foundation, to mention just a few[2].

There is also a misperception that finance is a cut-and-dried field full of boring bean counting and rote calculations. This is false. Learning accounting is like learning a language, except it is not the language of a country, but of business. Financial statements are a window into the underlying business dynamics. Numbers can tell you whether a business strategy is working or not, whether management is executing well or not. Numbers can serve as aspirational targets or benchmarks and help set expectations or milestones to track progress. Numbers keep you in the know and are critical to decision-making. *If information is power, numbers are its poster child.*

The paradoxical thing is, numbers are brought alive when they are interpreted, not when they are calculated.[3] Unraveling the narrative contained in the numbers tickles both the right (artistic) and left (analytical) side of your brain. And if you are in my neck of the woods—stock picking and money management—you will face some of the most cerebrally taxing and thrilling mind games. If you are up for an intellectual challenge, this profession won't disappoint.

---

2. For more global resources, try http://theglasshammer.com/top-10-professional -networks-for-women-in-finance/.

3. This rote calculation part is easily done in a spreadsheet. You don't even need to know complex equations or formulae as they come preprogrammed in Excel.

"Your job is what you make it to be."

I would especially encourage women to consider money management as a career because they can be well suited to it. Women tend to approach assignments holistically and weigh all sides; this is advantageous when conducting fundamental research. Also, digging up a lot of facts and figures can be tedious and messy. On top of that, the data gathered can be contradictory. Women tend to be both comfortable with and capable of dealing with such disorder and detail. Also, women are more likely to bring humility than hubris. They also tend to think about and plan far ahead into the future. These are all excellent traits in the wealth-management profession. Best of all, you get to help people in one of the most critical aspects of their life—looking after their savings or pensions. *You get to make a difference, not just a living.* This is how a career in finance can be morally aligned, emotionally fulfilling, and intellectually satisfying.

It can also be financially rewarding. Finance is a stepping-stone into many plum C-suite roles—chief financial officer, chief investment officer, chief risk officer, chief executive officer, and so on. And beyond helping you climb the corporate ladder, being numerate and financially literate also helps you better manage your personal financial goals and budgets.

If you are willing to give this profession a try, you should know that it is about learning on the job. So, your first step is to get your foot in the door. Once you are in, raise your hand to take on projects even if you are not qualified. That is how I got my first big break. In the late 1990s, when our analyst covering Japan quit, I stepped up and offered to take on the job of researching Japanese equities. I did not speak the language; I did not know Japanese accounting or business practices. But I applied myself and learned what I needed to know. Over the next decade, I went on to cover fifty countries and an equally large number of industries. I graduated from research analyst to portfolio manager. I became part of the senior leadership team. I was never "qualified" to do any of this, but then who is? Don't shirk from taking on additional responsibilities or difficult challenges; view them as opportunities to prove yourself or to learn something new.

I was fortunate that my mom gave me enormous freedom (which was and remains unconventional in India) to make my own decisions—and therefore mistakes, because things did not always work out as intended. Looking back, this was perhaps the most influential factor in my success. Early on, even though it was never pleasant accepting that I had fallen short, I owned my mistakes, because I had mostly myself to blame. As I fixed what needed fixing, my mistakes stopped turning into misgivings and more into opportunities to figure things out—*what would I do differently next time?* This is personal growth at its best, organic and experiential.

In fact, I could not have been better prepared to face the world of investing, where almost half your decisions can turn out to be wrong. Get used to making, acknowledging, and fixing your mistakes in your formative years; it is a prerequisite to building confidence and success. The more you put yourself out there, the more mistakes you are likely to make. The more you learn from your mistakes, the more proficient you become, because you now know what *not* to do. I think this is true of entrepreneurship as well, because most things don't go as planned. Instead of getting bogged down by missteps, you learn to iterate and pivot. Mistakes prepare you for the rough-and-tumble of the business or investing world. This explains why "fail fast, fail cheap" is a proven Silicon Valley pathway to success.

Which brings me to my next point. Many women don't raise their hand because they are afraid they are not qualified; they fear they will make mistakes or mess things up instead of sorting them out. Men, on the other hand, are more likely to suffer from over-confidence and believe they are qualified to do everything, so they readily take on responsibilities or projects that they could very well muck up. However, simply by doing more, they improve their odds of success, because every mistake becomes a source of learning for them, which they apply in the next project or role they take on. *Expertise is built on the shoulders of mistakes.*

There is another thing our gender would do well to learn from men: their knack for keeping it simple. Some might quibble they do it to the point of being superficial or even lazy, but I would reframe it as smart and thoughtful. Women think they are being sharp and diligent when they examine an issue from every angle and weigh all ramifications. However, in most situations, in-depth analysis or painstaking rigor is simply overkill. I myself was guilty of this in writing this book. Even after my final manuscript was ready, I had this urge to constantly finesse a phrase here or a thought there. I kept writing and rewriting because I wanted to make sure I had written the best book I could. After many late nights of doing this, an epiphany hit me: I was *falling into the trap of pursuing perfection instead of excellence.* That stopped me in my tracks. I let go and turned in the final manuscript.

If you dwell unduly on any one issue or challenge, it often comes at the expense of dealing with something or someone else. And there is only so much time and energy you can spare; best not to expend it all on any one thing. Our desire to go deep is often a cover to be perfect. But we can only pursue perfection, we can't be perfect. So, it's best to keep it simple and focus on being excellent instead. This means achieving *optimum* rather than *maximum* results. It is a liberating principle to live by. You will accomplish more than you ever imagined.

A deep-seated desire for perfection also makes us afraid of making mistakes. But life is all about making mistakes; otherwise there would be no experimentation, no risk-taking, and without it, no progress. You don't have to be right every time; only learn from what went wrong. The more you do, the more mistakes you will make, but the more you will learn. So, raise your hand to take on more responsibilities. Don't be bashful that you are not qualified; most people aren't. Don't think you need to have all the answers; most people don't. Just put yourself out there and let courage and capability work their magic.

> **"You don't have to be right every time;**
> **only learn from what went wrong."**

As I said before, I did not start out by plotting this path. In fact, I have never managed my life by goals but by principles. If you keep doing the right things in the direction of your destination, you get there. While I did not have anyone to lean on, I did lean in. I chose to work for bosses who were very accomplished and exacting. All my former and current bosses set the bar high and skewed the curve up on me. They did not cut me slack. I would not have it any other way. They helped me stretch and fulfill my potential in ways that I could not have on my own. My biggest advice to aspiring professionals is to look for the best firms and figure out a way to work alongside industry veterans, because you learn through osmosis. At work, as in life, it is all about the company you keep.

My fervent advice to any girl or woman is, even if you are not very career minded, please try working; it gives you optionality should you need to support yourself and financial security if needed. Also, when you enjoy what you are doing, work can be as emotionally rewarding as it is financially. If the mere act of organizing or cleaning out someone's home can be a full-time and fulfilling job, then any avocation can be turned into a vocation.[4] Because self-reliance and self-confidence are critical traits to thrive in today's world, the more you accomplish, the more confidence it

---

4. Watch the spiritual fervor and fulfillment that Marie Kondo feels when she declutters a client's space, on YouTube or Netflix.

will engender. You will be a better parent, partner, and person for it, if not a better professional.

Also, earning money means you must learn to manage it, from budgeting to saving to investing. This makes you financially literate in addition to making you independent. Women have surpassed men in getting more advanced academic qualifications, but they are woefully illiterate when it comes to managing money. *Understanding money is as important and easy as knowing how to cook.* Once you apply yourself and learn the basics, you will wonder what the fuss and fear were all about.

Last but not the least, don't give up. Be patient and know that your time will come, even if it feels interminably overdue. All of us go through some bad phases or experiences. For instance, there were times when I did not get credit for the good work I did; someone else hijacked it and got rewarded for it. I let it go the first few times, but I spoke up the next time. Things changed for the better after that. Don't feel bashful about doing this in a polite but firm way. If you don't speak up, you become complicit in the wrongdoing. Also, it is important to set the record straight so that your superiors can remedy the wrong.

I have walked into countless meetings where I was the only woman in the room and felt I did not belong. It was even harder for me to fit in because I am not into sports, which topic tends to be a natural bonding ground among men. I even bought a book called *The Smart Girl's Guide to Sports*, but I had little interest in the subject so I kept falling asleep every time I tried to read it. Instead of letting this be a handicap, I turned it into a joke, poking fun at myself for not knowing how defense could be the best offense or mixing up my sports metaphors to evoke a chuckle or a laugh. Once I had their attention, I was typically able to steer to a topic of common interest and become part of the conversation. If you find yourself in this situation—whether man or woman—try to be considerate and focus on topics of mutual interest rather than creating a divide where women congregate with other women and men with other men. Diversity and inclusion are known to improve decision-making and outcomes, so preach it and practice it.

On too many occasions, I have felt overlooked or snubbed. Often in meetings, men direct their pitches to my male colleagues instead of to me. Men consciously or subconsciously assume women are not the decision makers and simply ignore them. I have overcome this bias by making sure I ask good questions in those meetings. Some men get the point and pivot. Others remain dense and lose my attention (and my business).

Many women are diffident or introverted. Men would do well to gently strike up a conversation to make us feel at ease. A simple "what do you think?" would do the trick. Sometimes, merely making eye contact to acknowledge a woman's presence in a meeting can be a shot in the arm. Women, too, should transcend their fears and introduce themselves with a firm handshake, a warm smile, and a brief introduction to let people know who they are. A little goes a long way to break the ice for both sides.

I am a firm believer that it takes two to tango. The onus should not fall exclusively on one gender or the other to make the room more inclusive. Each side needs to get a little bit out of their comfort zone and not fall into familiar patterns of behavior. On balance, I have had a terrific experience working with my male colleagues. I find that often when men (or women) engage in biased or inconsiderate behavior, it is because they are not even aware of it. It is our job to sensitize them to this and help them sharpen their antennae.[5] Diversity cuts both ways, so I am not rooting for an all-women team but one in which both genders are equally represented and respected.

---

5. Watch the short Disney Pixar video at https://www.youtube.com/watch?v=B6uulHpFkuo for help on sensitivity training. Purl, directed by Kristen Lester and produced by Gillian Libbert-Duncan, features an earnest ball of yarn named Purl who gets a job in a fast-paced, high-energy, bro-tastic start-up. She tries to fit in, but how far is she willing to go to get the acceptance she yearns for, and in the end, is it worth it?

Index

Page numbers in *italics* indicate figures.